EMPIRE ADRIFT

The Portuguese Court in
Rio de Janeiro 1808–1821

PATRICK WILCKEN

BLOOMSBURY

First published in Great Britain in 2004
This paperback edition published 2005

Copyright © 2004 by Patrick Wilcken

The moral right of the author has been asserted

Bloomsbury Publishing Plc, 38 Soho Square, London W1D 3HB

A CIP catalogue record for this book
is available from the British Library

ISBN 0 7475 6869 3
ISBN 978 0 7475 6869 8

10 9 8 7 6 5 4 3 2 1

Typeset by Hewer Text Ltd, Edinburgh
Printed and bound in Great Britain by
CPI Antony Rowe, Chippenham and Eastbourne
All papers used by Bloomsbury Publishing are natural,
recyclable products made from wood grown in well-managed
forests. The manufacturing processes conform to the
environmental regulations of the country of origin

www.bloomsbury.com/patrickwilcken

For Andreia

CONTENTS

Map showing the flight
of the Portuguese court
to Rio de Janeiro 1807–1808

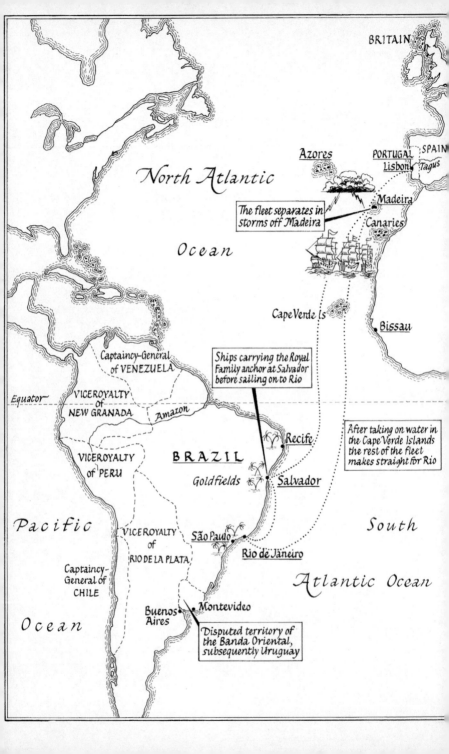

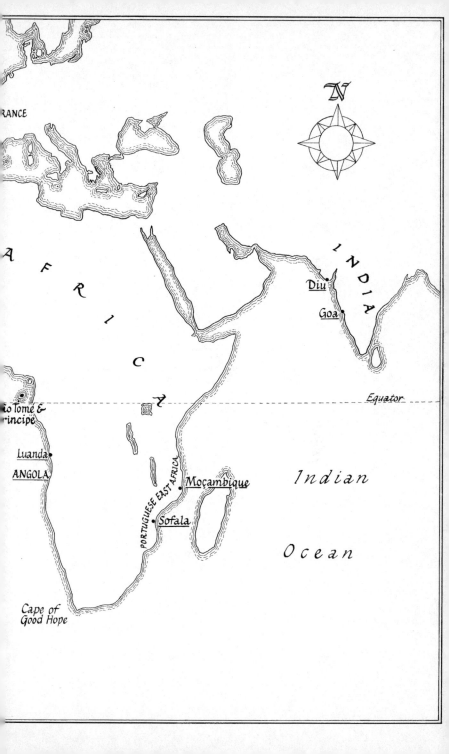

Preface

Twenty-five miles north of Lisbon, over the Sintra hills, lies the small town of Mafra. Its dwellings are dwarfed by an enormous eighteenth-century structure, an Italianate baroque monastery built during the reign of Dom João V (1706–1750). Spires and bulbous domes are visible for miles around; the imposing façade, flanked by two squat bell towers, dominates the area, but obscures the full extent of the complex, extending back, as it does, through 40,000 square metres of monk cells, chapels, apartments and banquet halls.

Yet the project started out small, when Dom João V ordered the construction of a modest convent in gratitude for the birth of an heir. It was originally meant to house just thirteen Franciscan friars, and in 1717 only a few hundred stonemasons headed out into the countryside to start work. Seven years later, 12,000 peasants were encamped in an area that was fast becoming the biggest building site in Europe. By 1730 the workforce was approaching 50,000, the equivalent of a large eighteenth-century city. Costs soared, but the royal treasury paid out, placing orders for Italian marbles in pinks, whites, blues, yellows and blacks. Bell makers in Liège and Antwerp were so surprised at the size of the order coming from Portugal that they queried the amount, but in time over a hundred bells would be cast and carted across Europe to Portugal.

Thousands of miles across the Atlantic Ocean to Brazil, and

then a further 300 miles inland to a region now known as Minas Gerais, was the ultimate source of revenue for the Mafra extravaganza. There, at the headwaters of the colonial system, men, their slaves and Amerindian 'helpers' were raking the topsoil, digging rudimentary mines and sieving the streams, in the world's first modern gold rush. In the early years conditions were horrendous – the gold fields lay in rugged, unmapped territory, and the waves of prospectors soon outstripped their supplies. But as work got under way on Mafra, gold dust crossed the Atlantic. Soon, diamonds and precious stones were being unearthed and shipped back to Europe, the tax receipts from their sale further swelling the Crown's coffers.

With ever increasing yields arriving from the colonies, architects met to redraw their plans for the monastery. The infirmary was redesigned to open on to its own chapel, so that bedridden patients could hear mass; a superb library, with an eighty-three-metre-long marble floor and towering bookshelves was installed. New antechambers, side chapels and dispatch rooms fed off into further passageways, and soon whole wings were sprouting from the building's original nucleus as the labyrinth spread outwards. Building works continued long after the death of Dom João V, and by the early nineteenth century the complex had become a favoured royal residence. From its inception as a small votive monastery, Mafra was now a palace, the command post of an empire to which it owed its very existence.

The grandeur of Mafra and the scramble for riches in Brazil, although in one sense intimately linked, never came together in the time of Dom João V. To him, Brazil was a welcome, yet mysterious benefactor, a generous donor from across the seas. The Portuguese Empire, born in the 'Age of Discoveries', then stretched from Macao in the East, through scattered Indian trade ports and African slaving centres, on to the sugar plantations and gold fields of Brazil. The king stood symbolically at its apex, but had no personal contact with and little knowledge about his distant dominions. Instead, Lisbon and its hinterlands became showcases of imperial wealth, while out in the empire – in Salvador, Rio de Janeiro, Mozambique and Goa – the king was celebrated *in absentia* with fireworks, parades and *Te Deum* masses.

Britain's George III was similarly fêted, from the cane fields of Jamaica to the penal colonies of Australia, worlds alien to the king's actual life in England. In the nineteenth century, Queen Victoria, the Empress of India, had the Durbar Room built in Osborne House on the Isle of Wight, an Indian fantasy done out in sandalwood, soapstone carving, ivory and marble inlay. But the queen would never visit the subcontinent, which remained throughout her life an imagined realm of fine art and costumed servants. Around the same time, Belgium's King Leopold II was closely identified with another colonial venture – Belgian Congo – and Brussels became the repository for the years of plunder that followed. The giant Cinquantenaire arch was erected, the royal palace and the château of Laeken renovated on the proceeds of Congolese rubber. Leopold became passionate about, even fixated on the Congo, yet he never set foot in Africa. It was not until the twentieth century, when the royal tour took off, that kings and queens finally moved out into their empires – and then, only in carefully choreographed visits that seemed to re-emphasise the gulf between metropolis and colony.

This is the story of the one time in history when this polite distance was breached. It follows Dom João VI – the great-grandson of the extravagant Dom João V – whose reign as prince regent of Portugal from 1799 to 1816, and then king until his death in 1826, spanned the Atlantic. At the height of the Napoleonic Wars, he and his entourage fled Mafra and sailed for Brazil, in a journey that would rupture the delicate membrane dividing the empire's centre from its periphery. This was no pre-planned royal tour – when the royals disembarked in the Americas they stood before their colonial vassals not as remote overlords, but as *émigrés* in need of succour.

The court had fled a Continent being torn apart in the afterglow of the French Revolution. Napoleon Bonaparte had ridden out the turmoil of the 1790s as a military commander, and then seized power in a daring coup in 1799. Through the next decade-and-a-half he would turn Europe into a string of battlefields, conscripting a generation into wars fought out on unprecedented scales. A series of coalitions would be built against him, only to be manipulated and eventually crumble before the might and tactical prowess of his ever-expanding *Grande Armée*.

The effects of Napoleon's campaign went far beyond just Europe – it was a clash of empires, a fight for supremacy over global trade, a battle in which Portugal, a small European state with extensive imperial holdings, found herself caught between Britain and France, the two superpowers of the day. Portugal had pursued a policy of neutrality through the Napoleonic Wars, determined to stay clear of the conflict, but in the autumn of 1807 matters had come to a head. With a French army advancing on Lisbon, the royal family, their ministers, religious leaders, assorted courtiers and servants joined a great caravan snaking its way down to the docks. As Napoleon's troops closed in on the capital, thousands crammed on board the royal fleet. At seven o'clock on the morning of 29 November 1807, the hastily provisioned convoy left the Iberian peninsula and floated out into the Atlantic, flanked by British escorts.

After almost two months at sea and a stopoff in Salvador, the court arrived in Rio de Janeiro, spilling off the fleet into an unfamiliar tropical city. The gold mines long exhausted, the colony had fallen back on its traditional role – as a slave-driven factory farm for Europe. Rio was then the largest slave market town in the Americas, its port busy with the comings and goings of slavers, its population one-third African. There, nestled between dramatic mountain ranges and sweeping beaches, the regent's ministers and advisers were forced to contemplate the effects of their policies and, worse still, to live in amongst their own colonial handiwork. The shock was mutual. For Brazilians the unthinkable had happened: mythical figures had materialised, unprompted, in the colony. The icons stamped on their coins, the people they knew only as statues and engravings, were now among them, in flesh and blood.

In the draining humidity, courtiers donned wigs, breeches and fitted jackets and went about their business, administering the Portuguese Empire from the tropics. Their presence brought great changes to a city that had been transformed from colonial outpost to imperial capital overnight. They oversaw the construction of a new theatre and government buildings, the remodelling of a planter's mansion into a palace and the transfer of the royal library to Rio, as a metropolitan façade was hastily erected. In the shadow of the Corcovado Mountain, the exiled prince regent Dom João founded a botanical gardens – one of the age's symbols of modernity and learning – carved out of the surrounding rainforest. And there he planted a new variety of palm which, over the next years, he would inspect at intervals as it germinated and climbed upwards.

While the court established themselves in Rio, Portugal was playing host to the early years of the Peninsular Wars. Mafra was transformed into an army barracks, given up first to French and then British troops, who were billeted in the chapels and apartments that had once been the preserve of royalty. Their stays were destructive – they left behind soiled living quarters, vandalised works of art and broken furniture. The wider country was also devastated, sucked into a conflict it had tried everything to avoid. This was the beginning of a long, dark period of Portuguese history, the first step in a process that would gut the nation and leave it politically unstable well into the nineteenth century. With the court and government went any semblance of Portuguese self-determination, any powers of negotiation or standing in Europe, as a once respected state sank deep into obscurity.

Although by 1815 Napoleon had been defeated, thrown into permanent exile on the South Atlantic island of St Helena, and Europe was finally at peace, there remained a sense of unease in Portugal. After the war the Mafra complex lay empty, derelict, its gardens overgrown and unkempt. Years passed with no word from Rio. There were rumours, off-the-record talk, vague promises, but no sign of the returning royal fleet. If anything, the traffic was now flowing in the other direction. Freighters set off from Lisbon carrying royal carriages, crates of rare books and sheet music destined for Brazil; courtiers who had remained in Portugal boarded vessels for the Americas; Portuguese troops fresh from the peninsular campaigns were packed on to Brazil-bound transports for operations in the colony, while from the dockside their compatriots looked on in disbelief.

By now Dom João's palm had grown into a magnificent tree, its slender trunk standing over thirty metres tall, as solid as a flagpole. Neat seedbeds furrowed the gardens, the testing grounds for exotic grafts that arrived from around the empire. In the city itself slaves were working on yet more buildings, paving streets and sculpting parklands from the hillsides which undulated around Rio. Foreigners – traders, diplomats and travellers – were flooding into the capital in ever-greater numbers as a colonial port grew into a vital South Atlantic metropolis.

Ten years into the royal family's sojourn, the idea of their return to Portugal had dissolved into a dream, a fantasy clung to by the more credulous. Because in Rio de Janeiro something remarkable was happening, unparalleled in the history of European colonialism. Dom João had left the mother country behind. His court and government had set down roots amidst the palm stands and banana plants of their one-time colony. The seat of the Portuguese Empire, cast adrift from the Continent, had come to rest in the New World.

ONE

Exodus

On 25 September 1807 a coach wound up through Lisbon's loosely cobbled streets. Once it had hauled its way over the hills which encircled the port, it broke into open countryside, and began rattling through rolling pastureland and citrus groves. Seated in the cabin was the twenty-seven-year-old Irish peer, Percy Clinton Sydney Smythe, sixth Viscount Strangford, the British envoy in Lisbon. As the carriage raced northwards, Strangford worked through the sheaves of diplomatic correspondence spread across his lap – letters from George III, recommendations from the British foreign secretary, George Canning, and his opposite number in Portugal, Antônio de Araújo – preparing for the most crucial meeting of his career. On flatter stretches of road Strangford would jot comments in the margins of his papers, otherwise he mentally rehearsed what he planned to say when he came face to face with the Portuguese prince regent, Dom João.

Strangford had arrived in Lisbon at the age of just twenty-two, as secretary of the British legation. After graduating from Trinity College, Dublin, he began his career as a foreign office clerk in London, but his passage to Lisbon would be an unconventional one. While serving at the foreign office, he had spent long evenings in his study of his apartment in Bury St, off Piccadilly, translating some of the lesser-known love poems of the Portuguese epic poet Camões, and it was the resulting book, rather than any diplomatic skills, that would secure him his post in Portugal. On publication, Strangford's collection was a runaway success, reaching the living rooms of the British court and marking him out as an expert on things Portuguese.

The collection would, however, also cast early doubts on Strangford's probity. Despite its popularity, the book drew criticism, partly for its uncertain rendition of the original Portuguese, but mostly because of its similarities to the work of the poet Tom Moore, who lodged upstairs from Strangford. In a damning review, the poet and critic Robert Southey called the book a literary fraud, while Strangford won a less than flattering role in Byron's own poem, *English Bards*: 'Mend, Strangford! Mend thy morals and thy taste;/ Be warm, be pure, be amorous, but be chaste:/ Cease to deceive; thy pilfered harp restore,/ Nor teach the Lusian bard to copy Moore.'

Once in Lisbon, Strangford had at first spent his time sleeping late and working on new translations until, with the departure of Lord Robert Fitzgerald, he was promoted to Britain's representative to the Portuguese court. Red-haired and with a fine-featured face, Strangford dressed for the part, wearing dandyish suits and cravats. In temperament, too, he was the man for the job – a diplomatic operator, a haughty defender of British interests at whatever the cost, an egotist who barely registered his own duplicity when circumstances required. He took up his post at the most delicate of times: Napoleon's conquest of Europe was well under way, and the Portuguese court, desperate to maintain its neutrality, was coming under enormous pressure to choose between the British and the French.

Strangford slipped easily into the role of shadowy agitator, using a network of spies and a combination of intrigue and bullying, but in the process came to be viewed with suspicion by all sides, even the British. The young lawyer Lord Brougham, part of a British diplomatic team which visited Lisbon in 1806, was so unsure about Strangford that he was reluctant to share intelligence with him. 'I would rather divulge it to another than

Lord Strangford, who is somewhat too flighty and uncertain in his movements to gain my confidence,' he wrote back to London at the time. Worse, he found the peer immature and untrustworthy, complaining about his '*total want*' of that 'first-rate quality which gives a man's word the right to be believed' and of 'respect either for common society or from those he has to do business with'. Brougham was also annoyed by the fact that Strangford had not bothered to introduce him to anyone in the court, forcing him to write to London for letters of introduction. Nevertheless, with characteristic self-deception, Strangford would later eulogise his relationship with Brougham, saying that they lived together in Lisbon 'like Helen and Hermione'.

Deep inside the Mafra monastery complex, the prince regent, Dom João, awaited Strangford's arrival. A portly man on the cusp of middle age, he sat at his writing table, working through a copy of the letter from George III that Strangford had sent him earlier, weighing up his response. The day before he had received a similar visit from the French *chargé d'affaires*, bearing a threatening letter from Bonaparte. The meeting had lasted just a few minutes – Dom João struggled in French, but in any case could do little at this stage to meet Napoleon's increasingly extreme demands.

The prince regent had now been living in Mafra for several years, removed from the capital and a good fifteen miles away from the rest of the royal family, who were installed at the rococo palace of Queluz. His estranged wife, the princess regent Dona Carlota Joaquina, daughter of the Spanish king Carlos IV, maintained yet another residence – a country villa of her own at Ramalhão. Dom João's love of Mafra was in part a religious one. There, with his Augustinian and Franciscan friars, he could indulge his passion for sung masses, benediction, pipe organ music and Gregorian chants. In the current circumstances, though, there was undoubtedly an element of siege mentality: the compound was bunker-like, its gridiron plan gave off a sense of solidity – as if its sheer extent could cocoon the regent from the anti-monarchist violence that was now spreading through Napoleon's Europe.

Mafra was a world in itself, a small royal city. Dom João could pace through its miles of corridors, visit its world-class library, and choose between two giant monasteries or a host of smaller chapels; in season he could go hunting in the adjoining range and feast on game in the banquet hall, all without leaving his home. But no trappings of royalty, no spoils of empire could protect the prince regent from what was now in train. For even as Dom João considered his options, two veterans of the Napoleonic Wars were receiving new orders that would spell the end of his European kingdom.

In the autumn of 1807 Admiral Sir Sidney Smith was recalled from his leave in Bath, where he had been taking the medicinal waters in the aftermath of a disastrous campaign in the Dardanelles. He was told to captain the flagship *Hibernia* and set sail with a fleet of nine battleships for Portugal. In France, Napoleon sent General Andoche Junot from Paris down to Bayonne, on the Atlantic coast. There he would take charge of a 20,000-strong French force, and lead them into the Iberian peninsula. Both men were ordered to head for the Portuguese capital, Lisbon.

The son of a prosperous Burgundy farmer, Junot was now in his mid-thirties. His face bore the marks of his military career, a clean scar working its way down one side, the result of a sabre blow received during the Italian campaigns; otherwise, he was a man of handsome, symmetrical features. He was known to be hot-tempered and although he had accompanied Napoleon on his rise to power, working as his trusted lieutenant, he had not been rewarded with a marshal's baton. A brief spell as ambassador to Portugal in 1805 made him the ideal choice for the Iberian assault – his first major campaign command. Smith had also played a vital role in the wars, roving Europe's waterways as an admiral in the British navy. He had ruffled feathers when he had taken over the command of Nelson's ships in the Eastern Mediterranean, but then proved himself in the bombardment of Acre (1799), during Napoleon's ill-fated foray into the Middle East.

When Smith and Junot began mobilising against Portugal, the war in Europe had reached a critical point. On the face of it Napoleon's crusade was at its high water mark. After earlier expansions into Holland, Switzerland and northern Italy, late 1805 had seen a showdown in the east. At Austerlitz (December 1805), in a winter battle fought against a backdrop of frozen fog, sheet ice and snow drifts, Napoleon's *Grande Armée* routed the combined Austrian and Russian armies. So devastating was the defeat that Britain and Russia considered suing for peace, but Napoleon drove onwards, quashing a Prussian uprising at Jena and Auerstädt in October 1806 and occupying Berlin. By spring 1807 Napoleon was in Warsaw and that summer he smashed the Russian army at Friedland, forcing Tsar Alexander I to the negotiating table. They met in June 1807, on a specially constructed raft at the mid-point of the River Niemen, and over two weeks of talks Napoleon ironed out the details. Eastern Europe was carved up; Prussia belittled; Britain isolated as far as possible from the Continent. In the three years since Napoleon had declared himself Emperor of France, the European landscape had changed radically. Through his web of client states, occupations and courts – the duchies and kingdoms that Napoleon doled out to family members and his marshals – Napoleon's empire now stretched from Poland to the Pyrenees, from the Low Countries down to Naples.

Britain remained beyond his grasp, but even on this front, the situation was looking promising. After the loss of the Spanish and French navies at Trafalgar, Napoleon had set about crippling Britain economically. In 1806 he issued the Berlin Decree – a blanket blockade of the British Isles that involved not just goods but all contact, commercial or otherwise, with Britain and her colonies. By 1807, Britain was left with just toeholds in Sicily and Gibraltar and a handful of underpowered allies or pliant neutrals: Sweden, Portugal and Denmark. This reversal of fortune bred uncertainty in Westminster. In parliament there were Whig sympathisers to the Napoleonic project, and with George III's mental deterioration evident to all, his reign was looking shaky. Next in line to the throne was the ineffectual, pro-Whig Prince of Wales, seen by many as unlikely to hold the line against France. Napoleon's rolling campaigns and the Berlin decree were also affecting the economy and privations in the north of England were turning manufacturers against the war.

As 1807 wore on Napoleon tried to impose his economic blockade and both Britain and France scrambled to take control of the few neutral ports remaining and the fleets that were stationed there. Copenhagen was the first to fall, in a pre-emptive strike launched by Britain in August 1807. The British entered the harbour and seized the Danish fleet, and in the battle that followed they fire-bombed the port and then stripped it 'down to the last nail and the minutest ropeyarn', leaving it in ruins for the French. Over a thousand Danish civilians died during the bombardment and in fires that followed the assault, making this a highly controversial action, even in Britain. The brutality, the underhand nature of the operation and the fact that it was carried out against a weak neutral state drew condemnation from across Europe. With the stakes rising, all eyes turned towards Lisbon, a strategic Atlantic port, vital to British shipping.

Up to this point, Portugal had maintained her neutrality, but some sort of engagement had long seemed unavoidable. Portugal stood at the edge of Napoleonic Europe, hemmed in by neighbouring Spain, an ally of France. Her seaports were ideally located for the Atlantic trade, Lisbon's prime position as a year-round, warm-water port making it particularly vulnerable. The city served as a beachhead to Europe for the British and for Napoleon it was the one remaining serious breach in his 'Continental System'. Lisbon was also the nexus of Portugal's empire, the clearing house of the Brazil trade from which Britain profited greatly, giving it an aura of importance in a war that was beginning to centre around access to trade routes. Portugal's fleet, small though it was, would be an added bonus in Napoleon's ongoing struggle to rebuild his navy.

Yet as General Junot prepared to cross the Pyrenees and start on the long march to Lisbon, Napoleon's battle for supremacy entered a new and less propitious phase. Although Napoleon could not have possibly realised it at the time, the decision to send this small division of troops into the peninsula would have far-reaching consequences. Hundreds of thousands of soldiers would follow Junot through the mountain passes in the years to come as Napoleon's operations became overstretched, split between distant fronts across Europe. The beginning of what would become known as the Peninsular Wars would, in time, turn the tide against Napoleon. His conquest of Europe would die in the east, but would initially falter where he least expected it – on the sun-baked plains of central Spain.

In Lisbon's central plazas people gathered to discuss the latest news, fatalism creeping into their every utterance. War seemed inevitable and around the city preparations were already under way. Shopkeepers erected makeshift barricades over doors and windows, flimsy defences against the looting that was sure to follow. Families bid farewell to their daughters and wives, who were being sent away into the countryside, out of reach of the marauding French regulars. And in the cobbled lanes which wound up through Lisbon's famous hills, order was already beginning to break down, thieves and vagrants sensing their opportunity.

Something else, though, even more subversive, was happening. There had been no sign of the Portuguese army taking up defensive positions. Instead, people were exchanging stories of unusual movements down at the Belém docks – the port area of Lisbon. The word was that repair work on the Portuguese fleet which had begun in August was being stepped up. High-ranking bureaucrats were milling around, personally supervising matters on board the fleet and past midnight, dock workers were loading large crates of goods on to the ships of the line. An air of secrecy pervaded these dockyard activities, but from the constant traffic of royal carriages ferrying government officials to and from the quays it was clear that the preparations were climaxing.

The better connected had at least some inkling of what would soon be unfolding across the city. In the midst of the

uncertainty, Pedro Gomes, a wealthy merchant, wrote to his
father-in-law:

> 'We have not as yet been able to secure a firm passage for there
> are many who wish to leave and the ships are few . . . We shall
> keep you updated with developments. In the meantime we are
> organising ourselves to leave the capital, for wherever, at the first
> sign of danger. They say that Dom Lourenço [the Portuguese
> ambassador to France] has brought hope of some accommoda-
> tion with the French, and that the row is now with the English.
> The ships continue under hurried preparation and all signs
> indicate some kind of embarkation.'

The truth of the matter was to be found in the complex
negotiations that took place between Britain, France and Portugal in the run-up to the French invasion. The diplomatic
build-up to the crisis began one month after the signing of the
Treaty of Tilsit, when Napoleon ordered the Portuguese court
to fall into line with the Continent-wide blockade against
Britain. Mid-August saw Napoleon backing up his demands
with an ultimatum: the Portuguese were to comply by 1
September, or face a French assault.

In a series of high-pressure meetings, Portugal's council of
state argued over how best to respond. Each path seemed
suicidal. Compliance would mean a repeat of the Copenhagen
action: a British bombardment of Lisbon, the loss of the fleet and
perhaps even the seizure of Portugal's lucrative Atlantic colonies.
Rebuffing Napoleon would lead to a scenario already familiar
throughout most of Europe: French occupation along with the
overthrow of the Portuguese throne. But there was one possible,
if drastic, way out – and as the discussions intensified it emerged
again and again as the front runner. While negotiators tried to
stall the French, an extraordinary plan was being finalised.
Towards the end of August, the council recommended to
the prince regent, Dom João, that he should ready his ships
for flight. The journey was to be an epic voyage to Portugal's
largest colony, Brazil. At first it had been thought that only the

heir to the throne, Dom João's eight-year-old son Pedro, would sail but the plan rapidly evolved into something much more ambitious.

It was decided that, if forced, the fleet would carry off not just the royal family, but the court along with the government, its functionaries and the apparatus of state – in short, the entire Portuguese elite – to the colonial city of Rio de Janeiro. Once there, the court and government would reconstitute themselves and continue their rule from the tropics. The British had long been pressing for this option and were offering to escort the Portuguese across the Atlantic in return for preferential trading status with Brazil. After the ignominious expulsion of British forces from Buenos Aires the previous August, and a failed second assault in June 1807, Britain was looking for a way back into South American markets to compensate for her loss of trade on the Continent.

Caught up in the political maelstrom was the middle-aged Portuguese foreign secretary, Antônio de Araújo, the Count of Barca, a former emissary to the Hague who had also held positions in Paris and Berlin. Araújo was a cultured man fluent in French, English and Italian, and had been a vocal leader of the pro-French faction within the Portuguese court. When Junot had last been in Lisbon as ambassador, Araújo had smoothed his way, exempting him from as much antiquated court protocol as possible. For his services Araújo had won plaudits from Junot's wife, the Duchess D'Abrantès, who adored his 'little grey-black wicked eyes and his delightful wit'. She found him to be the perfect gentleman – 'a man of very mild but resolute character'. At the current impasse Araújo was in an impossible position. Years of slavish diplomatic support for France were being repaid with invasion. As the autumn drew on, the realisation that he had backed the wrong horse dawned and he saw his political career dissolving before his eyes.

A few weeks before the all-important Mafra meeting, Strangford met with Araújo. 'I have had much conversation with M. d'Araújo respecting the unusual activity now pervading the Dock-Yards and Arsenal of Lisbon . . .' reported Strangford back to London, 'he declares that the preparations in question are undertaken solely with a view to that Emergency which may compel the Royal Family of Portugal to retire to the Brazils'. Putting a brave face on the crisis, Araújo told Strangford that once in Brazil, Dom João would establish 'a great and powerful empire, which protected in its infancy by the naval superiority of England, may rise, in time, to competition with any other Political Establishment in the Universe.' Araújo warned Strangford that time was running out, and that a 'simulated' war might need to be declared on Britain in order to delay the French invasion. Diplomatic prevarication had pushed the French deadline back through September, but it was clear that Napoleon could not be stalled indefinitely.

When Strangford alighted his carriage at Mafra after the twenty-five-mile journey from Lisbon, his goal was clear: to prevent any moves towards appeasing the French, and to recommend an immediate, British-assisted embarkation of the court for the Americas. He knew, though, that he would be fighting an uphill battle. Consensus on the move to Brazil was gathering momentum within the Portuguese council of state and the British delegation, but the final word was in the hands of the prince regent, Dom João, a man famed for his lack of initiative and indecisiveness.

Palace footmen escorted Strangford through Mafra's maze of corridors and delivered him into the half-light of the wood-panelled dispatch room. There he would spend the next hour-and-a-half with the prince regent in a meeting which, according to his own foreign office dispatch, included haranguing, threats and wounding personal allusions, all cloaked in the even-tempered tones of diplomatic politesse. Strangford began by warning the regent of the dire consequences that would follow if he became 'the willing, or at least unresisting Vassal of France'. He then ridiculed the regent's delaying tactics – 'surely His Royal Highness could not suppose that France would now be satisfied with any imperfect or temporising measures of hostility which Portugal might (in order to soothe her) employ against England.' 'According to our system,' he concluded darkly, 'the sword must be entirely sheathed, or entirely drawn.'

Dom João was upset by this line of attack – 'I do not wish that I ever saw any person under more strong anxiety and agitation than His Royal Highness evinced during this conversation,' wrote Strangford – but worse was to come. Appealing to what he thought was the regent's superstitious nature, Strangford reminded him that 'the two former occasions on which he had yielded to the Enemies of England were severely marked by a sad and disastrous event'. He was referring to a peace treaty with France, signed in 1797, which coincided with Dom João's mother, Queen Maria I's descent into incurable insanity, and the 1801 treaty with Spain and France, finalised at the time of the death of the prince regent's firstborn son. 'Such awful coincidences,' menaced Strangford, should be thought of 'as something more than accidental.' The regent was again taken aback, and even Strangford realised that he had crossed some sort of line with what he described as an 'unexpected, and, under other Circumstances, unjustifiable Allusion'.

Although rattled by Strangford's onslaught, Dom João evaded it in his typically roundabout fashion. On the question of leaving Lisbon he was noncommittal. He would agree in principle to the flight to Brazil in the event of a French invasion, but added that he would not give the order until 'the actual arrival of danger'. His concerns were with his subjects – 'duty forbade him to abandon his people until the last moment,' wrote Strangford – although there was also a suggestion that his worries might have been closer to home. Dom João was a timid man by nature and, according to Strangford, he feared the hostile reaction of the Lisbon mob. He was also said to have dreaded seasickness, and panicked at the prospect of an Atlantic crossing.

For all his foibles, Dom João was not naive. He was well aware of Strangford's hidden agenda, and spoke of his hopes that Britain did not 'intend to oblige him to sacrifice his European Possessions merely that she might have the advantage of trading with his Colonies, and of repairing in the new World the losses which her commerce had sustained in the old'. 'If England wished to aggrandise herself in the other hemisphere,' the prince regent countered, 'she ought to do it at the Expense of her Enemies in America [i.e. Spain], not of her friends in Europe.'

As Strangford's coach set out on the long journey back to Lisbon he knew he had failed, but nevertheless concluded his report to London in an upbeat fashion: 'Everything that I said, made the strongest Impression upon His Royal Highness, and though I obtained no positive promise of accession to my Demands, still I left His Royal Highness in a frame of mind from which I augur the most favourable results.' Back in Lisbon, Strangford swung into action. 'Notwithstanding the lateness of the hour,' he wrote, 'I went to M. D'Araújo and engaged him to write a letter to the Prince, urging in the strongest Forms the necessity of the Measure in Question. I then proceeded to employ some indiscreet but sure means of influence on the physician in whom the Prince has the greatest Confidence, and whom it was natural to suppose that his Royal Highness would consult on an occasion of much Importance.'

Soon after Strangford's meeting with the prince regent, French and Spanish ambassadors broke off diplomatic relations and stormed out of Lisbon. With Portugal now technically at war with France, Dom João rushed to reassure Napoleon by closing his kingdom's ports to British shipping. The prince regent was hedging his bets. While trying to mollify Napoleon, he was also signing a secret agreement with London, opening the Brazil trade to Britain in exchange for British naval protection if he was forced out of Portugal.

During October, the crisis deepened. The Portuguese ambassador to France, Dom Lourenço de Lima, abandoned his post in Paris and was *en route* to Lisbon. In an alarmist dispatch, he wrote ahead that Napoleon was far from satisfied with Portugal's stance, and was demanding the immediate imprisonment of all British citizens and sequestration of their property. What he did not know was that at that very moment French and Spanish officials were gathering to discuss the fate of Portugal. Their talks, formalised in the Treaty of Fontainebleau, carved up the country between them. On occupation, Portugal would be cut into three strips: the north – renamed '*Septentrional Lusitania*' – going to the house of Etruria (so that, in a bizarre exchange, Napoleon's sister could take over Tuscany), the middle swathe to the French, and the Algarve for the Spanish foreign minister, Manuel de Godoy.

Pressure was building from the British side, too. Dom João was furious to receive a note from Strangford warning that if he would not agree to exile, he should at least move his fleet to Madeira or perhaps even to the British station at Cadiz, so as to avoid Bonaparte seizing it. Were the regent to refuse, 'his Majesty's government will be most thoroughly and manifestly justified in any steps which it may think proper to pursue'. Right on cue, Sir Sidney Smith's fleet of warships appeared in blockade formation, clearly visible off the coast.

Mid-October brought more bad news: Junot had left Bayonne, and was now leading his troops at pace through Spain towards Portugal. The campaign had opened poorly. 'Junot . . . entered Spain on October 17,' recalled Baron de Marbot, a senior officer in Napoleon's army, 'and sent forward his columns along the roads where no preparations had been made to receive them. Our troops slept in the open air and got only half rations of food. Autumn was drawing to an end, the army was traversing the spurs of the Pyrenees, where the climate is severe, and very soon the road was covered with sick men and stragglers.' In atrocious weather, the remainder of the army pushed on, Junot force marching his troops across the peninsula.

To those in Lisbon it still seemed possible that the French invasion could be halted or at least delayed, and the prince regent's advisers pressed for full compliance with Napoleon's demands, including the imprisonment of British citizens and the seizure of their property. It was a decision Dom João had been dreading having to make, a move that would almost certainly drag Portugal into the wars that had already spelt ruin for the smaller kingdoms east of the Pyrenees, like Piedmont, Parma and Naples. Much to the prince regent's anguish, Portugal's long-term strategy of neutrality was unravelling, her delicate balancing act between Britain and France on the point of collapse. Seated at his writing table, the decree placed before him, Dom João suffered a last-minute bout of indecision. Five times he made to sign, before throwing his pen aside in exasperation, but in the end, goaded by his advisers, he forced himself to scrawl his name across the document.

The British were given time to get out of Lisbon, Lord Strangford among the many who were asked to leave. He initially refused, lingering for a further ten days in the city, until a brusque note from Araújo forced him out. Hiring a small fishing boat, he sailed down the Tagus and after two uncomfortable days at sea he reached the British fleet.

By early November Dom João had decamped from Mafra to yet another royal residence – the half-built Palace of Ajuda by the docks. A stone's throw from his chambers, over rows of terracotta rooftops and down to the banks of the Tagus, the provisioning of the fleet was proceeding apace. Palace officials moved discreetly through the dock area, issuing their instructions in whispers; great casks were being carefully lowered down on to waiting galleys, while on the quay courtiers sorted through books and paperwork, arranging them into wooden boxes for transportation.

French troops were now massing on the border, but still Dom João refused to give the nod. Instead he sent an envoy, the Marquis of Marialva, to Paris to deliver news of Portugal's total capitulation in person. Marialva took with him a sweetener – a cache of diamonds – and was to have offered up the regent's son Pedro for marriage into the Bonaparte clan, but his journey would end prematurely with the seizure of his passport in Madrid.

Meanwhile the merchant José de Oliveira Barreto was dispatched to the border to make contact with Junot. It was hoped that Barreto might be able to reason with Junot, or at the very least buy the court some precious time. They met on the banks of the Zêzere river, swollen by recent rains. Barreto found the French army in a deplorable state, 'impoverished, in want of everything' and Junot busy trying to requisition shoes for his troops from the surrounding countryside. The rain was sheeting

down, the river roaring, as the two began their negotiations
under the less than adequate shelter of a nearby tree. Junot said
that he had come to liberate Portugal from the British, dismissing
Barreto's protestations that the British had already been expelled.
In response Barreto tried to convince Junot of Dom João's
conversion to the Napoleonic cause, while at the same time
warning him that if the French invaded, the court would embark
for Brazil.

It was to be the last roll of the dice. With Junot four days'
march from Lisbon, and Smith's blockade in place, incontro-
vertible evidence of Napoleon's intent arrived in the capital. On
23 November, a copy of Napoleon's official organ *Le Moniteur*,
forwarded on an express packet boat from London, reached
Lisbon in record time. In it was the news that Dom João surely
expected, but had refused to believe – the announcement of
Napoleon's decision to end the Bragança dynasty and usurp the
Portuguese throne.

At midnight on 24 November, the court official Joaquim José de
Azevedo was woken by a messenger and told to report immediately to the palace. As Azevedo approached the council of
state's meeting room he saw through a half-opened door a group
of wigged advisers in agitated discussion. He was ushered into
the room and, unusually, was given orders by the prince regent
in person to start organising the embarkation of the royal family
and state dignitaries. Other officials briefed Azevedo on the
arrangements already in place. The Admiral of the fleet had
drawn up a set of detailed diagrams, outlining space allocations
for both people and goods on board the Portuguese fleet. Those
chosen to accompany the royal family to Brazil had been issued
with permits for themselves, their family and their baggage,
which they had to produce on boarding. The departure was set
for the afternoon of 27 November, giving Azevedo less than
three days to complete his task.

Before setting off for the docks, Azevedo made sure of his
own passage to Brazil, and then alerted key members of the
royal household – the Gentleman of the Bedchamber, the

Comptroller of Provisions of the Royal Household – church and treasury officials. When he reached the port, he found it teeming with bureaucrats, dock workers and crowds of onlookers. In the dawn drizzle, carriages were now arriving from all quarters of the city, negotiating their way between the crates, luggage and barrels of water which filled the dockside. Offshore, brigs ferried stores out across the broad sweep of the Tagus to the fleet, where tiny figures could be made out clambering over the vessels, carrying out eleventh-hour checks and repairs. Azevedo set up his stall on the quay, and there he worked all night, through the next day and on into the small hours of the morning.

The archivist Cristiano Müller was also roused on that night and told to pack up the voluminous records of the ministry of state which he had been preparing for possible removal for the last few months. Conferring with Araújo, Müller finalised arrangements for the thirty-four large crates of paperwork that were to be dispatched to Brazil on board the Portuguese frigate, the *Medusa*. Meanwhile the royal residences of Mafra and Queluz were evacuated. The corridors of Mafra bustled with scullery maids, pages and valets who worked through the night, dismantling palace trappings, stripping the basilica of its gold and silver, and carrying oil paintings out into the autumn rains. From there the monastery's contents were loaded into hundreds of carriages and sent down to the docks. Palace staff cleared out the second main royal residence, Queluz, stacking its antiques, porcelain, silverware and any valuables to hand on to yet more coaches. It was here that the other members of the royal family, Dom João's mother, the mad Queen Maria I, his diminutive Spanish wife, Dona Carlota, and their eight children, would join the exodus to the port.

Although the plans had been mulled over for some months, the evacuation quickly fell into disarray, as one courtier described:

'If you looked to one side you could see a mass of belongings lying exposed to the elements; on the other, ornate carriages, waiting for the [royal] family, rode about aimlessly abandoning the protocol usually accorded these occasions, some not wanting

to be separated from their luggage and servants . . . others eager
to get going . . . frightened they were running out of time . . . It
was like this we left Queluz . . .'

As the last carriage pulled out of Queluz's forecourt, what had
once been a hallowed seat of royalty began to take on the air of a
condemned building. From the slow-moving convoy, the
palace receded into the distance, its rain-streaked walls no longer
imposing, the trimmed hedges, intricate topiary, fountains and
statues drained of their symbolic power.

In the city, crowds moved through the maze of alleyways,
down the twisting stairways and narrow lanes which dropped
sheer from the hills to the port below. They accumulated at the
dockyards, where emotions were running high. After months of
covert preparations, goods were now being openly loaded on to
the waiting fleet and dignitaries were making their way through
hostile crowds to embark. Araújo was in a particularly vulnerable
position, well known, as he was, for his French sympathies, and
believed by some to have been conniving with Napoleon all
along. Spotted as he tried to enter the quay, his carriage was
pelted with stones, damaging his cab and wounding his coach-
man. Araújo emerged unscathed and was spirited on to a skiff
which delivered him to the *Medusa*.

Those who were about to be abandoned to the invading
French looked on, incredulous, as the scale of their desertion
became apparent. It was a massive exercise. The royal treasury –
half the coinage circulating in Portugal at the time – and a huge
quantity of Brazilian diamonds took priority. Countless boxes of
government files containing records stretching back hundreds of
years were loaded into the fleet's holds. A new printing press
which had been recently delivered from London was shipped
across to the convoy, still in its original packaging. Araújo's
personal library, an impressive collection accumulated through
his diplomatic travels, was hoisted aboard, while the 60,000-
volume royal library of Ajuda sat crated up on the docks.
Religious paraphernalia, heirlooms and furniture made their
way down from Mafra in the caravan. After long queues to

enter the port, the carriages reached the dockside where a mass of smaller items – trunks of personal belongings, food and bundles of linen – had begun to pile up. Continuing wet weather hampered the operation, the dockside was now saturated and the carriages struggled to carve their way through the mud.

Any hope that the flight might be averted was dispelled on the morning of 27 November, when Dom João himself arrived at the docks, accompanied by the Spanish Infante, Pedro Carlos, a favourite of the prince regent who had grown up in the Portuguese court. On advice from his counsellors who feared violence, the prince regent had travelled down to the port in a nondescript carriage, his driver dressed in street clothes. A farewell speech had been deemed inadvisable in the circumstances and instead the prince regent left behind written instructions as to how the French should be received when they entered the city. They were to be welcomed by a regency assembly – the council of governors – appointed by Dom João, which had strict orders to co-operate with Junot and quarter his troops. The prince regent's exit would be low-key, the boarding itself an unedifying experience for a sovereign used to lavish displays of devotion. Down at the port there were no silk canopies, damask drapes or flower-strewn pathways for the departing monarch, just a rudimentary gangway – a couple of planks of wood, laid across the mud – that led from his carriage to the dockside. Dom João was visibly shaken throughout the ordeal, and was holding back tears as he boarded his skiff in driving rain.

Dom João's wife, Dona Carlota, arrived soon after him in a more conspicuous figure-of-eight carriage with her two sons, Pedro and his six-year-old brother Miguel, along with servants and a wet-nurse for the Infanta Ana de Jesus Maria, at that time a month short of her first birthday. More carriages arrived with her five other daughters: the teenager, Maria Teresa and her siblings, Maria Isabel (ten), Maria Francisca (seven), Isabel Maria (six) and Maria d'Assunção (two).

Next came Dom João's seventy-three-year-old mother, Queen Maria I, a woman who had been insane for well over a decade, and was prone to sudden, irrational outbursts. As her carriage sped towards the docks, she is said to have cried out, 'Don't drive so fast, they'll think we are fleeing!' On arrival at the port, she refused to leave her carriage, forcing the captain of the royal fleet, in a momentary lapse of courtly decorum, to remove her bodily from her cabin, carry her across the quay and bundle her on board the waiting galley. Dom João's sister-in-law, sixty-one-year-old Maria Benedita and his seventy-one-year-old aunt Maria Anna completed the embarkation of three generations of the Bragança dynasty.

Out in the Portuguese countryside, Junot left the main body of his troops behind, abandoned his heavy artillery and made a dash for the capital with his advance guard. His troops were by now caked in mud, their uniforms beginning to disintegrate, limbs exhausted from weeks on the march. Yet their reputation ensured safe passage. Peasants looked on in silence as this unkempt column trudged through waterlogged fields on to-wards Lisbon.

With the news that French forces were just two days' march away, the last semblance of order and organisation in the port evaporated. Eusebio Gomes, the royal storekeeper, was caught up in the thick of it: 'Everyone wanted to board, the docks filled up with boxes, crates, trunks, luggage – a thousand and one things. Many people were left behind on the quay while their belongings were stowed on board; others embarked, only to find that their luggage could not be loaded.' Those with any chance of a berth jostled with officials; unseemly scuffles broke out between minor nobles staking their claims to a place on the already overcrowded fleet.

While many with only tenuous connections to the court and government had managed to force their way on to the fleet in the dying hours, others were not so fortunate. Among them was the sixty-seven-year-old Lourenço de Caleppi, apostolic nuncio of the Palace of Ajuda. He had been promised a place by Dom João, but found his way barred when he could not produce his permit. Bernardo José Farto Pachcco, Master of the King's Horses, was another one left behind on a bureaucratic technicality. A whole troop regiment which was supposed to accompany the court would also stay on in Lisbon as no room could be cleared to accommodate it. For some of these men, this would be a fateful day. They had been destined for the tropics, but would now be dragooned into the French army, and years later freeze to death on the battlefields of Russia.

Joaquim José de Azevedo himself was almost trapped in Lisbon by angry crowds, as he later wrote from Brazil:

'. . . on my return from the Belém docks I was overtaken by a swarm of citizens all speaking at the same time, asking for news of their leader, their prince, their father, and how he could be behind a plan which rebounded so badly on them. I offered official apologies, sincerely protesting that I had no influence over the events, but nothing could placate the crowd . . . Not managing to reach the barracks, I was borne along by the mob; in the middle of the tumult I caught sight of a guard heading outside and asking for his protection I tried to calm the people once more, saying that I was innocent and that I would not be embarking seeing as I had just been named Junot's chief of staff.'

Azevedo was lying. And through this ruse he managed to extricate himself from the mob. He boarded the fleet at midnight, leaving his hat, money and papers behind in his dockside stall.

In the midst of the surge of people, a young boy looked on. Of noble birth, José Trazimundo, the future Marquis of Fronteira, was just five years old when the court left Lisbon. He would stay on in Portugal, but several members of his family would be on the ships to Brazil. Later in life he recalled the emotional turmoil of that day, as families were split and friends separated, some never to be reunited again. 'My aunts immediately sent two carriages for us to be taken without delay to the Belém docks,' remembered Trazimundo, but they found their way blocked by crowds of people, other carriages and by the accumulation of the court's baggage 'virtually abandoned in the road'. 'Hearing a salvo from the squadron, we knew that the

Prince had boarded. My uncle, the Count of Ega, approached our carriages and told us that the squadron was going to raise anchor and try to cross the bar, but that he doubted whether they could succeed because of the stormy weather . . . I will never forget the tears I saw flowing, as many from the people as from the Royal servants and the soldiers who were in Belém square.' Devastated, Trazimundo's family withdrew to the Count of Ribeira's house, where 'the rooms were full of relatives who had shared our misfortune, not having been able to say their final farewells to those emigrating.'

Strangford stole ashore late on the evening of 28 November. 'I learned that the greater part of the Royal Family and of the Portuguese Nobility were already embarked,' he later wrote in a foreign office dispatch to London, 'that the French were in Portugal, and that his Royal Highness was extremely desirous to see me, in order to learn from mine own mouth whether it were the intentions of the English to treat him as a Friend or an Enemy.' He tried to contact Araújo, but found his house bolted and barred. 'Lisbon was in a state of sullen discontent, too dreadful to be described,' his dispatch went on. 'Bodies of armed and unknown persons were seen, roaming the streets, in utter silence, without any lawful or obvious purpose in view; and everything seemed to indicate that the departure of the Prince, if not instantly effected, would be delayed by popular tumults, until rendered impracticable by the actual arrival of the French.' Junot's forces were indeed fast approaching the capital, but a shore wind continued to blow, holding the fleet at anchor. The Portuguese ships, now dangerously overloaded, lurched from side to side. An unspoken fear spread through their decks – the very real possibility of being trapped in the port by the French advance.

Picking his way through the streets, Strangford returned to the docks and boarded the Portuguese ship of the line, the *Príncipe Real*. There, in his own version of events, he found the prince regent still undecided but managed to talk him round. 'Everything depended on the degree of encouragement and consolation offered to His Royal Highness,' wrote Strangford in this, his most controversial dispatch, 'to whose mind it was continually necessary to present the Measure under the most agreeable and captivating forms . . . to destroy all hopes of accommodation with the invaders, terrify him with dark and gloomy descriptions of the capital which I had just left, and then dazzle him suddenly with the brilliant prospects before him . . .' Others present at the scene would later dispute Strangford's testimony. At this late stage a definitive decision had undoubtedly already been made; all was now set to go but the weather was still delaying the departure.

On the morning of 29 November, the winds switched round. At seven o'clock the order was given to weigh anchor. The rains had cleared, and in bright conditions the boats made their way unsteadily down the Tagus towards the open sea. For those left in Lisbon, it was a heartbreaking moment, as José Trazimundo recalled:

'The wind swept in strongly from the bar, and because of this . . . we heard a salvo in the distance. It was from the squadron of the English Admiral Sidney Smith who was saluting the royal flag of the ship carrying the prince regent, and at that moment . . . they left the harbour. Even if, at my young age, I couldn't appreciate the scale of the crisis into which the country and above all the capital was thrown, with the French army two leagues from its gates, I recall being struck by the expressions on the faces of my relatives and those around us.'

The convoy passed close by a Russian fleet which had strayed into the port some time earlier, but whose gunpowder had been confiscated by nervous port authorities. Behind them, the royal squadron left a dismal scene: baggage, sodden papers and abandoned crates lay strewn about the quay side; the churned mud had begun to encrust, leaving an imprint of the recent commotion – a chaos of footprints, divots and swirling lines. Among the debris lay priceless artefacts from the royal patrimony, left behind in the rush to clear the port. Luxury carriages with beautifully maintained harnesses, many still loaded up with valuables that they had transported from the palaces, stood in the empty dock; fourteen carriage-loads of church silver were abandoned to the French and all 60,000 volumes of the royal library of Ajuda sat in the mud. Somewhere in this collection of crates, stacked haphazardly on the dockside, were rare sixteenth-century bibles, parchment maps dating from the 'Age of Discoveries', first editions of Camões's epic, *The Lusíads*, and exquisite illuminated scripts.

TWO

The Journey

We may never know how many had managed to board the fleet, but it seems that around 10,000 people would travel out to Brazil in the first wave – a huge number considering that the population of Lisbon was at the time no more than 200,000. A vast retinue of courtiers – royal surgeons, confessors, ladies-in-waiting, keepers of the king's wardrobe, cooks and pages – was joined by the great and good of Lisbon society – counsellors of state, military advisers, priests, judges and lawyers along with their extended families. From the original nucleus of the court and government functionaries, bribes and the calling in of favours had widened the group to include petty bureaucrats, businessmen, distant relations and assorted hangers-on. Many had never travelled by sea before, some had never left Lisbon.

The royal family itself was divided between four ships. The *Alfonso de Albuquerque* carried Dona Carlota and four of her six daughters. The two middle daughters – Maria Francisca and Isabel Maria – travelled on board the *Rainha de Portugal*, with the lesser members of the royal entourage, Dom João's ageing aunt and sister-in-law, on board the *Príncipe do Brasil*. On the flagship *Príncipe Real* was Dom João, the mad Queen Maria I and the male heirs, Pedro and Miguel – a floating throne room containing the entire line of Bragança succession. If the *Príncipe Real* had gone down in the stormy weather that awaited the fleet, the Portuguese monarchy, so recently saved from certain destruction at the hands of the French, would have met its end on the seas of the North Atlantic.

As the fleet crossed the bar, a twenty-one-gun salute boomed out from the British blockade. It was returned by the relieved captain of the *Príncipe Real* – in spite of Strangford's protestations, there were lingering doubts as to whether the British side of the bargain would be honoured. The *Príncipe Real* manoeuvred its way towards the British flagship, the HMS *Hibernia*. Then Strangford briefly transferred ships, returning to the *Príncipe Real* with Sir Sidney Smith. The mood on board was sombre, according to Strangford: 'It is not possible to describe the situation of these illustrious people, their lack of comfort and the patience and resignation with which they suffer the privations and difficulties arising from the move.' A three-hour conference took place between Smith, Strangford and Dom João in which the details of the voyage were discussed. Four British warships – the HMS *Marlborough*, the HMS *Bedford*, the HMS *London* and the HMS *Monarch* – would join the Portuguese fleet as escorts; the rest, after accompanying the fleet halfway to Madeira, would return to Portugal and resume their blockade of Lisbon. Sir Sidney Smith offered Dom João passage on board one of the British ships, but the prince regent refused, no doubt aware of the message that this would send out to his fellow exiles.

Relief at clearing the bar gave cause for a momentary sense of optimism on board the fleet. Whatever lay ahead, they would be spared the terror of French occupation, a prospect rightly feared by Europeans of the era. Those left behind were feeling its effects even before the first troops arrived in the city; the movements of population that would see Portuguese society buckle under the onslaught of the Peninsular Wars were already under way. Peasants, knowing their stores would be an early target for Junot's soldiers, poured into Lisbon from the rural districts, while others fled in the opposite direction. All waited in trepidation for the arrival of the French.

In the event, initial impressions of the all-conquering French would be disappointing. The first soldiers to enter the city were footsore and weary, some so weak that they had commandeered Portuguese peasants to carry their weapons. 'The state we were in . . . is hardly credible,' remembered Baron Thiébault, who took part in the campaign. 'Our clothing had lost all shape and colour; I had not had a change of linen since Abrantes. My feet were coming through my boots.' The streets of Lisbon were by now empty, and Junot's troops limped into town unopposed. They had arrived at the docks too late even to catch sight of the fleeing convoy. Junot rushed to man the Belém battery tower, but all that was visible was a lone merchant ship that had belatedly decided to quit the port. It was disabled by cannon fire which sliced through its rigging – a derisory prize for the invading French. The sack of the city began immediately. Material left behind on the docks was rummaged through, houses broken into and shops' stores looted, as more hungry, unpaid and undisciplined troops filtered in from the countryside.

Off the coast, the Portuguese convoy merged with its British escorts. Last-minute inspections, repair work, transfers of people and supplies between ships were carried out in anticipation of the long voyage ahead. At dusk the winds reversed. By nightfall they were gale force, blowing the fleet back towards Portugal. The ships were forced to strike out in a north-easterly direction, while their crews dismantled the top sections of the mast and lashed them below. Groups of terrified aristocrats and courtiers huddled together on the decks, their faces pale with anxiety and nausea, their souls already yearning for the country they had left behind.

The gales blew through the night and into the following day, but to general relief the storm abated on 1 December, and the boats regrouped for one last inspection. A small warship was deemed unseaworthy and sent back to Junot's waiting forces in Lisbon; another ship of the line was judged unfit for the Atlantic crossing ahead but, against British advice, continued with the rest of the fleet. A large squadron was to make the trip, consisting of brigs, frigates, ships of the line and merchant vessels, but it was dwarfed once it hit the open seas.

As this miscellaneous collection of ships bobbed up and down in the North Atlantic, Portugal's imperial history was held in suspended animation. The hub of empire had been cut adrift from its metropolis; its seat, following age-old colonial sea routes, was on the move.

The convoy set off, coasting south-westwards towards the Madeiran archipelago, into the cloudbanks of a gathering storm. As the fleet approached the islands, the mists descended and visibility was poor – 'the weather so thick that we could not see three times the ship's length,' wrote Captain James Walker from aboard the HMS *Bedford*. Labouring through the grey haze, the ships swayed on an uncomfortable swell, waves periodically dumping freezing water on to their crowded decks. For the many who had never set foot on board an ocean-going vessel before, these would be testing times. Even veteran sailors of the early nineteenth century feared stormy weather, but they at least had some idea of what to expect. From years of experience, they had become inured to the disorientating instability of a ship on open seas as she ambled up a wave, paused, and then pitched precipitously into the trough beyond. Their ears were by now attuned to the languid creaking of the woodwork, undercut by the more urgent sounds of screeching blocks, winches and wheels. For the uninitiated, though, it was a waking nightmare of whipping winds, sea spray, nausea and collective panic.

Even to the untutored eye, the vessels which had been chosen for the voyage appeared unseaworthy. They leaked copiously, their rigging was ancient, their masts and yards half-rotten. And it was not long before the passengers' fears were confirmed. There were frantic scenes on board the *Medusa* when the mainmast splintered and snapped off. Soon after, the mizzen-mast went down, leaving the ship floundering in heavy seas. The damage was eventually repaired, but confidence was dented. Other ships in the fleet were also forced to make repairs around Madeira. The *Rainha de Portugal*'s main yard broke off and she began losing sight of the other vessels in the fleet; the *Dom João de Castro* also lost her mast and, shipping water, would later be forced to make an emergency landing in the north-east of Brazil.

Even ministers with direct responsibility for the maintenance of
the navy were astonished at how poorly prepared the royal
convoy had been. Antônio de Araújo's report on conditions on
board the *Medusa* was sobering reading for anyone who still had
illusions about the state of Portugal's once great fleet:

> 'The mainmast broke . . . because it was completely rotten; the
> ropes were in disgraceful condition; everything conspired to put
> our lives in danger due to the conduct and the decisions made by
> the commander and some officials. For Your Majesty to have
> some idea of the miserable state of this boat it is enough to say
> that if by chance the servants of José Egidio had not brought
> some sacks of thread to make a piece of fabric we would not have
> had any thread to sew the sails.'

In swirling seas off Madeira, the fleet broke apart. Veils of dense
fog had disorientated the captains and crews alike and when the
air cleared they found themselves in two groups, many miles
adrift. Half the convoy, including the *Príncipe Real* and the
Alfonso de Albuquerque on which the bulk of the royal family
were sailing, had taken evasive action, veering north-west; the
rest emerged from the storm still on course for the agreed
meeting point of San Tiago, a Portuguese island possession in
the Cape Verde group, off the west coast of Africa. The royal
party decided that rather than tack back towards West Africa
they would head straight for Brazil's north-eastern port of
Salvador; the others, after stopping off at San Tiago, would sail
directly to Rio.

On parallel courses they headed south, cutting their way more
confidently through the settling seas. At one point they were
within striking distance – three boats were sighted by the
Bedford, the British escort of the royal group, but light winds
prevented her from investigating further. Instead, after nightfall,
a signal was sent out in the form of a blue lamp placed at the top
of her mast. At close to midnight, according to a log book entry,
a luminous blue speck was spotted on the horizon by the Rio-
bound *Marlborough*. After this cryptic exchange the two fleets

appear to have diverged and thereafter followed their separate paths to Brazil.

With the weather clearing, Dona Carlota paid a visit to the *Príncipe Real* on a gentle mid-Atlantic swell. Braving the open sea, she boarded a skiff with her daughters and went to visit her mother-in-law, Queen Maria I, her husband, Dom João and her sons, Pedro and Miguel, before returning to her vessel. It would be their last contact before Salvador – still, barring further mishaps, five weeks away over a rolling ocean.

Accounts of the crossing are frustratingly incomplete, court memoirs silent on what must have been a traumatic episode for all involved. Even the composition of the fleet is disputed: three (some say five) frigates, two (or perhaps four) brigs and a store ship would accompany the core of the royal squadron – eight sixty-four to eighty-four-gun ships of the line. Sailing with them was a 'crowd of large armed merchant vessels' in Smith's vague formula, or 'several armed brigs, sloops and corvettes, and a number of Brazil ships' in Strangford's, making up 'about thirty-six sail in all'. The four British escorts completed what was, whatever its precise composition, a sizeable navy. The flagship of the Portuguese fleet, the eighty-four-gun *Príncipe Real*, was sixty-seven metres long with a beam of sixteen-and-a-half metres, three gun decks and a spacious hold, yet there was little room to spare. Over a thousand people (perhaps 1,600 according to the highest estimates) are reckoned to have packed her decks. The *Minerva*, which joined the fleet at the very last moment, is thought to have sailed with more than 700 on board. The *Martins de Freitas* took on similar numbers, her passengers crammed in with the substantial cargo that spilled over from the holds.

In one respect, though, the convoy was travelling light. 'The fleet left the Tagus in such haste that very few of the Merchant Vessels are victualled or watered for more than three weeks or a month,' remarked Strangford, 'many of the Armed Ships are in the same condition, and Sir Sidney Smith is of the opinion that the greater part of the convoy must bear up for England, to complete its provisions.' This was not possible – the ships would

make for Brazil with what little they had. A report published on
the eve of departure listed the woeful shortfalls:

> '*Rainha de Portugal* – needs twenty-seven casks of water . . .
> *Frigate Minerva* – has only sixty casks of water . . .
> *Príncipe Real* – needs medicines, chickens, rope, wax, twenty
> barrels of water, tackle and firewood . . .
> *Príncipe do Brasil* – in need of olive oil, wax, rope, thirty barrels of
> water, firewood and tackle'

The shortages began to bite as the weeks wore on. Crates of
linen had been left behind in Lisbon, and most of the women
would cross the Atlantic in the clothes they stood up in. In
desperate cases, British navy sheets and blankets were issued and
fashioned into shapeless garments.

On the *Alfonso de Albuquerque* the miseries were compounded
by a plague of lice which spread through the tightly packed decks.
Nobles cast their infested wigs into the sea and the women, from
Dona Carlota down, lined up to have their heads shaven. Somewhere in the North Atlantic, bald ladies-in-waiting grouped
together on the forecastle after their ordeal. Their scalps were
then bathed and treated with powders to kill off the remaining
lice. It was a ritual humiliation, a theatrical act that summed up the
abrupt transformation that was taking place in the life of the court
as the convoy pushed on towards the New World.

As to day-to-day life on board the fleet during almost two
months at sea, the records are fragmentary. The mid-twentieth-
century chronicler Luiz Edmundo's romantic portraits of men
and women singing songs to the strum of a guitar and playing
cards on moonlit decks sound unconvincing. Another unlikely
story has the nine-year-old heir to the throne, Pedro, revelling
in the experience, scampering around the quarterdeck, helping
the crew to calculate longitude. In this version, the Mafra
librarian Friar Arrábida passes the time teaching the young heir
passages of the *Aeneid*, illustrating his lessons by drawing
parallels between Virgil's epic and Dom João's voyage to the
Americas.

For a more realistic picture, one has to turn to the few surviving primary sources. One, a letter from a Portuguese officer, describes something more akin to life on the Australia-bound convict fleets, the difference being that while the convicts stewed in the holds, many of the Portuguese were forced to brave the open decks:

> '. . . the number of persons who followed the fortune of their royal protectors was so great, and every ship was crowded to such a degree, that there was scarcely room for them to lie down on the deck; the ladies being . . . destitute of any apparel but what they wore. As the ships had but a small proportion of provisions, it was soon found necessary to apply to the British Admiral to admit a number on board his squadron; and fortunate it was for the individuals who were sent, as those who remained were truly objects of pity from Lisbon to Baha [Bahia]. The greater part slept on deck without a bed or any covering. Water was the principal article that claimed our attention; . . . our allowance of it was small, our provisions were of the worst quality, and so scanty . . . that life itself became burthensome. Our situation was so distressing, that I hope none will ever witness or experience. Men, women and children all exhibited a most wretched spectacle: yet Providence, in the midst of our distress granted us one blessing – few felt the effects of illness.'

Another account, anonymous but probably written by someone within the court, does make fleeting references to the emotional state of those on board. People were soon rueing the things they had abandoned in the rush to leave Portugal – 'One had left a teapot behind in Lisbon which made the best tea in the world; another had forgotten to bring a chest which contained many very important belongings.' From these small anxieties, frustrations boiled over, 'and it was concluded that the voyage had been very badly planned, and that they should have been given more time and the great number of ships which stayed in the Tagus should have been readied as transports.' In amongst the carping and backbiting, Dom João remained calm: '. . . His

Royal Highness had a heroic bearing,' continued the anonymous chronicler, 'a serenity that none of his vassals could emulate; his suffering was only revealed to a couple of his closest servants.' Yet such was the mood of recrimination that Dom João imposed a rule of silence, forbidding any complaints or discussion of the rights and wrongs of the decision to quit Lisbon. Thereafter, the anonymous chronicle concludes sardonically, the sea remained their only talking point.

A final anecdote reveals the tensions on board a fleet packed with politicians and nobles, as a struggle for power broke out on the high seas. Scattered across the decks of the Brazil-bound fleet, men jockeyed for position in this brief, liminal period which separated the old administration from the new. One of the key players was Dom Rodrigo de Sousa Coutinho, the Count of Linhares, who was travelling in the Rio-bound convoy. Stocky, with curly hair and a complexion so dark that many suspected that he had African ancestry, Sousa Coutinho had served a long career at court. After working as a diplomat in Italy, he had returned to Portugal determined to rebuild the languishing Portuguese navy, but he had ended up being sidelined in the years before the exile for his pro-British outlook.

On the Atlantic he sensed his opportunity. Sousa Coutinho's chief rival in the court, Antônio de Araújo, was disgraced, his policy of appeasing the French discredited. With Araújo out of the way, Sousa Coutinho looked forward to Rio with relish, eyeing up a ministerial position of influence at the right hand of the prince regent. As they crossed the equator, one of the passengers on board Sousa Coutinho's ship was taken ill with the beginnings of scurvy, his legs swelling up in the heat. The ship was running dangerously low on supplies and the sick passenger's family pleaded with the captain to change course and make for Salvador, where they could re-provision and seek medical help. Hearing of the possible diversion, Sousa Coutinho pulled rank. After a heated argument in which he insulted the family 'in the most violent terms' he forced the captain to hold his course. It is not known what happened to the ailing passenger, but in the end, Sousa Coutinho need not have worried about being beaten in the race to Rio. He would dock in the capital almost two months before Araújo, whose battered ship the *Medusa* lost its way on the equator and ended up becalmed off the Pernambucan coast.

For the most part, though, the historical record gives us little idea of the thoughts and experiences of the Portuguese royal family and their army of attendants in the long weeks spent inching their way across the Atlantic. One is left to imagine the smells that wafted up from the bilges – the columns of putrid air rising through the hatches of ships that, in many cases, had not been serviced in years; the long queues to use the 'heads', a platform fastened to the bow, suspended over the ship's wake, that served as an open-air toilet; the boredom, the shame and anguish of those who had forsaken their friends and family in their hour of need. Accommodations would have been primitive, privacy nonexistent, sleep difficult if not impossible on the open deck, with sea spray regularly showering over the rows of nobles stretched out on the timbers. And during the day, the constant roll of the vessels would have subjected respected courtiers to the indignity of public bouts of seasickness.

The voyage was reminiscent of that other, smaller-scale royal flight, when Nelson had overseen the evacuation of the king and queen of Naples ahead of a French invasion eight years earlier. Then, the *Vanguard*, stashed with gold and jewels and crowded with royalty, braved stormy seas off Naples. The weather was as bad as anything Nelson could remember. Two days into the voyage, the *Vanguard*'s topsails were in tatters. The king's confessor broke his arm when he was thrown from his hammock, while courtiers vomited over the sides. But the comparison falls well short – the *Vanguard* headed a small fleet and reached the refuge of Palermo in less than a week, the trial a brief, if unpleasant interlude.

The Portuguese, in contrast, had endured six weeks of shipboard life on the open sea, before dropping down into the doldrums and beginning the run in to Salvador. The convoy slowed to a worrying pace – in ten days it covered just thirty leagues, a day's journey in good conditions – but the

winds picked up again as they approached Brazil and for the first
time spirits began to lift. A brigantine, sent out from Recife,
was spotted in the distance, and when it hove to it was found to
be carrying much needed provisions, among the more mundane items, a selection of tropical fruits. The ship had been
dispatched by the governor of the north-eastern province of
Pernambuco after he had been alerted to the fleet's likely
position by the captain of the *Medusa*, already languishing in
Recife for repairs. Somewhere off the coast of Brazil, palates
dulled by more than a month of sea biscuit and rice rations
savoured the exotic flavours of *cajú* and *pitanga*, foretastes of
their future home.

Days later, from the decks of the fleet a low coastal outline
shimmered in the distance, its form tinged with deep green hues
of tropical foliage. Closing in on the port, a colonial city
emerged from the blur, with its red roof tiles and whitewashed
walls. Silhouettes of palm trees dotted the hilltops, and columns
of agricultural land – cane fields, tobacco plantations and citrus
groves – undulated into the distance. Chill November winds had
given way to the superheated air of equatorial Brazil. More than
seven weeks and 4,000 miles after they had escaped Lisbon, they
were approaching journey's end.

The vagaries of the weather and demands of a poorly equipped
navy had delivered the royal family more than seven hundred
miles north of its intended target. The original convoy had
found itself scattered along Brazil's vast coastline – some ships
had landed even further up the coast from Salvador, only a small
number successfully reaching Rio. There was, however, an
historical symmetry to the outcome, for the prince regent's
route roughly followed that of the earliest Portuguese voyage to
Brazil, and he would soon be disembarking just a little to the
north of the founding scene of Portugal's colonisation of Brazil.

On 9 March 1500, over three centuries before the royal
family's hurried exodus from Lisbon, thirteen ships under the
command of the aristocrat Pedro Álvares Cabral made a more
orderly departure, slipping down the Tagus and spilling out into

the open sea. The voyage was a follow-up to Vasco da Gama's historic journey to India (1497–1499), which had arrived back to a rapturous welcome the year before. Cabral was instructed to retrace da Gama's pioneering route around the Cape to India, but whether through miscalculation or intention, he would end up brushing the Brazilian coast on the way through.

The expedition began inauspiciously. Two weeks into the voyage, one of Cabral's ships disappeared 'without there being strong or adverse weather conditions for it to have happened'. The captain trawled the immediate area, but found nothing. The tragedy was unsettling, perhaps more so, in an understated way, than the trauma of a shipwreck in a raging storm. One hundred and fifty men had vanished, swallowed by calms somewhere off Africa.

Once on the equator, Cabral left the coast, swinging round into the South Atlantic in order to get on the prevailing winds to clear the Cape of Good Hope, but, pulled by transatlantic currents, the fleet drifted much further west than da Gama's original route. Some way out Cabral's fleet came across 'a great quantity of those long seaweeds sailors call "*botelho*"'. The following morning, there were 'birds they call "belly-rippers"'. Later that day, at around vespers, they sighted land.

On board, Pero Vaz de Caminha, a royal scribe, set down in a letter to the king what historian Capistrano de Abreu has called 'the birth certificate of Brazil'. Shorn of its colonial overtones which, with the benefit of hindsight, it is difficult not to impose, the letter depicts an earthy encounter, full of ignorance and misunderstandings on both sides, but devoid of malice. It is a strange document. In the main it is a detailed, often repetitive description, a setting down of the record, but beneath the surface Caminha's humanity broods, his own hopes and curiosity tempered by the sense of religious mission that all these early voyages shared.

Anchored just offshore, one of the ships' captains, Nicolau Coelho, a veteran of da Gama's voyage, was sent by Cabral to explore the beach and river. Tupi natives appeared 'in groups of twos and threes' and began gathering on the beach. Coelho tried to speak to them, but was drowned out by the sound of breaking waves. So, 'He merely threw them a red cap and a linen bonnet he had on his head, and a black hat. And one of them threw him a hat of large feathers with a small crown of red and grey feathers, like a parrot's. Another gave him a large bough covered with white beads which looked like seed-pearls.'

Dragged off their original anchorage, they sailed ten leagues up the coast in search of more secure moorings. The pilot, Afonso Lopes, was sent to take soundings inside a cove. He returned with two natives who were taken on board the flagship to be received by the admiral. They were treated to a medieval court reception: 'the admiral was seated on a chair, with a carpet at his feet instead of a dais. He was finely dressed, with a big golden collar around his neck . . . Torches were lit. They [the natives] entered. However, they made no gesture of courtesy or sign of a wish to speak to the admiral or anyone else.' Instead, they stared in fascination at the articles of gold and silver they saw, and, according to the Portuguese, fixated as they were with precious metals, pointed to the land to tell them there was gold and silver there.

What followed was pantomime:

'We showed them a ram, but they took no notice of it. We showed them a hen, and they were almost afraid of it and did not want to take it into their hands; finally they did, but as if alarmed by it. We gave them things to eat: bread, boiled fish, comfits, sweetmeats, cakes, honey, dried figs. They would eat hardly anything of all this, they spat it out at once. We brought them wine in a cup; they merely sipped it, but they did not like it at all and did not want any more of it.'

Finally they lay down on the carpet to rest. The admiral provided a pillow and a cloak: 'They consented to this, pulled it over themselves and slept.' The Portuguese spent little more than a week off the coast of Brazil. In that short period, they left their cultural mark on what they then called the Island of the True Cross (*Ilha de Vera Cruz*). Rounding off their visit, they staged what has become the iconic scene of the birth of the modern Brazilian colonial project. They planted a wooden cross, set out an altar on the beach, and to the rustle of coconut palms swaying in a warm sea breeze, said mass to a mixed congregation of sailors and natives.

The cross was made by two carpenters. While they worked, they were surrounded by natives captivated not by the Christian symbol itself, but by the iron tools that were being used to fashion it. The admiral marked a place in the sand and a pit was dug. Helped by natives, the cross was borne along the beach to its foundation place. Afterwards the Tupis sat uncomprehending through the mass. At the end of the sermon they were issued with tin crucifixes, leftovers from Vasco da Gama's voyage east: 'Many came for this. All who came, some forty or fifty, had crucifixes hung round their necks.'

Little genuine communication could have occurred between the Portuguese and the natives on this first, brief encounter. Caminha was nevertheless fascinated by the Tupi; his short letter contains detailed descriptions of them, their elaborate body decoration and their easy nakedness. He describes their lip plugs, the inner part of which was made 'like a rook in chess', and their bodies, which were coloured with vegetable dyes of vivid reds and blacks. He notes their extravagant feather headdresses and their hair, which was cut to a certain length and shaved above the ears. He makes repeated references to the women's 'tightly knit', 'well raised' and 'comely' genitalia. He wonders at their lack of shame, but in the last instance is embarrassed by it. At the final mass they throw a shirt around a woman to cover her nakedness, 'But she did not pull it down to cover herself when she sat down.'

Two convicts who had been condemned to death in Lisbon were left behind to learn the natives' language and ways. They were not wanted by the natives, who tried on several occasions to deliver them back to the Portuguese. Nor did the convicts wish to stay. When the fleet readied itself to leave they began to weep at their terrible fate, being left in a faraway land they knew nothing about. While preparations for the onward voyage were finalised, it was decided to send one of the ships back to Portugal with Caminha's letter. Caminha himself sailed on to India with the rest of the fleet, surviving a horrendous passage around the Cape in which several ships were lost. In Calicut he continued to work as a scribe, but he would not live to embroider on his experiences in Brazil. He perished fulfilling another role, as a foot soldier of the empire, on a battlefield in India.

His letter lived on only to suffer years of neglect, buried in Lisbon's labyrinthine archives. In the eighteenth century it resurfaced, but remained in obscurity, available to a handful of royal archivists and top government officials. There is some evidence that Caminha's letter made the return trip to Brazil in the holds of the royal family's fleeing convoy. Whether, three centuries after it was penned, it was actually there, coasting towards Salvador's harbour, in amongst the archives which had been stacked on board in the panic of the final days in Lisbon, we may never know.

There was a degree of trepidation on board as the royal fleet neared its destination. No reconnaissance vessel had been sent ahead and it was uncertain what impact the sudden arrival of the royal family would have in the colony. The exiles had expected crowds of well-wishers but the docks appeared empty as the ships entered the bay of Salvador. All they saw was a lone official – the governor – who stood on the dockside in an otherwise deserted port. As the Crown's colonial representative, he was about to preside over an unprecedented event for the times: the reception of a royal family in a colonial outpost, thousands of miles from the courts of Europe. He had been given no forewarning of this historic event and was evidently confused as to what the appropriate course of action should be. On boarding the *Príncipe Real*, he told the prince regent that it was he who had cleared the streets around the docks, unsure of the regent's desires. In response, Dom João said that he wished to see his New World vassals, and after the word was passed around, the streets slowly filled with curious onlookers.

As the fleet dropped anchor on 22 January 1808, an air of unreality descended over the bay area. For both those on board and the crowds that were gathering at the docks, this was an unexpected and somewhat bizarre event. The royal family and the elite of the mother country – remote figures of authority to all but the upper echelons of Brazilian society – had arrived out of the blue. And confounding all expectations they had arrived in a fleet in far worse shape than some of the shabby merchant vessels that docked in this normally busy port. Even more astonishing, there were requests for women's clothing to be brought on board to relieve passengers dressed in the tattered remnants of the outfits they had left Lisbon in, or draped in makeshift garments.

Something of the mystery of colonial power was destroyed for ever on that day. The almost religious regard in which royalty was held was also momentarily shaken. Those already exposed to the revolutionary ideas then sweeping through Europe and the Americas had pause for thought watching these high-class refugees arriving destitute in one of their own colonies.

Salvador was then the most populous city in the Portuguese Empire and in certain respects familiar to the *émigrés* – dual-levelled, similar in layout to Oporto, or to a lesser extent Lisbon itself. Its upper level was connected to the trade port by a counterpoise pulley system which hauled goods to and fro, and by steep tracks winding their way up the sixty-metre escarpment. Opulent churches, convents and administrative buildings were scattered around the city's hilltops, while a network of narrow streets wound its way around the port area below. This arrangement was a favourite around the empire – Macao, Luanda (Angola), Olinda (in Recife) and Rio de Janeiro were likewise situated on uneven terrain in what had been a medieval strategy of building fortified hill towns. Unlike the grids that had spread out through urban Spanish America, the typical Brazilian city had a random quality to it.

In other ways, though, Salvador was unsettling for those arriving from Europe, for the city lay at the crossroads of Portugal's transcontinental trade network. Its position at the tail end of the *carreira da Índia*, the round trip from Lisbon to Goa, had brought contact with the East. Although not permitted to trade *en route*, ships docked illegally on the way back from India to offload their wares. More markedly, the slave trade had bound West Africa and Bahia so intimately that in many ways Salvador was more an African city than a European one. A largely black and mulatto population peopled its streets. The smell of palm oil wafted from food vendors – bulky Afro-Brazilian women wearing turbans and swathed in white dresses – who lined the port. Street traders filled the lower city, balancing trays of sweets, fried fish or fruits on their heads. The wealthy circulated on litters borne by slaves, a practice picked up from the decadent days of early empire in the East. Salvador's hustle and bustle spoke of the city's historic role as a tropical clearing house – 'the port of Brazil', as it had once been known – sucking in slaves from Africa and sending out the products of their labour to Europe: sugar, tobacco and agricultural produce.

A subtle change of accent had developed, the broader, more open sounds of Brazilian Portuguese already diverging from the clipped speech of the mother country; an equatorial casualness smoothed over the rhythm of daily life. For those emerging from the beginnings of a European winter, the light was intense, broken only by the shade of mango trees, banana stands and coconut palms which sprouted from unpaved streets and squares. Light reflected off the familiar whitewashed walls and tiled façades of Portuguese architecture, but even the city's buildings were not quite what they would have been back in Lisbon; oriental latticework verandas were grafted on to the fronts of the houses, another influence from Portuguese India. It was, in reality, an eclectic landscape, an agglomeration of people, habits and foliage from around the empire.

After a day at anchor the royal family set foot on Brazilian soil for the first time. They stepped ashore to a rousing reception – the city's notables, its planters, even groups of slaves lined the streets, cheering on their unexpected guests. All were awed by what was a unique event in the history of European colonialism. Up until that point no reigning monarch had ever travelled to the Americas even to visit, let alone set up court there. The novelty value was compounded by the first sighting of Dona Carlota, an unusual looking woman at the best of times. She was short (under five feet) with dark Andalusian features, and on this occasion wore a curious turban to cover her shaved scalp. More of the court's women emerged into the light, sporting similar turbans, to the astonishment of the gathering crowds. Courtiers and their servants followed them out into the humid air, trussed up in fitted jackets, knee breeches and stockings.

It is hard to imagine what the royal family made of Salvador on that clear, breezy afternoon. They could, at least, be guided by hastily improvised royal protocol as they were welcomed by the city's viceregal representatives. The prince regent's first engagement was a *Te Deum* mass in the main cathedral. A group of Bahian musicians led the congregation through a litany of sacred music sung in Latin verse while the priest officiated at the first of the countless religious ceremonies that the royal family would attend in Brazil.

Four thousand miles away, out off the coast of Lisbon, the British blockade was still in place, their mission to starve Junot's forces out of Lisbon, irrespective of the effects on the capital's residents. Junot had styled himself as a liberator, proclaiming 'roads shall be opened, canals shall be dug to facilitate communications and render agriculture and industry flourishing', with the Portuguese army forming 'one single family with the soldiers of Marengo, Austerlitz, Jena and Friedland'. The reality, though, was quite different. French flags hung in the deserted streets, the port was a ghost town of empty warehouses and windswept quays. Shortages of all kinds menaced everyday life, the looting which had begun as French troops entered the city continuing to deplete the city's stores. Junot had imposed hefty indemnity payments and introduced further taxes to squeeze yet more from the population. Europe's oldest state had been dismissively broken up, laid waste by Spanish and French troops.

For those left behind in Portugal the prospects looked bleak. The remnants of the court and government who had not managed to find a place aboard the fleet were left destitute.

Some resorted to writing begging letters to Brazil for financial assistance for themselves and their families, but would receive no reply. Others ended up collaborating with the French – the Marquis of Marialva even heading a high-level delegation to Paris. With the British in control of the offshore waters, escape by sea was relatively easy, and many took up the option. If they could reach Britain they were offered free passage to Brazil, and in time crowds of Portuguese gathered in Plymouth awaiting outward bound shipping for the New World. Dom Domingos de Sousa Coutinho (Dom Rodrigo's brother), the Portuguese ambassador to Britain, found himself overwhelmed by the response, writing to the court in Brazil: 'Such a large number of people have come that I don't know how I can help them, because most of them have arrived with absolutely nothing, almost naked.' Even as the royal family disembarked in Salvador, hundreds more were already on their way to join them.

Lord Strangford was by now back in London, claiming credit for the success of the Lisbon operation, but not everyone was convinced by his version of events. In a dispute that would rumble on for the next thirty years, questions were asked about exactly how crucial Strangford's role in the evacuation had been. While Strangford tried to defend himself in the press, Lord Brougham wrote to Earl Grey Albany of his scepticism:

> 'Respecting the Lisbon business, Strangford complains bitterly that they have garbled his dispatch; but while he says this to me, and one or two others, who are likely to know the truth, as an excuse for the bragging which appears in his letter [to the press], he tells people whom he thinks he can take in, that if the whole dispatch had been published, it would appear how much more concern he had in the transaction.'

The position would get much worse for Strangford, with accusations that he had doctored the evidence, that the crucial dispatch from aboard the HMS *Hibernia* had actually been written at a later date in Canning's London office. Captain Graham Moore, commander of one of the British escorts, was suspicious, remarking some time later – 'I have . . . a perfect recollection of the surprise which everybody at Rio de Janeiro felt when the dispatch signed Strangford, and dated "His Majesty's ship Hibernia, off the Tagus, November 29 1807" appeared there.' The case would eventually end up in court (and be dismissed) but the controversy did not affect the steady progress of Strangford's diplomatic career. To the astonishment of Lord Brougham, he was appointed as the British envoy to the Portuguese court in Brazil. 'Everyone is agreed that the choice of a minister for Brazil is of infinite moment,' wrote Lord Brougham, 'and could not have been worse made. It is conceived that Strangford has been appointed in order to give *éclat* to the management of the affair on our part and to make the country think we did the business.'

Strangford would not arrive in Brazil until the middle of 1808, giving the Portuguese court valuable breathing space in their first months in Brazil. For a brief period, Dom João and his advisers were freed from the diplomatic pressures of the European superpowers, as they came to grips with their new life in the tropics.

THREE

The Lisbon Court

Arrival in the New World signalled a great upheaval for the Portuguese royal family, but its emotional dynamics would survive the Atlantic intact. An eccentric, dysfunctional family would soon be setting up in Brazil, their internal battles recommencing on a new continent. At first glance, the Braganças appear to be almost caricatures of European royalty of the age: the mad queen Maria I in perpetual mourning, the ineffectual prince regent Dom João, a man who, as a second son, was never meant to rule, and his scheming wife, Dona Carlota. Dig deeper into their histories, though, and one finds a family mired in unhappiness, distrust and frustration, fragmenting under the strains of the Napoleonic era.

At the core of the Portuguese royal family's problems was a marriage mismatch so disastrous that at times its consequences would spill over into the public realm. Dona Carlota had been drafted in to wed the then eighteen-year-old Dom João in 1785, at the age of just ten. Sealed for reasons of state, the union continued a tradition of intermarriage between the Spanish and Portuguese courts – seen as a way of cementing alliances with Portugal's more powerful neighbour. Even while still a child, though, Dona Carlota took a visceral dislike to her new husband. At the time of their wedding, in an incident that would set the tone for the next forty years, Dona Carlota bit Dom João viciously on the ear.

The move from her native Spain to Portugal was clearly traumatic for the young Carlota. When she arrived in Lisbon she spoke little Portuguese, and was the only child in what was an ageing court. The early years prompted a catalogue of complaints from her maidservant, Dona Anna Miquelina, who relayed her concerns in letters back to the court in Madrid. 'She doesn't do what she's told,' wrote Dona Anna. She got up late and 'took an age to get dressed', throwing tantrums because of 'clothes that were too tight or shoes that she didn't want to wear'. At the dinner table, she was disruptive, 'picking up food in her hands' or 'throwing food at the face of the Infante [Dom João] and at the servants'. Her teacher, Father Filipe, despaired of her un-cooperativeness when she spent 'two or three hours without saying a word' during his lessons. On one occasion she scandalised the Queen's confessor and Father Filipe when she yanked up the skirts of her servants.

Only her mother-in-law, Queen Maria I, at this time in full possession of her faculties, seemed able to handle the child. Each time she was out of control, Queen Maria would be called in to discipline her, the most effective strategy apparently being to tell her that if she didn't behave, she would not be allowed to go on her donkey ride. Before her mental decline, Queen Maria developed an intimate relationship with the young Carlota, spending time with her, taking her on outings to convents, churches and to the thermal springs of the spa town Caldas. The girl became an emotional substitute for her own daughter, Dona Maria Ana Victória, who had been married off into the Spanish court in exchange for Dona Carlota. 'Our beloved Carlota pleases me greatly for her good qualities and up till now has adapted well, thank God,' she wrote somewhat disingenuously to her counterpart, King Carlos III in Madrid (Dona Carlota's grandfather), 'making the separation from my daughter easier for me.'

In the early years, Dom João, a gauche and none-too-robust youth, played the role of an older brother. He tried to look after his unruly child bride, admonishing her when she was late for official engagements and complaining when she behaved badly in front of him. He wrote of his concern for Carlota, when, in events that would repeat themselves somewhere on the Atlantic twenty years later, her hair had to be shorn off after an infestation of head lice. At first he was impressed by her precocity, writing to his sister, '. . . she is very clever and has a lot of common sense for one who is still little', and surprised by her extrovert nature – she was 'very uninhibited' he wrote in another letter, 'without any shame whatsoever'. But later Dom João would learn to dread Dona Carlota's irrepressible personality.

From an early age, Dona Carlota was in character. As a child she strove to be the centre of attention, developing what would be her lifelong passions – Andalusian dance and riding. By early adolescence she was wearing the extravagant clothes and jewellery that would become her trademark. Dona Carlota the woman is nevertheless hard to pin down. So mired in controversy was she to become that even physical descriptions are varied and inconsistent. By turns exoticised and vilified, she bore the brunt of both anti-colonial abuse from Brazil and liberal hatred from Portugal. She was branded the 'witch of Cordoba', the 'Marie Antoinette' of the Lisbon court, the adulteress, but mostly, the conspirator.

Two famous and oft-quoted portrayals, both written by foreigners, span the spectrum of opinion about Dona Carlota: those of the British aristocrat, poet and travel writer, William Beckford and Junot's wife, the Duchess D'Abrantès. Beckford claims to have met Dona Carlota when she was nineteen, in a chance encounter in the gardens of Queluz palace. He had come for an audience with Dom João, but on arrival was invited to see 'the curious birds and flowers last sent from the Brazils' in the palace's grounds. 'The evening was now drawing towards its final close, and the groves, pavilions, and aviaries sinking apace into shadow . . . Cascades and fountains were in full play; a thousand sportive *jets d'eau* were sprinkling the rich masses of bay and citron, and drawing forth all their odours . . .' Intoxicated by his surroundings, Beckford spied Dona Carlota's entourage 'amongst the thickets', arranged in an early-nineteenth-century erotic tableau: 'the Infanta's nymph-like attendants, all thinly clad after the example of her royal and nimble self, were glancing to and fro, visible one instant, invisible the next, laughing and talking all the while with very musical and silver toned voices.'

The Marquis of Marialva appeared and told Beckford that Dona Carlota wished to see him, and there, in the gardens, he was introduced to the infamous princess. 'We sprang forwards . . . to an amphitheatre of verdure concealed in the deepest recess of the odiferous thickets, where, seated in the oriental fashion on a rich carpet spread on the grass, I beheld the Alcina of the place, surrounded by thirty or forty young women, everyone far superior in loveliness of feature and fascination of smile to their august mistress.' The narrative continues in the same vein, with Dona Carlota playfully ordering Beckford to race her Spanish girls to the end of the avenue, then to dance the bolero with an Andalusian attendant. This is the exotic Dona Carlota, the sensualist, the head of a flamboyant, Moorish-Iberian court-within-a-court and a woman already attracting comment, malicious or otherwise. 'Reports . . .' wrote Beckford 'had been flying about, numerous as butterflies, some dark-coloured, like the wings of the dead-moth, and some brilliant and gay, like those of the fritillaria.'

At the other end of the scale come the lengthy descriptions of Dona Carlota's physical appearance in the memoirs of the Duchess D'Abrantès. She came to Lisbon as the wife of General Andoche Junot, who served as French ambassador to the court in 1805, two years before he would lead the invasion force. The Duchess D'Abrantès was dismayed by the backwardness of the Portuguese court, put out by its old-fashioned etiquette which meant she had to buy a hooped dress to wear on formal occasions. She was appalled too at the sight of the royal couple. Her gossipy, often spiteful memoirs described Dona Carlota, now thirty years old, as a virtual freak-show exhibit – 'the most hideous specimen of ugliness' – with her dwarf-like appearance, her asymmetrical body (one of Dona Carlota's legs was shorter than the other as a result of a hunting accident) and her 'chest all awry'. She had, according to the Duchess, 'blood-shot eyes', '*vegetable* skin' and coarse, frizzy, 'dirty looking' hair. The Duchess was more impressed with Dona Carlota's clothes, marvelling at the fine India muslin, embroidered with gold and silver lamé, set off with ravishing pearls and diamonds, only to conclude damningly:

'The exquisite beauty of these jewels, combined with the extreme ugliness of the person who wore them, produc[ed] an indescribably strange effect, and made the princess look like a being scarcely belonging to our species'. And it was not just her appearance that disturbed the Duchess. She was shocked by the fact that Dona Carlota rode astride in mannish hunting garb, and registered her amazement that: 'When I entered the Princess of Brazil's [Dona Carlota's] drawing room, all the *dames of honour* were seated – guess, reader, where? On the floor! yes! on the floor! with their legs crossed under them, like tailors, or rather like Arabs, who have bequeathed this among the many other customs they have left to the Peninsula.'

The Duchess D'Abrantès's memoirs are the work of a snobbish high-society woman looking down on a provincial court, and Dona Carlota is by no means the only target of her caricatures. The endurance of the Duchess's lurid sketches, which have been uncritically reproduced in many Portuguese, Brazilian and English histories of the period, bears testimony to strength of feeling against Dona Carlota as an historical figure. Portraits of Dona Carlota are themselves varied. Some seem scarcely to be depicting the same woman, but none match the Duchess's baroque descriptions. Dona Carlota was certainly no beauty, and she was odd-looking, with an angular, almost masculine face, her stature marking her out in any crowd. Her flamboyant dress sense survives in a number of canvases, most famously the French artist Jean-Baptiste Debret's plate engraved in Brazil, in which Dona Carlota appears as a kind of early-nineteenth-century Carmen Miranda, bedecked as she is in an exuberant headpiece of jewels and feathers.

Perhaps this uneven iconography was appropriate for a woman of such contradictions. Passionate, poetic, with a sense of the theatrical, she could also be crude and vindictive. There was something driven about her. Politically, she was self-taught, her wide-ranging private library including works on Spanish colonial affairs, the French Revolution and Portuguese history, along with the theoretical writings of Rousseau, Chateaubriand and Condorcet. Yet she was confined to a role she would never be at ease with, as a royal consort, and a mother of the nine children that she bore (one of whom died in infancy) over a thirteen-year stretch of pregnancies. From the outset she rebelled against her situation, trying to carve out a position of power for herself within the Portuguese and Spanish courts.

While the Duchess D'Abrantès's descriptions do at least have a certain immediacy, Beckford's surreal account of his meeting with Dona Carlota was written forty years after the event, and is in all probability the romantic fantasy of an ageing *artiste manqué*. But Beckford lived for long periods in Portugal, visiting the court around this time (a year later than he claims in this account, in fact) and much of the rest of his memoir rings true. He described a rundown, bucolic country, picking out on the way to the palace a 'neglected quinta of orange trees with its decaying garden house' and 'a half-ruined windmill, with its tattered vans, revolving lackadaisically'. The court itself he found antiquated, the palace a dark, empty, mausoleum-like place, full of dismal servants. 'The beings who wandered about this limbo,' wrote Beckford, 'belonged chiefly to that species of living furniture which encumber royal palaces – walking chairs, animated screens, commodes and conveniences, to be used by sovereigns in any manner they like best . . . weather-beaten equerries, superannuated *véadors* [chamberlains], and wizened pages. The whole party were yawning over dusty card tables.'

Beckford met with the then twenty-seven-year-old Dom João, an affable man with a sense of humour, who, speaking Portuguese with a 'purity and elegance' and perfect diction, told him: 'Every dispatch from France brings us such frightful in-telligence, that I am lost in amazement and horror; the ship of state in every country in Europe is labouring under a heavy torment – God alone can tell upon what shore we shall be all drifted.' On his way out, Beckford came across another room filled with 'fifteen or twenty unhappy aspirants to court benefits still loitering and lingering about'. 'The sovereign, in their eyes, was chance personified;' explained Beckford, 'his decrees for or against you, modestly styled *avisos*, were pieces of advice to the judicial obeyers of his commands, which, if once obtained, were never slighted. Most of the victims of this system at this time in this great hall assembled, appeared visibly suffering under the sickness of hope deferred.' There were, indeed, many caught up in what was an impossibly centralised, absolutist system. The monarch's word was all-powerful, and Dom João, as regent, spent the bulk of his time listening to petitions for legal redress, money or jobs.

At the time of Beckford's visit (1795), the court was already well into its downward spiral that would end in November 1807, on the docks of Lisbon. In 1788, Dom João's older brother, Dom José, who for years had been groomed for the throne, died suddenly of smallpox at the age of twenty-seven. A year later, the French Revolution spread fear through Europe's royal families, and set in train events that would culminate in their complete loss of legitimacy in the Napoleonic era. The revolution broke out when Dona Carlota was fourteen, and through her teens she would follow the humiliation and even-tual execution of her Bourbon cousin, Louis XVI.

The early 1790s saw the confirmation of Queen Maria I's mental decline, made public by a hysterical outbreak one evening during a performance at the theatre in Lisbon. The first cracks in her sanity had come when she was forty-seven years old and related to a ruling in which several courtiers were cleared of involvement in an attempted assassination of Dona Maria's father, Dom José I, over twenty years before. Dona Maria was upset by the decision and at first refused to sign the edict, but was talked around by her confessor, the Bishop of Algarve. After signing, Dona Maria screamed that she was condemned to hell, and had to be carried to her apartments in a fit of hysteria. Over the next few years, a string of events loosened her grip on reality. She was devastated by the loss of her husband (and uncle, the younger brother of Dom José I), Dom Pedro (1786). Two years later, she suffered extreme guilt over the death of her first son, Dom José, whom she had refused to vaccinate against the smallpox that killed him. While she was still in mourning, the French Revolu-tion broke out, provoking bouts of paranoia. Whatever the causes of her insanity, Dom João, who had grown up a minor royal, second in line to the throne, was now forced to unofficially take the reins, as work went on behind the scenes to find a cure for the queen's increasingly erratic behaviour.

While Britain's George III would talk continuously for nineteen hours, bolt his food, and slip into prolonged bouts of melancholy, Dona Maria I's affliction had a more religious bent. Her outbursts were at first short and explosive – she broke icons, insulted her confessors and developed a terror of crucifixes and holy places. There were repeated visions of the devil lurking in every corner, and what was described at the time as a 'conviction that she was irrevocably doomed to everlasting perdition'. The religious manias were spiced with eccentric behaviour – 'she eats barley and oyster stew on Fridays and Saturdays,' wrote Beckford, 'and indulges in conversation of a rather unchaste nature.' Her spells of melancholia cloaked Lisbon itself in depression – royal festivities were banned and state visits became austere, almost religious occasions. In February 1792, the prime minister, Luís Pinto, was forced to write to his envoy in London:

'I have the displeasure to tell you that Her Majesty is now suffering from a melancholic affliction which has degenerated into insanity and is reaching the stage of a frenzy. This sad situation made me think that perhaps it would be useful for Dr Willis, the principal doctor who assisted His British Majesty in analogous circumstances, to come to this court as soon as possible.'

Dr Francis Willis, a physician who, as part of the Willis clan of doctors, had become famous for his sporadically successful treatment of George III, did make the trip to Portugal to administer to the queen. He is said to have been paid £20,000 – a staggering sum for the times – but struggled with his new patient. It seemed that Maria I's religious mania was immune to 'scientific' cures, a belief that she herself held: 'Her Majesty has frequently exclaimed, in the paroxysms of her disorder,' reported one contemporary source, 'that a skilful physician might occasionally cure madness, but could never reverse the decrees of heaven.' In the end, Dr Willis proposed taking Queen Maria back to England for further treatment, styling the voyage as a therapeutic sea journey, but his suggestion was turned down.

Dr Willis was not the only Englishman intent on curing the queen, whose condition became well known throughout Europe. Dr James Graham, the self-styled 'Conqueror, under God, of Diseases' who advocated 'earth-bathing' as a universal cleanser and healer, also made the journey out to Portugal. Graham had written a treatise on health for the court of George III, but had remained on the fringes of early-nineteenth-century psychiatric medicine. He may well have been less than fully sane himself – he claimed that he had been ordered in a vision to undertake the journey to Portugal. A fellow passenger spotted him in the fourth mess room on the Lisbon-bound ship and described him as 'either madly or hypocritically religious . . . He lives upon vegetables, Milk, Honey & Water, & reads from the bible from morning to night . . . He has demanded, though not obtained an audience with Chevalier Pinto, the prime minister here.' It is unclear whether Dr Graham ever had the opportunity to try out his idiosyncratic cures on the queen, but with or without the attentions of Britain's medical profession, Dona Maria I would never recover her sanity. By 1799, the court had admitted defeat and Dom João was officially proclaimed prince regent.

In the years between Dona Maria's first signs of insanity and the beginning of Dom João's regency, the royal family began to disintegrate. After a fire gutted the *Barraca Real* (literally: royal hut), a temporary wooden palace near the waterfront used while the royal palace of Ajuda was being built, the family moved into Queluz, a scaled down, Versailles-like retreat with formally laid out gardens, fountains and citrus groves. In the summer, royal parties would go boating in the *azulejo*-lined canals which cut through the grounds; on certain evenings, Portuguese bullfights were staged in the palace's courtyard. Life on the inside, though, was hardly ideal. Dona Maria's screams reverberated through the corridors, unsettling staff and visitors alike. Dom João, who was very attached to his mother, became progressively more introverted as he tried to come to terms with his position as acting head of state.

It was an unenviable job. Dom João had been thrown in at the deep end, and for years he felt his way on the advice of a small collection of trusted ministers and a conservative instinct. He was no natural leader, and by the time he officially assumed the regency, Portugal's position in Europe was dire. As Dom João was declared regent, Napoleon seized power in the daring coup of 18 Brumaire (9 November 1799). Two years later, Portugal suffered invasion from neighbouring Spain, now an ally of Napoleon's France, and on top of some territorial loss, was forced to make indemnity payments. In the years that followed the very existence of Dom João's realm would be under constant threat.

It is hard to overestimate the terror that Napoleon's rise inspired amongst Europe's hereditary monarchs, a fear cultivated by Bonaparte himself. Late in 1804, Napoleon had sent his troops across the border into Baden, seized the last Bourbon prince, the Duke of Enghien, and after a perfunctory trial in Vincennes had him shot for conspiracy against France. Monarchs across Europe were shaken by this calculated act of intimidation, which amounted to the kidnap and assassination of one of their brethren. Even those, like Dom João, who were then still well clear of the wars now feared for their lives.

In official portraits Dom João appears rotund, his face olive-skinned with large, sunken eyes. He was a man of simple, courtly tastes. Especially fond of ecclesiastical music, he enjoyed long banquets in which he consumed prodigious quantities of venison and game fowl. There was something touchingly old-fashioned about Dom João – he was one of the last European monarchs to practise the medieval sport of falconry and had the comical habit of referring to himself in the third person, as in 'His Majesty is unwell'. Despite rigorous adhesion to court etiquette, he would never look the part of a European monarch. He disliked new clothes, and wore favourite garments until they virtually fell apart. He also suffered from a variety of skin disorders – his wounds did not easily heal, especially on his legs, and itchy rashes spread over his body. In obvious discomfort, Dom João fidgeted and scratched incessantly, even while receiving important guests.

Emotional – he wept often during his turbulent reign – he was certainly no genius, but neither was he the dolt depicted in anti-monarchist propaganda. He spent much of his day reading state papers and in session with his ministers only to find himself in a series of impossible positions, destined to preside over almost a decade of diplomatic prevarication before French troops finally crossed Portugal's undefended borders. Plagued by indecision, he somehow shepherded Portugal through the political labyrinth of 1807–1808, one of the most complex periods in Portugal's national and imperial history, surviving as monarch while his counterparts across Europe were dethroned and humiliated by Napoleon.

No leader, no matter how strong or charismatic, could have avoided the fate that awaited Portugal as Napoleon strengthened his grip over the Continent, but Dom João's weak reign had important effects on the life of the court itself. In the period before the royal family's flight to Brazil, the court became split, top to bottom, into British and French factions. On the British side, there were those like Sousa Coutinho who supported what was a venerable alliance with its age-old commercial and maritime ties, viewing Britain as a bulwark against revolutionary France. On the other side, politicians like Araújo were pro-French through a combination of realism – it was beginning to look inevitable that Napoleon would prevail in Europe – and a profound cultural attachment to France. The divide was deepened by the aggression of successive French and British delegations who were engaged in a cold war for influence over the Portuguese court – a role that Strangford took up with alacrity.

It is in this context that Dona Carlota's political manoeuvring needs to be placed. She was in a court in which intrigue was the norm, even encouraged by powerful envoys like Strangford. Her unique position as a Bourbon married to a Bragança regent, tied emotionally to Spain, but living in the Portuguese court, made her a key player in the politics of the Iberian Peninsula. At first, she looked forward to a legitimate political role alongside Dom João, but when he assumed the regency she found herself excluded from all participation in his government. Shunned by her husband's advisers, who ignored her overtures and strictly policed her contacts with Dom João, it was not long before she was engaging directly in projects of her own. Her early attempts were subtle and unthreatening – she created the Order of Noble Women of St Isabel, enabling her to confer privileges on the wives of some of the most influential members of the Portuguese ruling classes, and hold palace *soirées* where she could mingle with Lisbon high society. But it was not long before her ambitions grew, and she began her quest for real power and influence within the court.

By early 1802 their marriage had collapsed, and Dona Carlota moved out of Queluz, buying, with Dom João's consent, the villa at Ramalhão set in the hills around Sintra. The move was officially justified on health grounds – the villa had spacious, well-ventilated rooms overlooking orange and lemon groves – but for Dona Carlota, now with her own house and staff, it was ideal for other reasons. At last she had her independence – a base from which to explore ways of directly challenging her husband's rule. There were several levels of her brinkmanship. A 'conjugal guerrilla war' broke out which would be waged for the duration of their marriage. All decisions which were connected in any way to the politics of the court were fought out, tooth and nail, with her husband. There were arguments over the arrangement of marriages, the treatment of servants, the appointment of courtiers and even questions of etiquette.

Dona Carlota also undermined Dom João's standing by conducting a series of affairs from her lavishly decorated villa. Here, controversy emerges again, with conflicting rumours as to the identities of Dona Carlota's lovers. The subject has become bound up in her mythology, but in the end, there is little hard evidence to prove Dona Carlota's amorous escapades one way or the other. The paternity of Dona Carlota's favourite son, Miguel, is an especially difficult area. That he was born out of wedlock is apparently confirmed by Dom João's own statement, reported in a London newspaper, that at the time of Dona Carlota's pregnancy he had not had relations with his wife for two years. Was Miguel then, as some argued, the product of a liaison between Dona Carlota and her gardener? Or was the father a storekeeper at Ramalhão, João dos Santos? Or was the resemblance between Miguel and another of Dona Carlota's consorts, the Marquis of

Marialva, concrete evidence of an affair? The truth is clouded by the virulent hatred of both Dona Carlota and Dom Miguel which developed in the later years of Dom João's reign, when their counter-revolutionary stance would engulf Portugal in a civil war over liberal reforms. There were also rumours about the paternity of her two youngest daughters, Ana de Jesus and Maria d'Assunção, who were unlikely to have been sired within the marriage, since by this stage Dona Carlota would meet Dom João only in public when ceremony demanded.

The 'Mafra Conspiracy' would be Dona Carlota's most ambitious play for the Portuguese throne before her exile to Brazil. When, in the early winter of 1805, Dom João was taken ill with intestinal complaints on a hunting season foray outside Lisbon, rumours abounded in the capital. The illness had also afflicted other members of the party – among them, Antônio de Araújo – but it was said in Lisbon that Dom João was suffering a similar ailment to his mother. Dom João did, in fact, develop psychological symptoms that echoed his mother's early paranoia. He had attacks of extreme anxiety, and at times was delirious. There were bouts of dizziness that were explained by the prince regent in a disturbing way – he said that he saw great chasms opening up in the ground around his feet. Dom João withdrew from public view. His prolonged absences from Lisbon, spent either in the Mafra monastery complex or in a country estate in the Alentejo, fuelled the rumours of his madness. The crisis was the cue that many within the court had been waiting for, and during the early months of 1806, a faction of disaffected courtiers formed around Dona Carlota. The coup was set for 25 April 1806, Dona Carlota's thirty-first birthday, at the palace *beija-mão* (hand kissing) ceremony. Dom João's non-attendance was to have been taken as a signal for the conspirators to reveal themselves by placing their hands on their hearts after kissing the princess regent's hand. But the plan was foiled, probably betrayed by one of Dona Carlota's ladies-in-waiting. Tipped off by his advisers, Dom João made an unscheduled appearance at the event. Dona Carlota was spared the attentions of the inquiry that followed, but several noblemen were charged with treason and sent into exile.

The backlash did little to dampen the enthusiasm of the Carlotist plotters. In August 1806, one of the conspirators who had escaped the purge, the Marques of Ponte Lima, wrote of the increasingly tense situation, hinting at French involvement in the attempts to overthrow Dom João:

'Our man [Dom João] is worsening by the day, and not much remains for him to be declared completely insane . . . the trips he concocts are motivated by a desire to hide himself away. No serious business is put before the said gentleman . . . An express is leaving for Paris, in all probability carrying something related to our case. It is absolutely essential that the Princess knows this and bides her time . . . the man is certainly mad – even the Count of Belmonte says so.'

A week later, Dona Carlota sent a letter to her father Carlos IV in Madrid, urging him to intervene in her favour:

'I write in the utmost anxiety to say that the Prince's mind is deteriorating by the day. As a consequence of this everything will be lost, because those around him are becoming more and more absolute . . . the time has come for Your Majesty to help me and your grandchildren . . . who now do not have a father capable of looking after them . . . this is the way to avoid much blood being spilt in this kingdom . . . the court wants to give me a chance and so do the people, because they see clearly that the Prince has lost his mind.'

But Carlos IV was deaf to his daughter's appeals; he was already in secret negotiations with France on the eventual break up of Portugal.

After the attempted palace coup, Dom João became a recluse. He holed up in the Mafra monastery, disappearing within its warren of monk cells and royal apartments, feeling himself under siege from without and within. His life was now sedentary, he put on weight and was no longer able to mount his horse.

Although not insane, Dom João was clearly depressed during this period, and his isolation was making him neurotic. Arriving in Lisbon at the end of 1806, the young diplomat Dom Pedro de Sousa e Holstein, the future Count of Palmela, found it impossible to arrange an audience with the prince who was 'mortified by domestic problems and by the storm clouds which were appearing on the political horizon, affected by a nervous disorder, perhaps in part imaginary, living . . . imprisoned in the palace of Mafra without any company except some priests and a handful of family members and receiving no one whom he did not know'.

Palmela was perhaps one of the few within the court who might have been able to help the prince regent steer his way through the involved politics of the age. As the son of a diplomat, from early childhood Palmela had lived on the broader European stage, spending periods in Copenhagen, Berlin, Rome and Geneva. He had grown up on the road, well used to weeks cooped up in carriages bumping over the Alps and nights spent in remote travellers' inns.

When he came of age, Palmela began travelling through Europe on his own. In Rome, he developed into the fine-wine-loving *bon viveur*, who smoked expensive cigars and moved in fashionable high-society circles. He had a passionate, two-month affair with the French novelist and critic Madame de Staël, before heading via Geneva for France, where he spent seven months in the Portuguese legation in Paris. It was 1806 and a new nobility, Napoleon's chosen, was spending lavishly in the capital, which was consumed by the cult of the emperor. Paris was a city of energy and new ideas – a kind of imperial metropolis of Europe – overflowing with the cultural spoils of Bonaparte's campaigns. From here Palmela visited Madrid, and saw Europe's other extreme: a decadent, absolutist court, backward looking, bankrupt of ideas. It reminded him of Portugal: 'The same ignorance, servile ambition and degradation, with the difference in our favour that the character of our prince deserved more consideration and inspired more respect than did that of Carlos IV [the then king of Spain].'

Palmela arrived back in Lisbon to a court in crisis, a country hopelessly unprepared for what lay ahead. At the time of the flight, Dom João offered Palmela a place on board the fleet, but he elected to stay on in Europe. It was a shrewd move, as Palmela would end up as the Continental lynchpin of the new Brazil-based government, going on to represent the exiled court's interests in Spain, Britain and at the Congress of Vienna in Austria. On 29 November 1807 he watched from his window as the royal fleet trailed down the Tagus and disappeared into the Atlantic. The very next day, he was at his window again, picking out the exhausted French regulars struggling into the city.

For Dom João, the flight to Brazil represented a way out, an opportunity to erase the memory of Europe and start life afresh. It was as if he had been plucked from a nightmare world – the endless meetings on the parlous state of the kingdom, the sense of impending collapse, and machinations of the court itself – and delivered into a dream.

Dona Carlota, on the other hand, faced oblivion – for her, exile was a personal tragedy. When she arrived in Brazil she was thirty-two years old, and although her intrigues had until then been unsuccessful, she had served a long apprenticeship and built an informal power base of sympathisers and fellow conspirators. All this was demolished at a stroke when the fleet pushed off down the Tagus and headed for a colonial outpost, thousands of miles from the courts of Europe. In the months leading up to the flight she had tried everything to avoid her coming exile, writing pleading letters to her parents in Madrid:

'Dear mother, I cannot willingly fling myself into a well – if I should go, it will mean my ruin, for if they have treated me here as they have done, how will they treat me there, far away from you? There is only one way of saving me. I implore you, write to the Prince [Fernando, Dona Carlota's brother] saying you wish me to go and stay with you, so as to be in safety – quite as safe as if we gave ourselves up to the English. And make it plain you will accept no refusal.'

'Mother of my heart, my life, my soul . . .' she wrote in another letter, trying a different tack, 'I beg Your Majesty to remember and have compassion for this poor daughter, because I am surrounded by eight children, and these poor innocents are blameless; have compassion for them, more than for me, because they are your grandchildren.'

But her appeals were in vain. Dona Carlota arrived in Salvador a broken woman. Embittered, she developed a hatred for the country and its people. She would nevertheless waste little time in her attempts to rebuild her political base in Brazil; and the first years, at least, would be revelatory, as Dona Carlota found that South America of the early nineteenth century afforded her new and potentially even more grandiose opportunities in her bid for power.

After the welcoming ceremonies in Salvador had died down, Dom João, his son Pedro and mother Queen Maria went ashore for a week's recuperation at the governor's palace. Dona Carlota did not join them, staying on board the fleet for a further five days, before moving into a law court building in the centre of town.

For all his relief at being spirited out of Lisbon, Dom João was to find that the problems that he had fled had followed him across the Atlantic. No cargo had been able to leave Salvador since the capture of Lisbon. The harbour was jammed with ships waiting to clear the port, laden with goods for Europe. The harvest had just come in and warehouses were overflowing with produce arriving from the countryside, much of which was starting to go off. Under the colonial arrangements, Brazilian commercial shipping had been strictly controlled by the Portuguese Crown. All trade had in theory been forced through Portugal, from where, after the payment of port duties, the bulk of the goods would be re-exported elsewhere, often to England. With France controlling Lisbon, the entire imperial system was paralysed.

By a single, historic decree, the prince regent eliminated Brazil's most onerous colonial burden: he opened the ports to all friendly shipping. It was a move that was unavoidable and was in any case stipulated in the secret convention he had signed with Britain the previous October. With this proclamation he also in a sense opened up Brazil itself, a country that had been cloistered by its colonial overseers, jealously guarded against Portugal's European rivals. Even in the midst of the trade crisis brought on by Napoleon's blockade, the decision was opposed by Portuguese shipping agents, who were forced to relinquish a privilege that dated back to the birth of the colony – their monopoly on all goods leaving Brazil. Traders were also only too aware of the subtext of the royal order: the opening of the ports 'to all friendly nations' at that point effectively meant Britain, the only maritime power that was not allied to Napoleon's Europe. Brazil was to be released from one colonial master, only to fall into the embrace of another.

The royal family rested in Salvador for a month. On outings with his son Pedro, Dom João took his carriage into the hills, followed by crowds of vassals. The orange groves were in bloom, leaving a sweet scent wafting across the outlying plantations. On one occasion they visited Itaparica, a large island in the bay of beaches, palm stands and forest trails, and spent an unscheduled night there when adverse winds prevented their return to the mainland.

Meanwhile, news of their arrival spread slowly to other parts of Brazil. Araújo, stuck in Recife while the *Medusa* was repaired, wrote in typically effusive tones of his relief:

> 'On the 20th of this month [January] my worries were ended with the happy news that Your Highness passed by this Captaincy on the 17th. Everyone hugged and congratulated each other here at such wonderful and hoped for tidings. The weather and the poor state of this ship has delayed us thirteen days in this port, and I am impatient with this delay, because I long for the honour to prostrate myself at the august feet of Your Highness; in the meantime I kiss them with the respect and loyalty of your vassal and servant.'

The other half of the convoy was by now in Rio, but, extraordinary as it may seem, after two difficult months at sea, most of the exiles would not disembark for a further month, while they waited on news of Dom João's intentions.

During his stay in Salvador, Dom João began to find his feet again and, in a very different setting, slip back into his role of absolute monarch. He handed out coins to those who followed his coach, granted pardons, awarded honours and listened to petitions. Colonial strictures were loosened with the issuing of manufacture licences and the establishment of a school of medicine and surgery. Requests for him to set up court and government in Bahia, though, were diplomatically declined. Salvador, it was feared, was more vulnerable to attacks from the French than the well-fortified and still more distant port of Rio de Janeiro.

Crowds flocked to bid the royal family farewell. In contrast to the conditions on the Atlantic crossing, the ships had been repaired and freshly provisioned in port, and they were to enjoy a smooth passage down to Rio. Anchoring in coastal inlets each evening, the convoy worked its way south on the final leg of its journey. In fine weather it made good progress down the Brazilian coast and just one week after leaving Salvador it rounded Cabo Frio. From out on deck, a trail of small, dome-shaped volcanic islands could now be seen protruding through the waters, some barren rock, others with gardens of palms and grasses. Up ahead were the forested mountain ranges which backed Rio – the *Serra do Mar* escarpments – receding in ever lighter pastels into the distance, like theatre sets stacked one against the other.

FOUR

'Emperor of the West'

Moving thousands of people along with tons of paperwork, books and royal treasure across the Atlantic Ocean to Brazil was certainly one of the era's most spectacular and epic undertakings. The Portuguese royal family's strategy, though, was in keeping with the times. The revolutionary wars and Napoleon's subsequent expansion had convulsed Europe's old order, and courts across Europe were resorting to extreme measures to survive the onslaught. By the time the Portuguese royal family had relocated to Brazil, Louis XVIII (brother of the executed Louis XVI) was renting Hartwell House, a charming estate near Oxford, after years on the run in Europe. Willem V, the last Orange stadtholder of the Netherlands, was not far away, sitting out the wars with his family in Kew. The Neapolitan Bourbons Ferdinand and Carolina had fled for the second time to Palermo, while the Savoy dynasty had retreated to Cagliari in Sardinia. Even the British had gone as far as building a fortress in the Midlands to which the king and government could flee should the south of England be overrun, a scenario that was thought to be a real possibility until Napoleon's turn eastwards and the British victory at Trafalgar had diminished the threat of a French invasion.

But there was something different about the Portuguese flight, immediately obvious from its scale and audacity. There were deeper reasons behind the elite's willingness to move *en masse* to a country thousands of miles from their homeland. The idea of relocation to the Americas had a venerable pedigree, dating back to the first centuries of Portuguese imperial expansion. Royal advisers to the Lisbon court had long portrayed Brazil as the promised land – a utopia to which they were destined one day to transport themselves. The argument began in a religious, millenarian vein, but soon evolved into a hardheaded analysis of where Portugal stood in relation to her colonies. Relocation emerged as a solution to the paradox at the heart of a failing imperial system: that Portugal herself was the empire's Achilles' heel, her position as a weak state constantly threatened by European rivals a liability to her own global network of colonies.

The Portuguese Empire had begun with seafarers' words, numbers and images. As pilots pushed their fishing-boat-sized caravels out into unexplored oceans and along rugged coastlines, they compiled detailed *roteiros* – running commentaries of sea and land conditions they observed along the way. The *roteiros* not only told of coastal landmarks, ocean currents and slicks of different-coloured water, but gave vivid descriptions of the marine life that they encountered – sightings of whales, seabirds, blooms of algae, and outcrops of sea grapes floating just offshore. Seated at swaying writing desks, the pilots set down columns of astronomical observations on to scrolls of paper. During their long months at sea they filled out tables of distances, elevations and angles, laying the groundwork for the naval handbooks that would soon be appearing in translation across Europe. In time, new, more accurate charts of Africa, India and beyond began appearing, the route maps of the coming imperial expansion.

This knowledge, backed by sea power, would drive the Portuguese on to their early successes. Just two decades after the completion of Vasco da Gama's famous voyage (1497–1499), Portuguese ships had made astounding inroads into the trade circuits of the East. Moving into largely unmilitarised waters, they swept through the Indian Ocean, the Persian Gulf, and the South China seas, sinking opposing fleets and capturing ports and offshore islands as they went. A vast archipelago of Portuguese trade ports – the *Estado da Índia* – resulted, its pivots, Hormuz (a barren island in the straits of the Persian Gulf), Goa, Malacca (at that time one of South-east Asia's richest emporiums) and, later, Macao, serving as the main way stations in what was then a revolutionary concept: a seaborne empire. And as physical reminders of what the Portuguese had achieved, a string of forts, so solidly built that many remain in good condition to this day, studded the new sea lanes.

While the East boomed, across the Atlantic the new colonies of Brazil were slow to emerge. In the early part of the sixteenth century, it was the French who were exploiting the new opportunities that Brazil offered. They sailed out of Brittany and Normandy, anchored off the coast and loaded up with brazilwood – a much sought-after commodity on the European markets which yielded a powerful dye across a spectrum of reds and burgundies. With French ships appearing in ever greater numbers, the Portuguese tried to patrol the coast, an impossible task given its extent. Finally, some thirty years after Cabral, they turned to settlement.

The coast was sectioned off. Fourteen horizontal lines were ruled across the eastern half of the South American continent. The lines divided Brazil into a series of elongated strips – called 'captaincies' – that drove through hundreds of miles of native settlements, uncharted forests, river systems and arid scrublands, ending abruptly when they intersected the 'Line of Tordesillas', the disputed frontier between Portuguese and Spanish America. The strips were then handed out as royal gifts for proprietary captains to develop as they saw fit. Hampered by lack of capital, a paucity of willing settlers and, most crucially in the early years, an aggressive response from the indigenous peoples – the Tupi tribes scattered along the seaboard – the colonies struggled to find their feet. Some of the captaincies were never occupied, some were settled and then abandoned, while others found themselves besieged by native attacks. In amongst the failures, two captaincies in the north-east – Bahia and Pernambuco – had begun to thrive.

In these captaincies, earlier experiments with slave-driven sugar plantations on Portugal's Atlantic possessions – Madeira, as well as São Tomé and Príncipe (an island group in the Gulf of Guinea) – would reach their fruition, only this time production would take on an industrial intensity that shocked those who witnessed the mills working at full throttle. Behind the rural façade of the cycles of farm life – planting, weeding and harvest – lay a complex process of refinement. Millstones or large wooden rollers driven by water or animal power pressed the cane, reducing its woody stalks to a dark syrup. This was gradually purified as it was boiled and passed through a series of cauldrons, then poured off into conical casts which were left for two months to crystallise into the sugar loaf. As a perennial, cane could generate prodigious yields; the clayey black soils preferred by the mill owners could be planted continuously for fifty years or more. During harvest sugar mills ran round the clock – twenty hours pressing cane, the other four spent repairing and cleaning equipment.

The continuously fired-up furnace, the great vats of boiling liquid, the constant grinding of the cane presses and the foul smelling by-products which polluted the countryside for miles around were disquieting foretastes of modernity. And for those who worked the mills – overwhelmingly African slaves who began pouring into Brazil well before the trade was established elsewhere in the Americas – these premonitions were borne out in their lives. Sixteen-hour shifts, unbearable heat and frequent industrial accidents created a scenario redolent of a nineteenth-century Midlands factory floor.

The Brazilian plantations added a new dimension to the Portuguese Empire. One hundred years after the voyages of da Gama and Cabral, this small medieval nation on the edge of Europe was trading globally. To the east, a stream of cargo ships rounded the Cape on the gruelling Lisbon–Goa *carreira da Índia*, arriving back in Europe laden with high-value spices – mainly pepper, but also cinnamon, cloves, cardamom pods, turmeric, nutmeg and mace. To the west, the classic triangle of exploitation that would come to dominate Europe's Atlantic trade was emerging. Cheap goods were freighted from Portugal down to Africa, while slave ships ferried Africans across the Atlantic to work the Brazilian plantations, sugar and agricultural produce filling the holds of transports on the return leg to Europe. The port of Lisbon had become famous – it was the Amsterdam of its day, serving as Europe's clearing house for products arriving from around the world.

But the roots of decline were already in evidence. Overstretched, from the outset unwieldy and impossible to control, the fledgling empire was racked with corruption. The new territories had also become a dumping ground for exiles – Lisbon's prisons were emptied into what were beginning to resemble a string of remote open penal colonies – a problem that would persist in one form or another throughout Portugal's imperial era. Even before the advent of serious military threats, the Portuguese Empire was decomposing from within. Over the years, official correspondence between *Estado da Índia* governors and Crown officials in Lisbon degenerated into a never-ending stream of pleas for resources and military assistance, as the governors sensed that their early gains were ebbing away.

By the late sixteenth century, the empire was coming under sustained attack. With the union of the Spanish and Portuguese Crowns (1580–1640), Portugal was dragged into a wider European conflict, one that would almost spell the end of her imperial aspirations. The union brought together two huge empires, a conglomerate that was truly global, stretching, in a tropical swathe, from South and Central America to the Philippines and Japan. The two empires were kept administratively separate, but for the Dutch, who were then entering the final stages of their war against Spain, they presented one enormous target.

Even after the restoration of the Portuguese Crown, the assaults continued. The Dutch took the wealthy Spice Island entrepôt, Malacca, in 1641. The defeat of Ceylon (Sri Lanka) followed in 1656, and Cochin a decade later. And the Portuguese were not just under Dutch attack – Mughal forces drove

them out of Hugli (Calcutta); Persia, with some British assistance, seized back Hormuz in the Gulf; and Muscat fell to the
Omanis in 1650. By 1666, over fifty Portuguese forts had been
reduced to just nine. When the Jesuit priest Manoel Godinho
travelled the empire a hundred years after Camões, he found
only remnants – 'mementoes from the great hulk of that state left
to us by our enemies, either to remind us of the great deal we
possessed in India [i.e. Asia] or to grieve us, considering the very
little we now hold in it'.

Portugal's imperial ambitions in the Atlantic were sinking fast,
too. After a long struggle to take Recife, the Dutch took control
of Brazil's sugar plantations in the north-east. By the 1630s, they
had extended their claims along a thousand-mile stretch of the
Brazilian coastline, from south of the Amazon's mouth down to
within striking distance of Salvador. In 1641 the Dutch captured
the crucial slaving port Luanda (in Angola), paralysing Portugal's
Atlantic system.

The empire was now on its knees. The slave trade was
disrupted, the *Estado da Índia* in ruins, the most lucrative parts
of Brazil under Dutch occupation. Portugal, indebted, her fleet
crippled, was powerless to defend what little she had left. The
position was so dire that towards the end of the 1640s the
Portuguese Crown was seriously exploring the possibility of a
negotiated settlement in Pernambuco, abandoning the north-
east to the Dutch for good, an act that would have changed the
course of Brazilian history. In the end, it was the Brazilians
themselves who saved the day for the mother country. A series of
local rebellions drove the Dutch out of Pernambuco in 1654,
and a fleet dispatched from Rio recaptured Luanda.

Brazil had been rescued, but the problem, as it was perceived
at the time, was how to exploit these enormous imperial
resources from the vulnerable European base of Portugal.
And from this dilemma came a radical solution: if the empire
was to be saved, argued the Jesuit priest António Vieira, one of
Dom João IV's (1640–1656) key advisers in the mid-seventeenth
century, its European headquarters had to be jettisoned in favour
of a new administrative centre in the Brazilian tropics.

Vieira had impeccable credentials for considering the role of Brazil in Portugal's failing empire. Born in Lisbon, at the age of six he had gone with his parents to Bahia where he spent his formative years studying at the local Jesuit college. He had been witness to the Dutch attack on Salvador (1624–1625) and was in Pernambuco on the eve of the second Dutch invasion. Returning to Bahia, he quickly built up a reputation as one of the pre-eminent orators of his time. In sermons which became famous for their lyricism and energy, he urged Brazilians to unite against the Dutch interlopers. It was in Lisbon, though, as court preacher, that his influence and stature would grow. There he counselled the king on matters of state through the difficult years of the 1640s, travelling around Europe on sensitive diplomatic missions in an effort to shore up Portugal's declining fortunes on the world stage.

After another long spell working on Jesuit mission stations in Maranhão, then a massive territory encompassing much of the north-eastern plantations and extending inland through the *sertão* (arid scrublands), Vieira's religious and political beliefs merged. In an idiosyncratic take on Sebastianism – the belief that King Sebastian, who was killed on a Moroccan battlefield in 1578, would return from the dead to save Portugal from its enemies – Vieira portrayed the Portuguese monarchy as the universal Fifth Empire of the Book of Daniel, an everlasting entity, destined to renew itself through relocation to America. Brazil, or more specifically Maranhão, held an aura for Vieira. It was a spiritual location that the Portuguese were meant to discover, explore and settle, a place where prophecies would be revealed. There the king 'would assign a place for a palace,' wrote Vieira, 'which would enjoy the four seasons of the year at the same time,' serving as the seat of the Fifth Empire. The New World was Portugal's destiny, the means by which the empire would rise up again after the humiliation of Spanish rule (1580–1640) and Dutch conquest. At the time these views were considered outlandish, and in the last years of his life Vieira would face unpleasant probings from the Inquisition. He was forced to travel to

Rome to clear his name and never regained the influence he once had within the court, but his ideas lived on.

Towards the end of the seventeenth century, Vieira's case for the relocation of the court to the Americas was strengthened when fate handed the Brazilian colonies a second lease of life. Colonial administrators had long looked on with envy at the wealth produced by Spanish America. With the Potosí silver mines in Upper Peru (now Bolivia) working overtime, expectations of finding precious metals in the Brazilian interior had initially been high, but after more than a century of colonisation, hopes had begun to fade. Report after report of spectacular finds had been proved unfounded; so when, in the 1690s, rumours of commercially viable strikes of alluvial gold began arriving in Portugal, the Crown was at first slow to react.

The Brazilian interior was little known in the late seventeenth century. Only a few, hardy men, known as the *bandeirantes*, had penetrated far inland. Using indigenous helpers, they had journeyed out from the captaincy of São Vicente (modern-day São Paulo) into the Brazilian hinterland on Amerindian slaving expeditions that could last months or even years. It is unclear when they first struck gold, but by the early 1690s finds proliferated throughout a region that would become known as Minas Gerais (General Mines).

The closing years of the seventeenth century saw the world's first modern gold rush. 'Nothing like it had been seen before,' wrote the historian C. R. Boxer, 'and nothing like it was seen again until the California gold rush of 1849.' Soldiers abandoned their garrisons, priests their parishes, and, more worryingly for colonial authorities, slaves the plantations, in the stampede west. According to a witness to the early years of the gold rush, André João Antonil, the prospectors cut across Brazilian colonial society, their numbers made up of: 'Whites, Coloured, and Blacks together with many Amerindians enslaved by Paulistas . . . men and women; young and old; rich and poor; nobles and commoners; laymen, clergy, and Religious of different orders.' Access routes were tortuous, the land around the gold fields difficult to cultivate, and many who had been goaded on by dreams of instant wealth were reduced to starvation. The prime sites lay in land that had never been mapped, between the jurisdictions of several captaincies. As more and more people flooded the area, anarchy spun into open warfare.

For authorities in Lisbon, the news that they had longed for precipitated a crisis. Brazil's main ports were now poorly defended, her plantations suffering a severe shortage of labour, and the mother country herself was haemorrhaging vassals who were boarding Brazil-bound ships in their thousands – all this while news of the gold rush spread through Europe to Portugal's imperial rivals. There were fears that Portugal might be invaded, or Brazil seized.

The gold years brought a new urgency to discussions about the reorganisation of the empire. With revenue pouring across the Atlantic from Brazil, Luís da Cunha, a career diplomat in the reign of Dom João V (1706–1750), re-examined Vieira's ideas of relocation. Da Cunha had spent forty years outside Portugal working in London and Paris and travelling widely through Europe on diplomatic missions. Although he had never been there, he was knowledgeable about Brazil, having been one of the negotiators of the Utrecht Treaty which strengthened Portugal's claims to disputed territories in the Amazon and in the far south. Above all, da Cunha was a realist, inculcated with the modern world view that was then emerging in European circles, one which was secular and trade orientated.

In a secret memorandum to Dom João V, da Cunha outlined ideas that were decades ahead of their time. He was brutally honest about the state of affairs in Portugal. The disproportionate influence of the church, with its ranks of clergymen and its vast, unproductive properties were a drain on resources; the Inquisition was a throwback to a bygone age. He suggested opening up Portugal to its empire, declaring Lisbon a free port and creating Dutch-style trading companies. The colonies themselves should be developed, with land routes through Southern Africa connecting up Angola and Mozambique and the exploration of the potentially productive tropical forests of the Amazon. Even these sweeping reforms could not hide the basic vulnerability of the mother country. For da Cunha, Portugal was but 'an ear of land', dwarfed by her holdings in America.

Breaking free from his closely argued text, da Cunha envisaged, in almost biblical terms, a scenario that would eventually come to pass, albeit several generations after his words were penned:

> 'I consider, perhaps dreamily, that it is about time for Your Majesty to see that immense continent of Brazil as a resourceful and well-populated country. And in Brazil you would take the title of 'Emperor of the West', establishing your court, taking people of both sexes who wanted to follow you – and there would be many – including a large number of foreigners. And in my opinion, the most suitable place for your residence would be the city of Rio de Janeiro which would soon become more opulent than Lisbon.'

His argument was at heart economic: anything produced in Portugal could be easily made in Brazil, safe from military and political interference from hostile European powers. It was also territorial. The Portuguese could come to some sort of mutually beneficial arrangement with the Spanish, exchanging the Algarve for Chile and the rest of Portugal for the Río de La Plata region (modern-day Argentina). The change of climate would not be a problem, according to da Cunha's brother, who had stopped off in Brazil on his way back from Goa – 'he assured me that it was not only very healthy and similar to ours, but that the country is a very suitable place to cultivate European crops, already having those of India and Africa.'

Da Cunha realised that Portugal had become unsustainably dependent on Brazil's resources. While shiploads of sugar continued to cross the Atlantic, the unexpected influx of gold and diamonds harvested from the Brazilian interior was propping up Dom João V's profligate reign, much of the revenue squandered on extravagances like the monumental monastery complex at Mafra. But when the gold rush petered out towards the middle of the eighteenth century, Portugal's position in Europe slipped further.

The gold years left an important legacy for Brazil. They opened up the interior to settlement, eventually extending Portuguese claims well beyond the original Line of Tordesillas. Portuguese cartographers drove deep into the interior, their work, formalised in the Treaty of Madrid (1750), establishing the basis of modern Brazil's western borders. The treaty doubled the territory under Portuguese rule, giving the Crown control over roughly half of the South American continent – an area larger than today's United States, minus Alaska.

In other ways, though, the gold cycle retarded development in the colony. Portugal, fearful of losing her most valued colonial possession, tried to isolate Brazil and ensure its dependence on the mother country. The Crown banned printing presses, and stopped the import of books and the establishment of universities. Lisbon suppressed nascent cottage industries in Brazil, its colonial authorities destroying looms to protect the import of poor quality Portuguese wools; native trees were even uprooted to prevent possible competition with certain types of timber. There were systematic attempts by the Crown to cripple Brazil's internal communications where they did not serve the export trade. Laws were passed restricting riverine navigation and the development of a land-based postal system was discouraged. Roads – the few that existed – were in terrible condition. Mud tracks only marginally aided the mule trains that ferried goods between captaincies. Rather than wind up through mountains, they scaled them precipitously; on flatter terrain small obstacles were circuitously bypassed instead of removed. Poor planning sent tracks off in the wrong direction altogether, going round in giant arcs or even circles. And some paths trailed off in the middle of nowhere, gradually becoming indistinguishable from the forests and scrublands they divided, barely visible reminders of works abandoned.

It was left to Sebastião José de Carvalho e Mello, the Marquis

of Pombal, a dictatorial figure at court in the mid-eighteenth
century, to try and breathe new life into the empire. Years in
London had given him an insider's view of the superpower of
the day and Portugal's growing subservience to British interests.
He realised that while Lisbon was lumbered with the administration of her colonies, all too often the profits derived from the
empire wound up, via the international markets, in London or
Amsterdam.

Pombal came into his own in the aftermath of the Great
Earthquake of 1755. The earthquake, striking on a Sunday
morning while the bulk of the population attended mass, razed
one of Europe's most famous cities in hours, and was thought by
many to be more than just a geological accident. Preachers saw
God's hand in the disaster, punishing Portugal for its decadence
and moral decay. With Lisbon in ruins, thoughts again turned to
transferring the capital to Brazil, but Pombal opted to tackle the
crisis head-on. He took control of the city and rebuilt it to a
more modern, rational plan, modelled, in part, on London's
Covent Garden.

Pombal took an equally aggressive approach to the reform of
the empire. The Jesuits, who throughout the colony's first
centuries had fanned out into some of the most inaccessible
regions of Brazil and established mission stations, were suddenly
expelled and their property expropriated in 1759. The reasons
were in part economic – the Jesuits were believed (wrongly as it
turned out) to have hoarded vast wealth in Brazil, but the move
was also prompted by a irrational hatred of the order. The Jesuits
practised 'abominable, inveterate and incorrigible vices', read the
edict against them, and 'have clandestinely attempted the usurpation of the entire state of Brazil'.

In other policies, Pombal was more surefooted. Brazil was
fortified, and its capital moved from Bahia to the wealthier and
more easily defended port of Rio de Janeiro in 1763. The
education and promotion of local elites was encouraged,
whether they be white, mulatto, or in some exceptional cases,
even black. Pombal tightened the tax system and set up monopoly companies to try and stimulate Brazil's export trade. The

same underlying ethos remained – Brazil was restricted to primary products, exchanged, Pombal hoped, for Portuguese manufactures. But while Brazil revived in the late 1700s, Portugal fell back further in relation to the rest of Europe. However much trade was directed towards Lisbon, Portugal remained a way station, a conduit between her Atlantic colonies and Europe's economic powerhouses in the north.

Towards the end of the eighteenth century, as Napoleon began his ascent, the time of reckoning was at hand. With Dona Maria's madness and Dom João's shaky regency, never had Portugal looked so vulnerable to events beyond her control. It was at this point that the case for the transfer of the court to Brazil – with Rio now the frontrunner as the probable destination – began to be argued for most forcefully by the minister who would soon be leading Dom João's new government in Rio, Dom Rodrigo de Sousa Coutinho.

In a presentation to the court in 1798, Sousa Coutinho laid down the unpalatable truth, that 'the dominions in Europe' no longer formed 'the capital and centre of the Portuguese Empire'. Reduced to itself, he concluded, Portugal would soon be 'a province of Spain'. Following Pombal, he went on to propose an enlightened, federal idea of empire, in which Brazil would be shorn of its colonial status and developed in tandem with the mother country.

In 1801, a further Spanish incursion, The War of the Oranges, added urgency to Sousa Coutinho's arguments. 'Your highness should order all your warships to be armed without delay, and all your transports which are by the *Praça de Lisboa*,' the Marquis of Alorna had written at the time, 'into which you should place the princess [Dona Carlota], your children, and your treasures, and put all this ready to leave at the Bar of Lisbon . . .' Again it was a false alarm, the Spanish being bought off by indemnity payments.

Two years later Sousa Coutinho was returning to the theme once more. In a prescient address, he foretold in detail the events of 1807. His advice, delivered to the prince regent in a formal presentation in 1803, was radical and unambiguous:

'The only way left to defend the Crown's independence . . . and to have any hope of defending the realm is to create a great empire in Brazil and to secure for the future the complete reintegration of the Monarchy and all its parts. There might be dangers in taking this course, but they are far less than if you let the French enter the kingdom's ports, bringing about your abdication and the abolition of the monarchy . . . and the tearing apart of your vast dominions in the islands near Europe, in America, Africa and Asia which are sought by the English as compensation for their loss of trade with Portugal.'

Pressures for the move were now coming from other quarters. A British diplomatic team, headed by Lord Rosslyn, which arrived in Lisbon late in 1806 to monitor what was already a tense state of affairs in Portugal, looked into the idea of offering to transfer the royal family to Brazil, but found few supporters for the plan. 'The reluctance to remove was universal and deep-rooted;' wrote one of the team's members, Admiral Lord St Vincent, 'nor could any arrangement the expected invader might offer prove less palatable than expatriation and banishment for life across the Atlantic to pampered voluptuaries the extent of whose excursions had hitherto been the distance between the town and the country palace.' Lord St Vincent suggested what amounted to kidnap – Dom João would be invited on board the British ship the HMS *Hibernia* which, after rounding up ministers and the other members of the court, would then set sail for Brazil, with or without the regent's consent.

In the end, the court and government ignored all the warnings, only to be pushed off the peninsula by the invading French. But their misfortune, as past thinkers had pointed out, had an upside: Brazil offered sanctuary, potential wealth and a chance for renewal. The move put an end to the blackmail, the bullying and aggression, that the court and government had long suffered in Europe and pointed the way to a new imperial age.

Soon after the flight, these ideas were fleshed out in an anonymous pamphlet which was published in Lisbon some time in 1808. In it, its writer described the creation of a futuristic New World empire. A city, named 'Nova Lisboa' would be built in the jungle, somewhere in the centre of Brazil; roads would fan out through the dense foliage, connecting the colony's coastal cities to its new capital.

Everything would start from scratch – even a new calendar would be created. 'And it wouldn't just be the names of the months that would change,' the anonymous pamphleteer went on, 'the names of cities and rivers of the Kingdom of Portugal will replace the names of the rivers, cities and provinces of the Great Empire. The river closest to "Nova Lisboa" will be called "Novo Tejo" [New Tagus].' In this new world, all traces of French influence would be erased: 'We will create a type of Inquisition to root out all French people by birth or by their customs, anyone who speaks French and any book in French (except translations from other languages).' And from his new seat the prince regent would wreak a terrible vengeance 'punishing France for its crimes and Spain for its perfidy with a sceptre of iron'.

The court had in a sense been primed for their exodus from Europe all along. And as they prepared to disembark in Rio, the historical arguments seemed to be ringing true. The flight, dramatic as it had been, fitted into a preordained plan, reiterated down the centuries by the likes of Vieira, da Cunha and Sousa Coutinho. The New World beckoned, an open road leading away from an exhausted, war-torn Europe.

Brazil was certainly a great deal safer than Europe when the court arrived so unexpectedly in early 1808, but the colonies had not been untouched by the ideas of the age. The anti-monarchist creed that had driven the royal family from Portugal had travelled on ahead of them, brought across the Atlantic by Brazilian scholars forced to study in European universities. Through the dense fog of Crown censorship, new ideas were passed by word of mouth, smuggled books exchanged. The American War of Independence (1775–1783) was avidly discussed in literary groups and amateur societies. North America's post-revolutionary development provided mental tools with which to think the unthinkable; models of what life could be like and how society could be organised outside colonial arrangements, without a monarch.

As early as 1786, Thomas Jefferson, then the United States envoy to Paris, had a mysterious encounter which revealed the strength of feeling amongst disaffected Brazilians abroad. As the autumn of that year closed in, Jefferson received a strange letter from Montpellier, a university town in the south of France. It was signed with the pseudonym 'Vendek', its contents urgent yet obscure. 'I have something of great consequence to communicate to you,' wrote Vendek in rough, accentless French, 'but the poor state of my health does not allow me to have the honour of going to Paris to meet up with you.' Vendek went on to explain that he was a foreigner and as a consequence was 'not familiar with the ways of the country' but that he could be reached via M. Vigarons, a professor of medicine at the university. Jefferson responded and the two struck up a correspondence.

Vendek's second letter was more direct. 'I am Brazilian,' he revealed to Jefferson, 'and as you know my unfortunate country is caught in an appalling slavery which becomes more unbearable each day since the time of your glorious independence.' Portugal gave Brazil nothing, for fear 'that we will follow in your foot-steps'. It was time, he went on, 'to follow the striking example that you have given us' and 'break our chains', throwing off the yoke of European colonialism once and for all. He ended by claiming a pan-American fraternity, and asked Jefferson for assistance in the coming Brazilian revolution. The two later met near Nîmes, where they exchanged ideas. Jefferson offered vague encouragement but shied away from concrete assistance.

Even without US help, on the eve of the French Revolution there were stirrings in the Brazilian interior. A plot hatched by wealthy ideologues, aiming at a North American-style break from the mother country, was uncovered in the exhausted gold mining districts of Minas Gerais. The movement was betrayed before it could even begin to realise its aspirations, but the ideological threat that it posed was taken sufficiently seriously by Crown authorities for the staging of an elaborate show trial in

Rio. One of the conspirators, Luís Vieira, was captured with a clutch of banned books from Montesquieu through to Turgot and Raynal, while their leader, Tiradentes, was caught in possession of a French edition of the US constitution. The initial sentence was draconian: the conspirators were to be hung, drawn and quartered. Tiradentes would be singled out for special attention. His head would be put on display in Minas, the rest of his body dumped at the border of the captaincy. But at the eleventh hour a pre-planned royal pardon was issued and although Tiradentes was hanged, the rest were allowed to continue their lives in exile in Africa.

The French Revolution set different precedents – worrying ones for the Brazilian elite. A decade after the Minas conspiracy there was trouble in Salvador, but this time the cry came from below, in a passionate adaptation of Paris mob sloganeering. The rhetoric touched on issues that remain relevant to the Brazilian polity to this day. The kind of change that one of the rebels, an impoverished mixed-race tailor, João de Deos, wanted was root and branch. Come the revolution: 'everyone would become Frenchmen, in order to live in equality and abundance . . . They would destroy the public officials, attack the monasteries . . . open the port . . . and revolutionise everything so that all might be rich and taken out of poverty, and that the differences between white, black and brown would be extinguished, and all would be admitted to positions and occupations without discrimination.' These echoes of the violence in France prompted another extreme response from the Crown: the conspirators were strung up, their bodies left rotting on public display.

Although these rebellions were exceptions in a largely con- servative colony still loyal to the mother country, no one was yet sure what effect the royal family's presence at the heart of the colonial system would be. Nor did they know how Spanish America would react to the wars in Europe, as Napoleon's armies spread out through the Iberian peninsula. Past thinkers had eulogised Brazil as the arcadia of their times, but Dom João was preparing to sct up his court in a continent on the cusp of revolutionary change.

FIVE

A New World

The man in charge of Rio de Janeiro, Dom Marcos de Noronha e Brito, the Count of Arcos and the viceroy of Brazil, had received a bewildering array of orders before the royal fleet finally pulled into Rio's spectacular Guanabara Bay. On 11 January 1808, news had come through of Dom João's attempted appeasement of Napoleon, and the Count of Arcos had been told to close Brazil's ports to British shipping and prepare his troops to repulse the likely British attacks. Three days later the brig *Voador* had docked, bearing the sensational news of the royal family's departure for Brazil, sending the Count of Arcos into a frenzy of activity. He had vacated his seat, overseeing much-needed repair work to convert his colonial headquarters into something approaching a royal palace, and ordered food to be sent in from the provinces. Soon, consignments of beef, pork, poultry, manioc, sweet potato and tropical fruits had started their journeys from Minas Gerais, São Paulo and the districts around Rio. All through the city, workers cleaned out churches, polished altars and swept streets and squares. Preparations were also set in motion for the music, dance, fireworks and processions that would feature in the welcoming ceremonies.

But for a few, agonising hours, it seemed that Rio would face the royal family, as Salvador had, unprepared; for just three days after the *Voador* docked, word came through via the coastal semaphore system that the fleet was on the horizon. It was a false alarm. When the ships entered the harbour, they were found to contain only Dom João's aunt, sister-in-law and two middle daughters.

The delays and false starts had heightened tension in the city. Slave dressmakers worked round the clock; the prices of ribbon, lace, velvet, damask and satin soared. When, seven weeks after the first party had docked, news came through that the fleet was off the coast, fishing boats filled the harbour and well-wishers lined its shores. In the crowd was the slight figure of Luís Gonçalves dos Santos, a fifty-year-old Brazilian priest. He was a small, wiry man, and from his large head flowed a crop of fine grey hair, giving him a cerebral demeanour. He had in fact been a Latin scholar before joining the priesthood, and would end up writing a lengthy account of the royal family's stay in his home town.

'It was two minutes to three in the afternoon,' wrote dos Santos, '– a very fresh, beautiful, and pleasant one – on what will always be a memorable day, 7 March [1808], which since dawn, the sun had announced itself to us as one of the luckiest for Brazil . . . how it rejoiced to witness the triumphant entry of the first sovereign of Europe into the most fortunate city in the New World.'

Dos Santos captured the intensity of feeling at the first sight of the royal squadron, as the convoy passed through the heads to the roar of cannon fire echoing off the rock faces:

'. . . at the sound of these booming salutes that could be heard for miles around, and of the joyful pealing of the church bells, the spirits of everyone were lifted, and men, women, old people and children ran through the streets, anxious to see the extra-ordinary entrance of the Royal squadron.'

Smoke from the cannon fire rolled across the harbour, picking out shafts of sunlight angling across the bay; the smell of spent gunpowder mingled with the tang of the sea air. To general commotion, the fleet manoeuvred in towards the royal arsenal, anchoring close to the city centre. There were emotional scenes when the ships had docked as families, split between ships in

Lisbon and then separated by the storms on the Atlantic, were finally reunited. Dona Carlota saw her two middle daughters, Maria Francisca and Isabel Maria, for the first time in over three months. Husbands embraced wives, and relatives and friends hugged each other in relief – some not knowing up until that point if their close family had managed to make it out of Lisbon. The viceroy and the city's notables, donning their best stockings and wigs, were granted an audience on board Dom João's vessel, where they kissed his hand, welcoming him to the city.

The royal fleet lay at anchor in grandiose surroundings. Ancient volcanic activity had pushed granite rock formations from the seabed; other-worldly shapes and volumes rose out of the ocean, their rock faces blackened and smoothed over by millions of years of erosion. On their upper reaches, in an otherwise lush environment, only the hardiest vegetation managed to find footholds – scrub, clumps of ferns and cacti. Down below, combinations of beach and forest, hill and bay, lagoon and ocean, spread out in an over-abundance of natural effects; the *Pão de Açúcar* (the Sugar Loaf Mountain) leaning gracefully back, as if it had been sculpted into position at the harbour's entrance.

On a clear evening the refugees from Napoleon's Europe stood out on the decks and looked over towards the small enclave that was then the city of Rio de Janeiro – a two-mile stretch of land forming a corridor of frontage between bay and mountain. As they watched, a brief but extravagant firework display lit up the low houses and narrow streets in flashes of colour. Muffled sounds of celebrations drifted across the bay, punctuated by irregular cannon fire, echoes of festivities which continued through the night.

The following day, the royal family disembarked. There was a reverent silence as the brigantine made its way slowly from the fleet to the wharf. It docked in front of the main square – a granite-paved clearing – which gave on to the bay where, at the head of a ramp, an altar had been set up. Reaching the altar, the royals prostrated themselves and were showered with a light spray of holy water. From there, under the cover of a silk canopy, the entourage walked in a slow procession across the square to the Carmelite cathedral where prayers were said and thanks given for the successful completion of such a long and dangerous voyage. The entire city had turned out and taken up vantage points in the streets, on hillsides, some even climbing on to rooftops. They looked on with a mixture of amazement, deference and curiosity – the royal family was held in awe by many, its sudden appearance in the New World akin to some kind of religious revelation.

When the royals emerged from the cathedral the crowds erupted in spontaneous applause, bands of musicians struck up in the streets, competing with the church bells which pealed throughout the town. Shredded mango leaves, flower petals and cinnamon, strewn across the city's thoroughfares and trampled under foot, perfumed the air, a sprinkling of sand cushioning the way. That evening lamps were spread out to all corners of the city and cartwheels of fireworks sprayed vivid colours against the night sky. Week-long festivities had begun – heartfelt celebrations from *cariocas* (natives of Rio) astonished by the turn of events that had brought the royal family amongst them and in the process elevated their city at a stroke from colonial to imperial capital.

It was a momentous occasion, not lost on those charged with the commemorative decorations in the city. A triumphal arch was erected in the main square, its centre filled in and painted over with an allegoric scenario aimed at giving a laudatory gloss to this complex moment in Portuguese history. At the painting's centre was a portrait of Dom João held aloft by spirits on clouds; round the bottom were vassals from around the empire paying homage; off into the distance was the Portuguese fleet, captained by the prince regent leading his ships not in retreat, but on some unspecified heroic journey, while on the periphery the abandoned Europeans wept at their terrible fate. Lusitanian coats of arms and selected verses of Virgil added historical gravitas to a structure bathed in the glow of coloured lanterns. And in an exotic touch, an inset had Dom João receiving the natural treasures of the tropics from a native Brazilian, kneeling in obeisance to his monarch. No historical parallel was spared in an effort to capture the sense of occasion felt on that day. Dos Santos likened Dom João's journey into exile to Vasco da Gama's voyage to India, the court arriving in Rio, in a famous quote from *The Lusíads*, 'from the far off Tagus'.

Dom João remained serene throughout the opening proceedings, but Dona Carlota could not contain her disappointment. She was dressed simply in black, wearing no jewellery and exposing her close cropped hair. According to one anonymous eyewitness, she wept during the reception. Another perhaps more believable account gives her a regal demeanour, maintaining etiquette but hard faced, betraying her alienation from the city and its jubilant crowds. Queen Maria I disembarked two days later. The long voyage had apparently had a calming effect and her 'usual anxieties' had abated. To further displays of affection, she was borne on a litter across the square to the door nearest to the room that had been prepared for her. Her new home was in the Carmelite convent that adjoined what was to be the royal palace.

The arrival of the Portuguese in Rio collapsed the vast distances which had in the past worked to temper imperial relations. At close quarters, the royal family could scarcely live up to the idealised portrayals – the religious allegories, the flattering portraits and engravings – through which they were known in the colonies. There could well have been disappointment, even dismay, at the first sight of Dom João; a short, stout man, with a large head and stocky arms and legs. Even on ceremonial occasions, such as this one, he cut an unlikely figure for an absolute monarch.

The women, many virtually bald after their ordeal on the Atlantic, filed through Rio's streets as curiosities. Once over the fantastic sight of a troupe of shaven *dames d'honneur*, their Paris-inspired fashions were noted, from the high waistlines and intricate embroidery of the empire style, to the long silk gloves. Those who had not travelled aboard the lice-infested *Alfonso de Albuquerque* could show off another fashion: elaborate, piled-up hairstyles, with wisps of hair hanging down around their faces.

As for the men, their silk stockings, wigs, fitted coats and square-toed shoes looked somehow out of place in the tropics.

Facing them were their colonial cousins, whose dress was for the most part simple and practical – and with good reason. In Rio temperatures regularly reached over thirty-five degrees Celsius and rarely dipped below twenty. While the city's dignitaries battled on in European-style clothing, most others chose looser-fitting garb. Women went about in sleeveless dresses, all-enveloping capes and mantillas, their hair left down, with little affectation. In their homes they wore as little as was decently possible, given that, with the poor ventilation of *carioca* houses, temperatures soared indoors. The colours were, on the whole, vibrant – lime greens, vivid blues and *sangue de boeuf*, set off by bulky necklaces and earrings featuring the diamonds and precious stones which were still being mined in the interior. Male fashion had also evolved in a more practical direction – open shirts, unfastened waistcoats, baggy trousers and sandals with no stockings were the norm for street wear. The enslaved wore virtually nothing at all, going about bare-chested and unshod, although those who carried the sedan chairs of the affluent were done out in wigs and embroidered coats. There were also many freedmen and women in Rio who had begun emulating European habits and dress. As the exiles surveyed the gathering crowds, they were taken aback by the sight of Afro-Brazilian women wearing jewellery and African men sporting top hats, walking canes and snuff boxes.

While most of those stepping off the Portuguese fleet knew little of their new colonial home, a handful would not have arrived in a state of ignorance. There was a small contingent of Brazilians who had been living in Lisbon at the time of the invasion and were now returning home. There were also bureaucrats who would have read a great deal about the capital of their largest colony, absentmindedly signing forms relating to the business of Rio, developing an accountant's-eye-view of the city as a distant, but going concern. Few, though, were prepared for what they saw. The *émigrés* were coming into an intensely ritualistic society – like Lisbon, but with an African twist. Ornate religious processions, commonplace in early-nineteenth-century Portugal, were mixed in with other traditions – the thunder of African drumbeats in the Afro-Brazilian dance, the *batuque*; *capoeira*, a provocative martial art practised in slave communities, no doubt unnerving to European onlookers; as well as more subversive rituals like the burning of the effigy of Judas, eventually banned by frightened colonials. The streets were colourful, carnivalesque even; but they were also brutal and menacing, riven as they were with the underlying tensions of a slave society.

The exiles spent their first weeks in cultural and emotional shock. In letters back to Lisbon, they expressed their horror at their new life in Rio. The climate, the unhealthiness of the city and the vulgarity of the resident Brazilians ran through letters infused with a bitter-sweet yearning, an intense nostalgia, a *saudade* for Europe. A nobleman, the Marquis of Borba, pleaded with his family to write often 'and not just short letters' or he would die of homesickness ('*morro de saudades*'). He was frightened by the frequent tropical storms: 'Every day,' he wrote back to his family in Lisbon, 'there is thunder like I have never heard in my life . . . and lightning strikes constantly in the mountains which surround the city.' But it was the perceived immorality of his new home that made the greatest impression on him. It was, he wrote, 'a new world, but one for the worst', one that had forgotten 'religion and the fear of God . . . I never thought I would end my days in a land of such abomination and scandal.'

For the royal family, too, the early days would be difficult. They were lodged in the hastily converted viceroy's palace, on the city's main square. In the few months of preparation time available, the smallish building had been expanded by being joined to a neighbouring Carmelite convent and a prison via makeshift covered walkways. The palace had been spruced up, its outside walls freshly painted and its inside lined with silk, but the whole unwieldy conglomerate was far from ideal. It was an austere set-up, made worse by its location, so unpleasant that one former viceroy had moved his headquarters to a nearby hillside, rather than suffer the noise and smells of central Rio. Servants were housed in rooms that months before had been prison cells,

Queen Maria quartered in the convent overlooking the square. The rest of the royal family and their inner circle of attendants – three hundred in all – were crammed into the converted offices and meeting rooms of the original building.

It was, indeed, a far cry from the court's accustomed surroundings – the limitless space of the Mafra complex with its miles of corridors leading off into banquet halls, libraries and chapels, all set in hundreds of acres of countryside; or the French-designed Queluz palace, its walls hung with fine art, its cabinets filled with crystal. The sheer claustrophobia of Rio's euphemistically renamed *Paço Real* (royal palace) underlined the exiled status of the royal family and its court. It was the first time in years that the whole family had shared the same residence. For a brief period, Dom João and Dona Carlota slept in rooms across the corridor from each other, but this arrangement would not last long. Soon, they were living at opposite ends of the city, with their family split between them.

Out on the streets, the court was forced to improvise, scaling back the lavish effects that had accompanied their outings in Lisbon. Even so, some locals were impressed. For the Brazilian priest, Luís Gonçalves dos Santos, the early religious processions were events of poise and splendour, displays of 'pomp and magnificence never seen before in the city'. He described the brilliant religious garments, the columns of crosses and the rows of horsemen wearing fine cloaks stamped with the royal insignia. But perhaps he had a certain audience in mind – his book was written as a dedication to Dom João, and rarely a page goes by without some laudatory reference to the prince regent and his triumphant arrival in the New World.

For those on the sidelines, like the clothier John Luccock, a very different picture emerges. Luccock had come to Rio from Yorkshire, then devastated by the effects of the war. So hopeless were the commercial prospects for mill towns in the north of England that substantial numbers had petitioned the government to enter into peace negotiations with Napoleon. In the past, when European hostilities had disrupted business, many traders had travelled to cities like Philadelphia or Baltimore to open up new markets. But now even the United States was barred. US complaints against both Britain and France for the harrying of American shipping had escalated into a trade war, culminating in the adoption of the Embargo Act (1807), which was replaced by the Non-Intercourse Act in 1809. Spurned by the United States, large numbers of British traders would eventually make it out to Rio, but Luccock was one of the first, arriving a few months after the court and staying on and off for almost a decade. He wrote a long and detailed memoir of his experiences there, an outsider's view of an eventful period in the city's history. An everyman, a British patriot, he was aghast at many aspects of Rio and Brazil, but by no means hostile to a country that after his first, difficult years, he came to love.

Luccock described a dispirited court, struggling to keep up appearances. Queen Maria, although perhaps unaware of the decline in standards, toured the city in something less than what was expected of royalty: 'The best vehicle which the rich colony of Brazil could afford its sovereign was a small chaise,' wrote Luccock, 'brought out by the same vessel in which she [Queen Maria] arrived. It was drawn by two very ordinary mules, and driven by a servant in old and discoloured, if not tattered livery.' The prince regent's outings were no more inspiring. He appeared in public in 'much the same miserable state as his mother', his 'exceedingly shabby' carriage a 'common Lisbonian one'. Dona Carlota went about on horseback, while the children were rarely seen in the open 'until a good strong family-chariot arrived, a present, it was said, from the King of Great Britain [George III]'.

The British trader was no less harsh on the city itself. Beneath the decorative veil laid on for the arrival of the royals was an urban environment very much in the colonial mould. It was heavily fortified, but in other respects poorly equipped, 'a garrison town, though without walls' according to Luccock. There was wealth in the city. As the administrative centre of Brazil since 1763, and a well-placed port in relation to the empire's sea routes, Rio had recovered well after the collapse of gold mining in the interior had brought a temporary decline to its fortunes. Economically, it was on the up, but the rich had long since abandoned the city centre to those who serviced them, moving to hilltop mansions and farmhouses in the outlying districts.

Rio's problems were in part topographical, its low, swampy terrain proving difficult to drain, leaving pools of stagnant water to gather around the town. Mountain cliffs shut off ventilating breezes, trapping humid air in the city's centre. Roads were unpaved, sanitation nonexistent. When it rained, raw sewage was thrown out into the streets in the vain hope that it would be washed away. The modern panoramic aspect was not generally accessible to early-nineteenth-century *cariocas* who lived mainly in the low-lying central districts. Nor could they travel with any ease to the Atlantic beaches (now Copacabana, Ipanema and Leblon), which were hidden behind thickly forested mountains and backed by lagoons.

At that time smaller than Salvador, Rio was nevertheless a sizeable colonial port by the standards of the day. Captain Cook, who had passed through in 1768, had likened it to Liverpool. Twenty years later, Watkin Tench, a lieutenant captain on the First Fleet to Australia, had somewhat less generously compared it to Chester or Exeter, though he added that its population was far greater. It had grown to 60,000 by the time of the arrival of the royal family – a population comparable to early-nineteenth-century New York. The port was busy, and would become an important international harbour after the Napoleonic Wars, but by land the city was cut off. Within a few hundred metres of the last houses, roads disintegrated into jungle and marshlands. In a short walk from the cramped streets of the central districts Luccock soon found himself in wilderness: 'Beyond these limits there where a few scattered houses, but within a few hundred yards of them, we were completely in the woods, or among marshes. From Gloria to Bota-Foga [Botafogo] was only a narrow mule track . . . the woods thoroughly hid the sea from our view, and the road terminated upon the beach, where we had no expectation of finding one.' The city centre, which contained less than fifty streets, had a rustic feel to it. Goats, swine and chickens roamed free; naked children played in the dirt tracks that trailed off into the jungle.

The sudden arrival of thousands of Portuguese represented a substantial increase in Rio's population (perhaps from 60,000 to 70,000 overnight), and had an immediate impact on the city's residents. There was a chronic housing shortage, and draconian measures were needed to accommodate the Portuguese. Even before the arrival of the fleet, the viceroy had invoked an unpopular law which gave the Crown the right to sequester private houses with little in the way of formalities. Officials toured the city, arbitrarily picking out suitable lodgings and chalking 'PR' (*Príncipe Regente*) on their front doors – the sign for the occupants to vacate their properties forthwith. As the requisitions went on, the initials became popularly known by the embittered *cariocas* as '*Ponha-se na Rua*' (Get Out!). In the short term this only worsened the crisis. In the uncertain climate that prevailed, plans for the construction of new houses were scrapped and those already under construction were left half-built. The wealthy became 'prudently poor' and withdrew their investment from the city. The mass eviction went on, though, creating bad feeling towards the exiles. It was a seminal act, a kind of re-colonisation, a casual seizure of property in the name of a metropolitan ideal, as the new wave of colonists displaced the old.

Through the exiles' first South American winter, the wheels of government turned swiftly, the royal press – the first allowed in Brazil – churning out laws, revoking colonial restrictions and issuing edicts. What emerged at the other end was something novel and in its own way quite extraordinary: a full-scale European bureaucracy, with all the trappings of an absolute, imperial monarchy had wound up in the tropics. From 1808 onwards, the court would run its still substantial empire from within one of its own colonies.

A sense of urgency accompanied the first weeks, courtiers making strenuous efforts to restore normality to a government that had almost met its end only a few months before. Just three days after docking in Rio, Dom João named a new set of ministers. After the Lisbon debacle, Antônio de Araújo was passed over and his nemesis, the pro-British minister Dom Rodrigo de Sousa Coutinho, was chosen to head the new government. He was a wily operator, a man not beyond using court intrigue to his advantage. He could at times be brusque, and he was renowned for his occasional outbursts of anger, as his behaviour on the journey over had shown. His family all held powerful political positions – most vitally in the coming years, his brother Dom Domingos, who was the Portuguese ambassador to Britain. Sousa Coutinho would be in his element in the first years in Rio. He was a workaholic, and threw his considerable energies into the mountain of administrative problems that the relocation to Brazil entailed.

While Sousa Coutinho's star rose, Araújo ended up taking a modest house near the *Passeio Público*, a pleasure garden in the city centre, then one of Rio's few metropolitan touches. Rebuffed, he went into semi-retirement, installing his huge library, the printing press and his mineral collections in the spare rooms of his new home, passing his time reading and writing translations of Gray, Dryden and Horace.

At the royal palace the work went on apace. Packing cases filled with the archives, state papers, ministerial correspondence and books which had made the journey on board the fleet were housed, a whole institutional framework created. The prototype was Lisbon, and it was not long before a full apparatus of state was in operation. The early months saw Dom João establish by royal order a series of bodies – a high court, a court of appeals, a military council, an exchequer, and a board of trade, industry and navigation, most of them replicas of Portuguese institutions with '*do Brasil*' tacked on to their names. By September 1808 the newly created royal press was turning out the official *Gazeta do Rio de Janeiro*, a facsimile of the *Gazeta de Lisboa*.

Advisory positions were handed out almost exclusively to Portuguese nobles, many of whom had little or no knowledge of Brazil. Whole departments with tenuous relevance to Brazilian realities were faithfully recreated. In the end the arrangements were more about providing jobs for thousands of refugee bureaucrats than serving the needs of Brazil. From 1808, the business of government – the meetings, the form-filling, the shuffling of papers – resumed in the humid airs and tropical foliage of Rio de Janeiro, as if the court were still in Lisbon. Grey bureaucrats sweated their way through their days, applying the rigid systems which had served for decades in Europe to the New World; courtiers held interviews in dispatch rooms over-looking palm groves, trying to maintain their poise through violent downpours.

Amidst the flurry of royal orders, Dom João moved out of the city centre. On his arrival, a wealthy planter had donated his neoclassical mansion at São Cristóvão in the Quinta da Boa Vista, three miles to the west of the city. It was there, set in countryside backed by mountain ranges, that Dom João, accompanied by his sons Pedro and Miguel and his eldest daughter, Maria Teresa, would eventually spend most of his time. Dona Carlota stayed on in the centre of town with the other daughters, before moving into a series of villas in the surrounding hills.

Dom João's retreat to São Cristóvão was in keeping with his increasingly reclusive lifestyle in Lisbon which had seen him move from the city palace of Ajuda, out to Queluz and then further away still to Mafra. He preferred the tranquillity of the countryside, and in São Cristóvão he gradually grew accustomed to a very different environment from the temperate landscapes of Portugal. Large palms, coconut stands and jacarandas filled the mansion's grounds, while beyond, the subtropical rainforest – dense foliage punctuated by orchids, bromeliads and tree ferns – ascended into the mountains. There, squirrel-sized marmosets and golden lion tamarins rustled through the canopy while red-breasted parrots and toucans winged overhead. In the other direction a bucolic trail led down to the bay, past the ruins of an abandoned church. The only aspect of his new home that gave Dom João problems was the sweltering heat and Rio's deafening electrical storms – so frightened was he in the early days, that he is said to have disappeared into the recesses of the palace until they passed. But the rains brought relief – cool airs wafting off

the mountains, bringing the smell of the jungle down into the
very heart of the city.

At first the mansion was cut off from the centre, but a
connecting road was built, passing through brackish swamplands
which dominated the outskirts of Rio. For those not used to the
marshes, the smell was unbearable. On humid evenings convoys
of carriages would leave the city and move slowly through the
tropical bogs. Inside the carriages, Portuguese noblemen and
women sat with white handkerchiefs clamped to their faces,
making their way out to see their monarch.

Cariocas who had gathered in expectation of catching their
first glimpse of their rulers would soon be familiar with the royal
family in their midst. Sightings of Dom João taking to the streets,
his officials in train, or Dona Carlota galloping out into the
countryside were soon commonplace. Dona Carlota's eccentri-
cities became the talk of the town, her unwomanly habit of
riding astride with a rifle slung over her shoulder, her hunting
expeditions into the hills, as well as her obvious estrangement
from her husband shocked the conservative colonial society.

Every day Queen Maria was lifted into her carriage in the
city's main square, before making her way through the city
centre for her outing. She was invariably dressed in black silk, in
extended mourning for her long-dead husband. Trailed by two
horsemen, one to carry water, and the other a set of steps
covered in red velvet for when she wanted to get out, the
convoy set off through the city. Sometimes the procession
would snake up into the hills, beating its way along half-cleared
jungle paths, and from one of the numerous lookouts over the
harbour, Dona Maria would count the mountains in the distance, over and over again. At other times they would end up on
the bay at Botafogo beach, an arc of fine-grained sands in the
shadow of the Sugar Loaf Mountain, and the queen would slip
into profound contemplation, watching the waves break against
the shore. In this state, she was difficult to rouse, but on occasion
there were paranoid outbursts. She would claim that the devil
was lying in wait somewhere further down the track, or that he
was hidden behind the Sugar Loaf, spying on her from on high.

Slave attendants became accustomed to these episodes, indulging her fantasies and reassuring her. Back at the palace she was also volatile – either comatose, or extremely awkward, screaming at her servants or telling distinguished visitors to go away and leave her alone.

What had been a sleepy colonial backwater was now subject to an involved protocol. Ahead of Dom João's carriage ran royal attendants who brusquely cleared the path, forcing those at the roadside to take their hats off. Dona Maria travelled with escorts whose job it was to force all passersby to comply with royal etiquette. Riders had to dismount, those in carriages stop, alight and kneel by the side of the road, heads bowed, until the queen had passed. As for Dona Carlota, her outriders went as far as whipping bystanders for not showing the appropriate respect. At certain times of the day, the city was paralysed by the movements of the royal family as the commotion of those paying deference rippled down roads and through squares.

The *beija-mão* – a hand kissing ritual, a particular favourite of Dom João – was a regular event. The ceremony was meant to open up a channel between the king and his vassals and was, in theory at least, open to all. Those admitted to the throne room queued up to touch the royal person, and amidst a series of carefully choreographed genuflections and bows, kissed the prince regent's outstretched hand while asking for royal favour. The *beija-mão* was the one, very public, occasion on which the uniqueness of what was happening in Rio was there for all to see. A European monarch would never be more intimately in touch with his colonial subjects – black and mulatto Afro-Brazilians, part-indigenous peasants and recently freed slaves were all in the queue. 'It is very curious to notice,' wrote one traveller, 'amongst the gentlemen with bows and ensigns, men of all colours, in coloured cotton jackets or provincial clothes.' 'They explain . . . their request, and it is always listened to graciously.'

Outside of these set-pieces, Dom João was petitioned directly as he toured the streets, with his carriage waylaid by vassals kneeling before it to ask for pardons or help in financial distress.

He had an excellent memory for faces and was soon greeting many of his colonial subjects by name. The prince regent also set up an honours system, out of which a Brazilian nobility rose. Planters, slavers and wealthy merchants were dubbed marquises, counts, barons and knights, further cementing Dom João's popularity.

Rio was a vibrant but rough colonial port. Royal litters shared byways with vendors touring the centre, advertising their wares with hoarse, rhythmic cries. Courtiers jostled low-grade surgeons bloodletting patients by the side of the road. There was a rawness to the central square. Beggars, gypsies, monks and soldiers mixed promiscuously, camped outside the royal palace. Around the fountains, where water carriers queued and slave women washed their masters' clothes, fights regularly broke out to screams in different African dialects, only to be violently suppressed by soldiers on guard. Early-nineteenth-century Lisbon would certainly have been no idyll – but there the court had been safely cloistered inside palace complexes, shielded from the nastier aspects of the port.

It fell to one of the few Brazilian-born appointees in the new administration, Paulo Fernandes Viana, to attack the problem of overhauling Rio and converting it into a city fit for royalty. He was put in charge of the 'Police Intendancy' (a type of mayoral office, modelled on a similar institution in Lisbon) and given sweeping powers over not just the city's security arrangements, but its expansion and remodelling through a far-reaching programme of public works. He was an intelligent man, energetic and dedicated to the task. Meeting often with Dom João, he set about transforming a garrison town into a showy imperial capital.

Moorish latticework verandas which fronted many houses in the centre were outlawed and replaced by windows or iron grilles. Their removal uncluttered some of the smaller streets, letting light in and allowing air to circulate more freely. The city's squares were emptied out, converted from ad hoc camping sites for the mule trains arriving from the interior, to empty

Iberian parade grounds. Roads were paved, marshes drained and a series of infrastructural works planned. House building, encouraged by generous tax concessions, gradually got under way to the north of the overcrowded central districts; and in time the *Cidade Nova* (the New City) rose out of earthed-over swamplands.

The creation of a botanical gardens was approved, Dom João inaugurating the *Horto Real* – the royal gardens – on a plot set back from a large lagoon, at the foot of the Corcovado mountain, several miles from the city centre. In front of the lagoon stretched a tract of ocean-facing beachfront. At that time this thin strip was wilderness, but in the following century it would become known by an evocative native name – Ipanema – as it made its transition from a rural outpost to a world-renowned beach corridor for the *carioca* elite. The gardens would eventually become a laboratory of empire, where acclimatisation experiments would be run using seeds and grafts transported from Angola, Mozambique, Goa and Macao.

The defining feature of the gardens came not from one of Portugal's many tropical colonies, but, perhaps more fittingly, as a result of European hostilities. Shipwrecked off Goa, a group of Portuguese officials ended up as prisoners on Île de France (modern-day Mauritius). One of them escaped, pocketing cuttings from the island's famous gardens at Pamplemousse. He brought with him an array of seedlings: avocado, nutmeg, cinnamon, breadfruit, sago and litchi and, more significantly for the future look and feel of Rio, the royal palm, a slender, towering tree topped by an elegant crop of fronds. At the official inauguration of the gardens, the first – the *palma mater* – was planted by Dom João himself. A year later, the gardens benefited from another play in the Napoleonic Wars: a joint British-Portuguese fleet was sent north and took French Guiana, and a new collection of Asiatic plants, cultivated in Cayenne's *Jardin Gabrielle*, arrived. The shipment included cuttings from a faster-growing variety of cane plant which would eventually spread through Brazil's vast sugar plantations.

From time to time Dom João would set out on tours of

inspection, some days making his way out to the gardens that he loved, and with which he would become strongly associated. On arrival, he could take his lunch at the very heart of the gardens, in a small pavilion designed for the prince regent and his servants, before walking the rows of vegetation, remarking on the origins and relative progress of different plant varieties. Once back in the city, he would inspect new buildings, fountains and repair work on church interiors before returning to the palace in the evening.

On these outings, the prince regent was venerated, his New World vassals shouting *vivas* as he approached, showering him with praise and affection. The same could not be said of the rest of the court, who came to be viewed with suspicion by their colonial cousins. Many sources testify to the generosity of the Brazilians on the court's arrival in Rio, but it was not long before relations soured. Those 'who had parted with their houses, and friends, and servants,' wrote Luccock, '. . . were indignant at the sight of inferiors favoured and advanced above them, [and] withdrew from the city to their farms . . . Others followed their example, because the expenses of living were so much increased by the influx of new inhabitants, and the manners of the times altered, as they thought, for the worse.'

Corruption had always been a feature of life around the empire but it came in a concentrated form to Rio. The sudden influx of thousands of displaced bureaucrats created fertile conditions for abuse, and mysterious fortunes were duly built up by court insiders. While life for many of the more peripheral courtiers was a struggle, government ministers were soon living well beyond any means they could have earned legitimately. Joaquim José de Azevedo, the court official who had overseen the embarkation of the royal family, became so wealthy in Brazil that he ended up as the court's banker, and according to one *émigré*, providing 'a free loan to the treasury . . . that filled five carriages full of silver and eleven slaves weighed down with gold.' Beyond the staves, the robes and wigs, beneath the formal ceremonies and edicts pronounced in courtly language, theft in the name of the Crown became widespread.

*   *   *

The Lisbon court faced many difficulties in the early months in Brazil, but there was one consolation. News from Europe painted a remorselessly bleak picture. Violence was erupting across the Iberian peninsula, the war rushing to fill a vacuum that Napoleon himself had created. Under the pretext of supplying reinforcements for Junot, Napoleon had moved huge numbers of troops over the Pyrenees. They were soon seen entering territory that lay well off any conceivable road to Portugal, and began taking up positions in strategic towns around Spain. A large column of troops set out for Madrid. With ironic symmetry, the Spanish royal family, headed by Carlos IV, began to weigh up the option of flight to Mexico, should it be forced by the French to quit the country. In the end the Spanish court was trapped by its own people. Hundreds besieged the royal palace outside Madrid in protest against the regime which had betrayed Spain to the French.

Under pressure, Carlos IV dismissed his foreign minister, Manuel de Godoy, who was widely (and rightly) perceived as a French collaborator, and then abdicated in favour of his son, Fernando (Dona Carlota's brother). Fernando VII, dubbed *el deseado* ('the desired one'), was the popular choice, but he found on his return to Madrid that he was not recognised by the French. Summoned, along with his father, to Bayonne to negotiate his position with Napoleon, he walked straight into a trap – once on French soil, father and son were both forced to abdicate in favour of Napoleon's elder brother Joseph. Robbed of his crown, Fernando was detained in French foreign minister Charles Maurice de Talleyrand's château in Valençay, where he would remain for the rest of the war.

It was a series of characteristically high-handed manoeuvres which Napoleon would live to regret. On 2 May 1808, Madrid exploded in violence. In a swirl of short daggers captured by Goya's dramatic *Dos de Mayo*, the French faced the first of the many uprisings in their troubled occupation of Spain. Their response was immediate and brutal. Hundreds of Spaniards were rounded up and executed, in scenes that Goya also committed to canvas in *El Tres de Mayo*. Against a blackened sky a man kneels, his loose white shirt glowing, lit up by a cube-shaped lantern, the only light source in an otherwise dark-toned tableau. His arms are outstretched in surrender, he holds an expression of half entreaty, half defiance as a row of trench-coated French soldiers prepares to end his life. In the shadows other Spanish prisoners await their fate, covering their faces in horror. Below them lies a corpse, its blood already congealed into craggy globs of red paint. The war had begun. News of the Madrid massacre reverberated throughout the Spanish provinces. Revolts broke out in Andalusia in the south, Asturias in the north and neighbouring Galicia. And in an action that set the tone for the brutality of the coming conflict, Valencia's French merchant community – over 300 men, women and children – was slaughtered by a mob led by the friar Baltasar Calvo.

Napoleon's seizure of the Spanish throne had opened up a costly front, but the coming war would impact far beyond the peninsula. The imprisonment of Fernando VII created a constitutional crisis throughout Spanish America. Across Spain, regional assemblies, called *juntas*, had begun springing up to fill the gap left by the absent monarch. They coalesced into a provisional patriot government, the Supreme Junta, based first near Madrid in Aranjuez, but later beaten back to Seville, which coordinated resistance to the French. The American viceroys, whose legitimacy derived from the Spanish Crown, now faced an acute dilemma: were they bound by the new government in Seville? Or should they, following the mother country's example, set up their own *juntas*, pledging their allegiance directly to the imprisoned Fernando VII? There were even fringe Bonapartist factions willing to align themselves with Napoleon's brother Joseph, now on the Spanish throne.

As the situation in Spain evolved, the questions multiplied – colonial understandings which had been in place for centuries were blurring, and creole (i.e. American-born) elites, unsure of where they stood, began taking matters into their own hands. The results were complex and varied. Revolutionary rips ran under a powerful loyalist tide, eddies of popular unrest swirled, only to disappear, vanishing beneath a surface of deceptive calm.

The year 1808 saw the staging of a *coup d'état* against the wavering Mexican viceroy, Iturrigaray, by loyalist Spanish merchants; the following year there was rioting in favour of the creation of semi-autonomous creole *juntas* in La Paz and Quito. They too were suppressed by loyalist forces, but as the crisis deepened in the mother country, the colonial bonds were straining.

Back in Europe, reports of the Spanish uprising electrified Britain. The winter of 1807–1808 – one of complete and, in the long term, debilitating isolation – was over. Hope returned to Westminster. Delegates from Asturias arrived in London in June 1808 to petition the British government for money and arms. Officials from all over Spain followed, asking for assistance, but – wary of wider British motivations – refusing direct military intervention. In July, Sir Arthur Wellesley, the future Duke of Wellington, was sent out from Cork with a flotilla of troops and equipment. He set his sights on Lisbon, where Junot's once solid occupation was turning into a French outpost in a hostile peninsula.

SIX

The War Years

In July 1808 Lord Strangford arrived in Rio 'after a tedious voyage of seventy-seven days' to a court finding its feet in the tropics. It had been a nightmare journey. Months before, he had written the first of a series of letters to Sousa Coutinho's brother, Dom Domingos, in an attempt to speed up his passage: 'We are still here [Brixham, Devonshire], my dear Friend, & are likely to continue so for many days. All our hopes are placed in you. For Heavens sake, try to save us! *Même à force d'importuner.* We shall not be at Rio de Janeiro before the end of August . . . p.s. We are all impatience for your Answer. Speak to Mr. Canning, I implore you. *Don't shew this letter.*'

Strangford was to travel within a large convoy heading for the Cape, from which he would peel off in the mid-Atlantic, and make for Rio de Janeiro. It was an arrangement with which he was far from happy, as he protested in another letter to Dom Domingos: 'Prevail upon Mr. Canning to make one attempt more, & represent to him the indecency of sending me with sixty-seven Sail of Merchantmen and with transports filled with troops for the Cape of Good Hope, which are such bad sailors that the last India company would not allow them to sail with their Fleet.'

The long journey had at least given him time to study foreign secretary Canning's instructions as to how he should handle the court in Rio. 'You will endeavour on all occasions to direct the

attention of the Brazilian Government to the care and cultivation of those ample and improvable resources which its American Dominions afford,' Canning had written to Strangford in a
secret annex, 'rather than encourage them in looking back with
unavailing regret to their European Territory, or indulging an
Expectation, not likely to be realised, of recovering it from the
grasp of the Enemy.' Strangford was to stress the advantages that
the prince regent would derive from staying on in Brazil,
particularly in the area of trade with Britain, which 'should
be wisely and judiciously placed on such a footing, as to induce
the British merchant to make the Brazils an Emporium for the
British Manufactures destined for the consumption of the whole
of South America.'

On arrival, Strangford went immediately to see Dom João and
found he had nothing to fear on the question of returning to
Europe: '. . . He had almost made up His mind to remain in
South America,' Strangford reported back to Canning, 'and . . .
he doubted not that time and Reason would reconcile Him to
His situation.' Strangford had some good news for Dom Domingos back in London. 'I hope that soon I will be writing to you
as a Count . . . The Prince [Dom João] has promised me that he
will award you some brilliant title.' After signing off he scrawled
the postscript: 'The women are awful in this country.'

In the following years Strangford would play a controversial
role in Rio, as the enforcer of British will in South America. The
city was soon familiar with his upright figure, strutting around
town in sharp suits, cravats and buffed leather shoes. Britain was
now the court's military protector and Strangford did not
hesitate to use his leverage over the prince regent. He quickly
established himself as the most powerful presence in the court,
able to bend Dom João's will to whichever objective he wished
to pursue.

His early months would be perplexing, though, as he grappled
with a set of problems for which Canning's instructions had not
prepared him. Against the backdrop of Napoleon's conquests,
the position of the court in the tropics was a peculiar, but
potentially advantageous one – as the only European govern-

ment removed from the theatre of war, it had a strategic edge. Before Strangford's arrival, Sousa Coutinho had been sizing up the opportunities, floating the idea of British-aided attacks on the Philippines and the Pacific coast of South America. In conversation with Francis Hill, the British *chargé d'affaires*, he had suggested that the Spanish American colonies could be pressured 'to declare in favour of the Prince Regent, who would by that means become the sole Sovereign of this Immense Continent'. The idea was far-fetched, but underlying it were certain political realities: Spain was disintegrating, its capacity to protect its American colonies virtually nonexistent; the Portuguese, backed by the British, were now based in the very heart of South America.

It would be in the south, though, that Sousa Coutinho would focus his energies. The conquest of a disputed territory known then as the Banda Oriental (subsequently Uruguay) – a block of land which started across the river from Buenos Aires and extended 250 miles up to the Brazilian border – would dominate the court's imperial policy in Rio. Disagreements over the Banda Oriental dated back to the very beginnings of Portuguese and Spanish colonial expansion in the Americas. They stemmed from the original Treaty of Tordesillas (1494), which marked out the pole-to-pole border splitting the world into Spanish and Portuguese hemispheres. The impossibility of accurately measuring longitude generated claims and counter-claims, disputes involving vast columns of imaginary land that cut through the centre of the newly discovered continent.

The Banda Oriental's importance grew in the sixteenth and seventeenth centuries as shipments of silver began to be ferried from the mines in Upper Peru (Bolivia) down the River Plate and out into the Atlantic. For the Spanish, it was a buffer zone, protecting their lucrative port activities in Buenos Aires. The Portuguese countered that the River Plate marked a natural frontier – an unambiguous endpoint to Brazil's southern pasturelands – but it was the access that the northern banks of the River Plate gave to the flourishing contraband trade in Spanish American markets that was always paramount. The region had

changed hands several times down the centuries, but since the
1770s it had been held by the Spanish. With the Portuguese
court now located in Rio, and Spain embroiled in the early
stages of the Peninsular Wars, the way now appeared open for a
renewed Portuguese offensive.

Just five days after the court's arrival in Rio, Sousa Coutinho
had fired off an intimidatory letter to the viceroy in Buenos
Aires, claiming that the threat of French attacks necessitated
Portuguese military protection of the Banda Oriental. Aware of
the predatory subtext, Buenos Aires refused all military assistance
from Brazil and an uneasy stand-off ensued. Strangford was at
first unsure of what to make of Sousa Coutinho's ambitions, but
after referring the matter back to London he was ordered to keep
the peace between Spain and Portugal, a difficult task in a court
primed for expansion.

Strangford's efforts would be complicated by the presence of
another British heavyweight. Two months before Strangford
disembarked in Brazil, Sir Sidney Smith, fresh from manning the
blockade on Lisbon, had pulled into Rio's Guanabara Bay to
take up his posting as the Admiral of the British fleet in Brazil.
Smith was flamboyant – in the Middle East he had taken to
wearing flowing Turkish robes – even a little eccentric ('half
mad' according to Napoleon). Earlier in his career he had been
captured and imprisoned in Paris, only to stage a daring break-
out, a story that became a favourite at high-society *soirées*. It is
unclear what exactly Smith's orders were, but from the outset he
would work at cross purposes with Strangford, a man he already
loathed for his exaggerated accounts of the part he played in the
evacuation of Lisbon.

The news of Napoleon's seizure of the Spanish Crown and
the popular revolt that this had prompted further muddied the
diplomatic waters. Overnight, Spain had become an uneasy ally
of Portugal. What was more, the imprisonment of both Carlos
IV and Fernando VII gave Dona Carlota a theoretical claim on
the Spanish throne. She was Carlos IV's eldest daughter, and in
the current circumstances, the closest Spanish Bourbon heir still
at liberty. At a minimum she now wielded enormous symbolic

power in what was a fast-moving and fluid situation in both Europe and South America.

Dona Carlota's first thoughts were for her imprisoned family. 'Mother of my heart,' she wrote to France, 'I prostrate myself at the feet of Your Highness to express the consternation at your plight, caused by those two infamous men: Bonaparte and Godoy. What my heart feels, neither my mouth, nor my pen can describe . . .' In more defiant mood, Dona Carlota consoled her brother Fernando: 'I am your sister, I am the Spanish Infanta, the Princess of Brazil, and I have enough strength to uphold the high dignity to which these roles correspond, but I am not able to hold back the tears that the most tender sisterly love wrenches from my soul at the memory of your unhappy situation.' All the while, Dona Carlota weighed up the new possibilities now open to her, as she began her campaign to defend the Spanish Bourbon monarchy in its time of crisis.

Dona Carlota's newfound relevance posed a problem for the Portuguese court. Sousa Coutinho viewed her with undisguised contempt for her record as a conspirator and interferer in court affairs, but he was not about to let a political opportunity slip through his fingers. Dom João was also nervous about his wife's ambitions, while mindful of the boon she might turn out to be for the court in Rio. As the cards currently lay, the Portuguese court had the tantalising possibility of proposing an Iberian Union of Crowns, run from Rio, by a Bourbon-Bragança royal house. Other players had different perspectives on what Dona Carlota's pretensions to the throne might bring. For Sir Sidney Smith, a Dona Carlota regency could legitimise moves against Beunos Aires. He had already begun planning a pre-emptive attack on the city, so as to block any French ambitions in the region, and capture another gateway into the South American markets for the British. Were Dona Carlota accepted as a Spanish monarch, he might be able to sail unopposed down the River Plate, and establish her as queen of South America.

Amid these grandiose schemes, Sousa Coutinho put forward a compromise. He drew up a manifesto, proposing both Dona Carlota and her cousin Dom Pedro Carlos, who had been brought up in the Portuguese court in Lisbon and fled with the royal family to Rio, as temporary regents while Fernando VII was imprisoned in France. The inclusion of Dom Pedro Carlos was meant to dilute any power that might accrue to Dona Carlota – his claim to the Spanish throne was tenuous in comparison to hers, but he was firmly allied to Dom João.

The issue of Dona Carlota's proposed Spanish regency split the palace once more, and the intrigues which had characterised the court in Lisbon before the flight returned with a vengeance. It was a familiar tale: 'Your brother and I are the best possible friends', Strangford wrote to Dom Domingos in London. 'We are (as you can well understand) ranged on the side of the Prince [Dom João], who is furiously tormented and harassed by the Princess [Dona Carlota] and her Admiral [Smith].' What was going on between Dona Carlota and Sir Sidney Smith was, according to the account Strangford sent to Dom Domingos, a full-blown affair: 'You have no idea of the things that these two people get up to . . . The secret conferences until two in the morning, five days a week, the intimate suppers, the nocturnal visits, the rings given and received, the locks of hair exchanged.' 'In truth, you could not have any idea all we have suffered here,' Strangford complained in another letter. 'To imagine how far the audacity and insolence of Sidney Smith goes, you have to recall the Ambassadors Lannes [who preceded Junot in Lisbon] and Junot.'

Dona Carlota had unexpectedly found herself in her element. She now had a grandiose goal, a court brimming with intrigue, and a powerful ally to work with. Her campaign for the Spanish regency was tireless. It began with the backing of the court but soon evolved into a personal quest – an obsessive search for a way out of her exile in Brazil. She was aided by her private secretary and confidant, José Presas, a renegade from Buenos Aires and Smith's former interpreter. Presas seems to have spent the bulk of his time under Dona Carlota writing letters. Towards the end of 1808, he was sending out a stream of correspondence to the viceroy of Peru, political and religious figures in Buenos Aires, the governor of Havana, and agents in Mexico, Chile and Guatemala, pressing her claims to the throne.

Her letters reached viceroys across the continent at a critical time. Officials throughout Spanish America were struggling to respond to events in Spain, weighing up both the opportunities and the dangers that the sudden loss of the sovereign had brought. Although there was the possibility of greater autonomy from the mother country, many feared for their safety without the protection of the Spanish Crown and her armies. In the circumstances, Dona Carlota's dynastic claims were by no means outlandish, although she would receive little clear-cut support with her first attempts. Her letters to Peru, Chile and Mexico went unanswered, but promising signals came from agents in Buenos Aires, the political centre of the viceroyalty of Río de La Plata, then a sprawling conglomerate of what are now Argentina, Bolivia, Paraguay and Uruguay. The situation there was unstable. Breakaway factions in Buenos Aires were beginning to explore the possibilities of autonomy from Spain; and uniting under Dona Carlota as regent was one route being discussed by some agitators.

As Dona Carlota continued her campaign, the conflict in the peninsula was shifting. What had begun as Napoleon's arrogant manipulation of the Spanish and Portuguese Crowns was degenerating into an all out war.

At Mondego Bay, on Portugal's Atlantic coast, shallow-bottomed troop carriers shipped water as they worked their way in towards the shore. Thousands of British soldiers huddled together within them, bracing themselves for what would be a difficult landing. A sand bar had formed across the harbour. Rips and counter-currents confounded the approach routes, and beyond the swell waves broke unevenly along the beach. Men, horses and equipment queued up to pass through the surf. Heavy artillery rode the waves on rafts and thudded into the shoreline's sands. Several of the flimsy transports went down; a handful of soldiers lost their lives – non-swimmers who drowned within striking distance of land. Most, though, made the short passage without incident and began setting up their encampment on the beach. After an arduous week, over 13,000 troops and their equipment had been landed.

They were soon on the move, heading down the coast towards Lisbon. This was to be a formative campaign, not least for the thirty-nine-year-old Sir Arthur Wellesley. At that point only recently promoted to lieutenant-general, Wellesley was embarking on his first high-profile military engagement. Because of his relatively junior status he had only been given provisional command of the army until more senior officers arrived − a plan, driven more by internal military politicking than strategic sense, that was to prove disastrous. Wellesley had been waiting in Cork to head an expedition to Venezuela when his forces were switched to exploit the growing unrest in the peninsula. Setting out on 12 July 1808, he had sailed on ahead first to La Coruña, in north-west Spain, and then further south to Oporto where he had explored the possibilities of a Portugal landing and had settled on Mondego Bay, halfway down the coast towards French-occupied Lisbon.

In the capital, Junot's position had deteriorated. Communications had been severed with Spain by the popular uprisings, leaving him stranded on the Atlantic coast with no prospect of assistance from France. Portugal, like Spain, was in open revolt. Oporto, which had been garrisoned by the Spanish, was now liberated, and even in Lisbon, civil disobedience was loosening Junot's hold. That year, the Corpus Christi parade had degenerated into a riot. 'While the procession was walking a great tumult arose,' wrote eyewitness Harriot Slessor, 'Legs and arms were broken. Poor ladies . . . with their clothing half torn off their backs were screaming for help; others fainting.' Junot had even contemplated withdrawing, but had decided instead to concentrate his forces in and around Lisbon. French troop regiments stationed in the provinces retreated, looting and killing as they fought their way back towards the capital.

Two light skirmishes started what would end up being Wellesley's half-decade long campaign on the peninsula, as the British army met French forward positions on its way down the Portuguese coast. The armies first engaged at Roliça but it was at Vimeiro, a small town three days out from Lisbon, that the decisive encounter took place. There, Wellesley distinguished himself, outmanoeuvring Junot and scoring Britain's first significant victory on the Continent in over fifty years. The French retreated in disarray and Wellesley regrouped to march on Lisbon, now an open target, but at this very moment he found himself relieved of his command. The incoming Sir Hew Dalrymple and his deputy Sir Harry Burrand opted for caution. Junot, sensing a way out, cut his losses and on 22 August 1808, he surrendered. Tactical errors on the British side were compounded by the signing of the Convention of Sintra – an armistice which allowed Junot's crippled army to leave intact with its kit and artillery, transported on British boats back to France.

There was an uproar when news of the agreement reached London. The Convention, wrote the London *Observer*, was 'honourable only to the enemy'. A 'total ruin of a great cause', was the *Edinburgh Review*'s conclusion, while William Wordsworth was so enraged that he wrote a passionate treatise on the cynicism of the agreement. Wellesley was also attacked in the press – 'all England has been deceived in its opinion of Sir Arthur Wellesley' declared *The Times* – although he would emerge relatively unscathed when, at a later stage, he faced an official enquiry in London.

Lisbon's residents were forced to look on as the vanquished French forces loaded up British boats with goods they had stolen during their stay – a farcical rerun of the Portuguese court's precipitous departure less than a year before. Once more the docks were piled high with crates; once more choice artefacts from the city's rich cultural heritage were stashed in the holds of an outward bound fleet. In the city itself Junot's troops had left their mark. French flags could be pulled down but buildings had been defaced – royal arms chipped from their façades, official emblems removed from palace gates and statues vandalised.

There was consternation, too, in Rio. The British had not waited for clearance from the court in Brazil where Dom João and his advisers first heard of the Portugal campaign and its aftermath through newspaper reports and private correspondence, weeks after the event. They were nervous of British intentions and complained about the number of foreign troops now on Portuguese soil, but there was little they could do other than file official complaints and wait for further month-old dispatches from the front.

With the liberation of Portugal, more British troops were sent in and the Peninsular Wars began in earnest. These were a series of complex and often inconclusive engagements – chaotic affairs that took their toll on all involved. Over the years the French threw enormous military resources into the peninsula, only to become mired in an unwinnable conflict. They were faced by a disorienting array of forces: poorly trained and sometimes erratic Spanish regulars, more professional British-trained Portuguese forces, the British army itself and the constant, but shadowy presence of guerrilla insurgents. To make matters worse, the French were often divided by petty disputes between marshals who were given too free a rein by Paris.

What had originally been envisaged as a rapid, pushover campaign, ground on. Time and again, the French found they captured territory, but could not hold it. They pillaged the countryside, but unlike in other parts of Europe, could not gather enough to feed their armies. Non-battle casualties soared; famine and disease killed thousands. Roving through a regionalised country, Napoleon's armies became enmeshed in local disputes, ambushed by warlords defending their own hastily claimed fiefs against all comers. The French had prepared for set-piece battles in open plains, but were dragged into a guerrilla campaign run by peasant fighters armed with far superior local knowledge.

It became a dirty war, even by the standards of the time, with the atrocities carried out by starving French forces more than matched by the Spanish and Portuguese guerrillas. The French tried to spread fear through the rural population with example executions, murders and rapes, but found themselves terrorised in turn by some more imaginative, not to say medieval, practices. Well-founded stories of crucifixions, garrottings and burnings at the stake haunted Napoleon's men as they advanced through the unfamiliar backlands. There, they were met by peasant fighters armed with pitchforks, fowling pieces, even kitchen utensils. It was a template for many future wars of this type, a tragedy, an unheeded lesson from history.

Junot's invasion was but the first of three assaults which Portugal would suffer at the hands of the French. The second came at the end of March 1809, in the wake of Sir John Moore's evacuation from La Coruña. The forty-eight-year-old Moore had taken over the command of the British forces in Portugal from Dalrymple, and in October 1808 was ordered to take a 23,000-strong army into Spain. He had got as far as Salamanca, and with news coming through of delays in the arrival of reinforcements, as well as a major French counter-offensive, Moore had set off at pace on a exhausting winter retreat to the Galician port of La Coruña. He was pursued, for a time, by Napoleon himself in his one and only, cameo role in the peninsular campaigns, but once the Emperor realised Moore's army could not be cut off from the port, he handed the chase over to Marshal Soult.

On the night of 11 January 1809, the British arrived destitute in La Coruña: 'Our beards were long and ragged,' recalled rifleman Hibbert Harris. 'Almost all were without shoes or stockings; many had their clothes and accoutrements in fragments with their heads swathed in old rags.' Embarkation took place against the sound of French cannon fire reverberating through the city's streets. The British rearguard held them off long enough for the boats to set sail, but only a fifth of Moore's original forces made it out of Spain. In one of the last stands, Sir John Moore was felled by a cannonball and bled to death on the battlefield. The remnants of his army arrived emaciated at Portsmouth, shocking a public recently buoyed by the recapture of Portugal.

Marshal Soult's forces wheeled south, and headed for Oporto. The city was attacked towards the end of March 1809, its makeshift defences crumbled and those fleeing from the advancing troops fell in a hail of grapeshot as they retreated back across the River Douro. Soult's battle-weary troops regrouped in the city, but their conquest would be short-lived. Wellesley arrived back in Lisbon on 22 April 1809 with orders to recapture the north, and after a stunningly successful surprise attack, Soult's army was driven out of Oporto in May.

The second French occupation had been brief, but destructive. An English officer, returning to the house of a Portuguese nobleman where he had stayed in 1808, described what he found:

> 'the fine balustrades [were] broken; the chandeliers and mirrors were shattered to pieces . . . the choice pictures were defaced, and the walls more resembled a French barrack than the abode of a Portuguese *fidalgo* [nobleman] from the obscene paintings that were daubed on them. The beautiful garden was entirely ransacked; the charming walks and fragrant bowers torn up and demolished; the fountains broken to pieces.'

Out in the countryside was the gruesome evidence of the revenge killings that had taken place during the French retreat: soldiers nailed to barn doors, corpses with their genitals sheared off. Only a year-and-a-half into the war, the Portuguese had already been brutalised by the violence visited upon them.

With news of the chaos in Europe filtering through to Rio, Dona Carlota redoubled her efforts. The British had recaptured Portugal, but Spain remained under French occupation, with reinforcements streaming over the Pyrenees. If she could somehow exploit the uncertainty that was now gripping the colonial authorities in Spanish America, she could turn her back on Rio for good.

Within the court there was a mixed response to her Spanish American ambitions. Sousa Coutinho was still aiming to use Dona Carlota's claims as a pretext to seizing the Banda Oriental. Dom João was characteristically indecisive, wary of his wife's obvious ambition, even scared, according to Presas, of what might happen if Dona Carlota achieved her own power base in the Americas. Under pressure from Sousa Coutinho, Dom João initially gave his wife permission to go to Buenos Aires '. . .

when Your Highness is called on in a formal and authentic manner,' wrote Dom João to his wife, 'you may undertake your voyage . . .' But he withdrew it just one month later: 'Your plan of appearing in Río de La Plata, to secure those provinces for the Spanish Monarchy, besides breaking my heart because of the fact that we will have to be separated from each other for some months . . . is absolutely inadmissible, not even if the state of those provinces demands a decisive resolution.'

Dom João's reference to the pain caused by their impending separation was disingenuous – they only met when they had to in Rio, the prince regent not even visiting his wife when she fell ill. But it is in keeping with their correspondence, which, curiously, is littered with tokens of affection. Dona Carlota would address Dom João as 'my love' or 'my darling sweetheart' (queridinho do meu coração) and sign her letters 'your loving wife'; Dom João, in turn, would finish his letters: 'Your husband who loves you dearly – João'.

Dom João's objections to his wife's ambitions were partly due to their troubled relationship, but more a response to pressure from Strangford, who was eager to safeguard Spanish-Portuguese relations. But Dona Carlota persisted, passing her days plotting with Smith in her beach house in Botafogo.

In October 1808, a messenger arrived at the country retreat of Santa Cruz outside Rio, where Dom João and Sir Sidney Smith were staying. He delivered letters from Dona Carlota to the prince regent and the admiral, informing them that she was leaving for Buenos Aires with Miguel and her daughters. The letters were in Dona Carlota's handwriting, but had evidently been concocted with Smith's help. They presented her plans as a fait accompli – Dona Carlota had nominated herself as the sovereign of Spanish America with Smith as her plenipotentiary, and had even removed her jewels from the palace in preparation for her trip. When Strangford next met Dom João, the prince regent was fuming: 'He felt himself deeply wounded by the utter want of Respect and Consideration which was manifest in this Transaction,' wrote Strangford back to London. 'He said that although He had borne with great patience the perpetual

Interference of unauthorised Persons in every Department, and in every measure of His Government, still he thought that he had a right to regulate his own Domestic Arrangements.'

Back in Rio, Dom João called a meeting with Strangford and Smith to try and put an end to his wife's scheming. It was then that Smith played what he thought was his trump card, revealing that he was not merely a renegade, but was operating under orders so secret that even Strangford was not privy to them. While Strangford referred the matter to London, Dona Carlota was ready to leave under just about any circumstances, even if 'the batteries of Rio de Janeiro should fire on her' according to Strangford. The key to her confidence was Smith's naval backing: 'Sir Sidney Smith is utterly convinced to carry off the beautiful Helen [Dona Carlota],' wrote Strangford, 'and to establish her as a provisional queen in Buenos Aires.' She did, in fact, try to leave at one point. When the Spanish warship, the *Prueba*, docked in Rio de Janeiro that November, Dona Carlota demanded to be taken on to Buenos Aires, but in a humiliating rebuff, the captain of the vessel refused her orders.

She suffered a further body-blow when Sir Sidney Smith was recalled to London in May 1809. Strangford had prevailed in the diplomatic tussle, convincing the foreign secretary, George Canning, to remove the troublesome admiral. In one last sleight, he managed to block Smith's claims to a share of the prize money from the capture of French ships after a joint British-Portuguese naval expedition had taken French Guiana. Smith left Rio with a bitter taste in his mouth, writing to his successor Michael de Courcy: 'I have not found His Majesty's Minister Plenipotentiary [Strangford] to act frankly and cordially with me, as the Admiral on this station, and . . . my experience does not warrant my giving you any ground for expectation that he will do so with you.' On reaching London, Smith claimed that the War Office had instructed him to ferment uprisings in South America. Canning was forced to curb his anger at Smith's apparent insubordination, and apologise.

Even without Smith's backing, Dona Carlota was still in with a chance. In Spain, where the gifted diplomat the Count of

Palmela was fighting her case before the Supreme Junta, the tide was gradually turning in her favour. Her claims had initially been held up on a technicality: the Sálica law, passed by Filipe V in 1725, prevented female succession to the Spanish throne, but had been revoked in a secret session in 1789. The Junta claimed it needed concrete evidence – the word of a member of the committee present at the session – that the law had in fact been struck from the books. Delegates to the Supreme Junta dragged their feet on the issue, but after showering waverers with money, 'diamonds of little value and other cheap stones', Palmela secured enough votes to carry his resolution. In January 1810 the Sálica Law was revoked; Dona Carlota's path to the throne was now in theory cleared. In the spring of 1810 a French offensive on Andalusia drove the Supreme Junta from Seville. It regrouped as a regency council in the besieged city of Cadiz but it looked, for a moment, as though France might overrun all of Spain. Across South America, semi-autonomous *juntas* were setting up, bypassing the Cadiz government, and allying them-selves directly to the imprisoned Fernando VII.

But Napoleon's campaign unexpectedly foundered in Anda-lusia, and the Cadiz government consolidated itself. It convoked a *cortes* – an ancient parliament, long sidelined by the absolutist monarchy – and called for delegates from both the Spanish provinces and the South American colonies. The moves shar-pened the choices in Spanish America. The Cadiz government was liberal and progressive, it favoured a constitutional mon-archy and in the years to come would draw up Spain's first written constitution. It would, however, grant the colonies only limited representation. To some within the colonial elites it seemed like the worst of both worlds. The undermining of the monarchy robbed them of their legitimacy, while at the same time they were still bound by deliberations in Cadiz. Rioting broke out in New Granada (modern-day Colombia and Ecua-dor); the Captaincies-General of Venezuela and Chile pro-claimed revolutionary *juntas*.

Dona Carlota's moment had arrived, but it would soon pass. Her hoped-for La Plata kingdom fell apart when Buenos Aires, baptising the revolutionary age that would soon engulf the rest of Spanish America, opted for a break with Cadiz. The rebel government in Buenos Aires soon took on a radical Jacobin hue, and Dona Carlota's supporters were rounded up and imprisoned. Loyalist resistance spread through the interior, and wars which would see-saw in the coming years broke out in Upper Peru (now Bolivia), Paraguay and the Banda Oriental. It was a foretaste of things to come in the whole of Spanish America, as civil strife alternating with loyalist backlash rumbled across the continent.

Her position weakening, Dona Carlota launched a series of last-ditch initiatives. Refocusing her energies on Montevideo in the Banda Oriental, Dona Carlota sent money, arms, her own jewellery, even a printing press for propaganda purposes to the Spanish royalists. By now her health was failing. Brought down by a series of respiratory illnesses that would plague her coming years of exile, she began spending long periods outside Rio recuperating in Santa Cruz. In reality, there was little more that she could do to further her aims. Her fate was now being decided thousands of miles away, on the battlefields of Europe.

Back in Portugal, Wellesley was embarking on one of the most elaborate long-term strategies of the Napoleonic Wars. Through a thirty-mile sweep around Lisbon, the countryside was cleared. Ten thousand Portuguese peasants were hired, and under the instruction of a team of royal engineers they began moulding the landscape into a series of intricate defences: valleys were walled off, hills were scarped, water was diverted from rivers to form swamplands, earthworks made subtle but decisive changes to the topography. Slowly, a series of defences emerged from the countryside – three concentric arcs, which would become known as the Lines of Torres Vedras, shutting Lisbon off from land attack. Wellesley was given more time than expected, and with each passing month the lines gained new ramparts, observation posts and redoubts. Over a hundred forts were built, linked by a semaphore system that could send messages up and down the lines in minutes. At one stage, there was even a plan to build an artificial canal to enable ocean-going transports to penetrate deep into the countryside.

The Portuguese were at first sceptical of these works – the defences, especially the innermost, seemed designed to aid escape should the French overrun the city once more. But with the works expanding outwards, confidence returned, and the lines became something of a tourist attraction for day trippers from the city.

Military historians have marvelled at the technical sophistication of Wellesley's defences, and the creative combination of landscape and built fortifications used to secure Lisbon against the French. There was, though, another, less edifying side to the whole operation, for the Lines of Torres Vedras involved destruction on a massive scale. British-led work parties demolished outlying farms, broke up roads and cleared forests. 'We have spared neither house, garden, vineyard, woods or private property of any description,' commented Major John Jones, one of the overseers. Not surprisingly, there were protests from those who were losing not just their possessions and livelihoods but their whole environments. Inhabitants pleaded with Major Jones with such vehemence not to cut down a beautiful avenue of old trees that he relented. The reprieve, though, was evidently short-lived: 'As I have trustworthy men with axes in readiness on the spot, there is no doubt of their being felled in time.'

With another huge French army, this time led by Marshal Masséna, entering Portugal in July 1810, Wellesley instituted the final and most ruthless element of his plan. His idea was to lure Masséna and his 60,000-strong army into a wasteland while the British, provisioned from the sea, dug in behind the lines. Troops retreating towards Lisbon destroyed crops, grain stores, mills, livestock – anything that might be of use to the French – as they went. Fires burned all around the countryside, which began to resemble a war zone even before the arrival of enemy troops.

Wellesley successfully engaged Masséna's army in the north before falling back to Lisbon. The British were joined by streams of refugees fleeing the French advance. August Schaumann, a commissary in the British army, described the procession: 'Old people, lame and sick people, women just risen from childbed, children and whole families with all their belongings . . . were to be seen mixed up with all kinds of beasts, among which pigs, owing to their unruliness and horrible cries, were the most conspicuous. Now and again the cry would arise that the French were coming, and then the young girls would implore all those who were riding to help them upon the saddle with them. Ladies who, according to the custom of the country had never perhaps left their homes except to go to mass, could be seen walking along, three in a row, wearing silk shoes and their heads and shoulders covered only with thin scarves.'

Masséna marched his troops unopposed through deserted fields but came to an abrupt halt in sight of the Torres Vedras defences. There he paused and as the extent of the Lines was revealed to him through French reconnaissance missions, the possibilities of attack dwindled. Tension ebbed away; both armies sensed a stalemate.

For five months, through the winter and into the spring, Masséna held out. Although it was forbidden, troops fraternised across the lines. British and French soldiers drank wine together; higher up, the French sent out invitations to British officers to plays that they were staging in their camps and an illicit trade brought luxury goods from Lisbon to bolster the diminishing stocks in the French officers' mess tents. All the while Masséna's position was deteriorating. Foraging expeditions worked the Portuguese interior, only to be harassed by peasant fighters. Food began to be scarce, morale sank. By early spring Masséna had lost almost a third of his men without a shot being fired. Leaving their night fires burning, the French stole away in the early hours of the morning of 6 March 1811. Wellesley set out in pursuit and after a series of futile stands at the border, Masséna's force was broken.

It was a decisive moment in the Iberian campaigns. The British never again looked like being forced off the peninsula. There would be many reverses – through the next year the fate of the peninsula would hang in the balance. But, with his port base of Lisbon secure, Wellesley eventually gained the upper hand and by the summer of 1812, he would be entering Madrid in triumph. The war was still far from over. Up ahead he faced heavy concentrations of French troops who had fallen back towards the Pyrenees. Elsewhere, though, there were already signs that Napoleon's grip on Europe was slipping. Hundreds of miles away, the *Grande Armée* was advancing on Moscow. That winter, over 300,000 troops under French command perished on the frozen steppes of Russia in a catastrophic retreat that would begin the unravelling of Napoleon's European empire.

For Portugal, the expulsion of Masséna's army was the end of three-and-a-half years of alternate occupations; three-and-a-half years of chaos, looting and violence. The war had brought suffering to all parts of the country. Lisbon had filled with refugees, subsisting on British handouts of wheat and salt fish shipped in from London. Out in the countryside, towns had been successively overrun, the French and the British becoming indistinguishable to traumatised peasants. Both came, looted and then pushed on. First French, then British soldiers had used the Mafra monastery complex as barracks, bivouacking in the halls and apartments in which Dom João and his courtiers had once worked, eaten and slept. Portugal, like many of the smaller states caught up in the Napoleonic Wars, had been humiliated, its culture and traditions derided, its people treated at best as an irrelevance in their own land. Up to a quarter of a million Portuguese had been killed during the hostilities, one twelfth of the entire population.

The country survived the onslaught, but what emerged at the other end was something quite different from its pre-war persona. Portugal became a kind of military protectorate of Britain. The British Major General William Carr Beresford took over the running of the Portuguese army. Like Wellesley, Beresford was of Anglo-Irish aristocratic stock. A large man who had lost an eye during a hunting accident in America, Beresford had pursued a chequered military career, culminating in a failed assault on Buenos Aires in 1806. He was selected for his proficiency in Portuguese (he had served as governor of

Madeira for a year) but later admitted that he arrived with only a
rudimentary grasp of the language. Using translations of British
drill books, he managed to turn round the Portuguese army,
which was already proving a dependable addition to British
forces. His contributions on the battlefield would be controversial, but he would end up being more political broker than
military man. Beresford would play a pivotal, but ill-defined role
in the coming years, acting on orders from London and Rio and
working with great difficulty with the un-cooperative council of
governors left behind by Dom João.

Liberation brought new fears for Portugal, when the long-
hoped-for return of the court and government did not materi-
alise. Even before the expulsion of the French, there had been a
growing unease in the capital, a sense that the court was settling
in for a far longer stay in the tropics than had initially been
envisaged. After the recapture of Lisbon from Junot's army,
Dom João had begun ordering the shipment of bulky court
paraphernalia to Brazil. As Soult took Oporto in the second
French offensive, officials in Lisbon were writing to Rio that
they had 'almost finished the embarkation of the Royal House's
treasures'. With the third invasion pending, more crates headed
across the Atlantic. Expensive paintings, rare books for the new
royal library in Rio and even a set of carriages were loaded on to
Brazil-bound ships, as yet more valuables were freighted out of
Lisbon. The carriages, dating from Dom João V's wedding
celebrations, were ornate and wide-gauged, so big in fact that
they could not be driven in Rio's narrow central streets. Some
were returned, but others sat for years in the city's royal arsenal,
where they gradually fell into disrepair.

In the aftermath of the wars, Portugal entered an unpleasant,
purgatorial phase. The mother country now found herself ruled
by her one-time colony, and the unwieldy division of officials and
powers between Portugal and Brazil brought decision making to a
standstill. Minor matters could take a double crossing of the
Atlantic to resolve. Petitioning the court – the most effective
way to overturn decisions made by other bodies – could take years.
In one epic case, the Marquis of Loulé, sentenced to death for

collaboration with the French, travelled all the way out to Brazil to seek royal pardon. After over a year in Rio he managed to waylay Dom João: 'I waited for my king and at a distance that appeared appropriate. I knelt in the middle of the road. His Majesty arrived and ordered [the carriers of] his palanquin to stop.' He was pardoned, his position and privileges in the court restored, but only after months on the Atlantic and a year in Brazil.

Many would embark on expensive and time consuming round trips to Rio just to complete some arcane paperwork or arrange a brief interview with a minister or court official. In a phenomenon that resonated with the bureaucratic overreach of early empire, orders issued by Dom João were often out of date by the time they arrived in Lisbon. It was a psychologically punishing position for those left behind in Portugal – a mix of reverse colonial relations with Brazil and virtual British occupation. And as with all long-distance colonial arrangements, slowly but surely the court and its advisers in Rio began to lose touch with the reality on the ground in Portugal.

Ironies abounded in this new transatlantic relationship. As Wellesley flooded the fields around Lisbon to stop the French advance, slave workers were draining Rio's swamps for new building works; country houses and farms were being destroyed in the area set aside for the Torres Vedras defences at the very time that Rio's outskirts – Catete, Flamengo and Botafogo – were beginning a new lease of life, with the building of villas for courtiers and government officials. British soldiers were digging up roads around Lisbon just as Dom João was turning his attention to improving communications between Rio and its hinterland. Rio was resurgent, while Lisbon crumbled. It was as if the store of wealth and prestige that the Brazilian colonies had invested in its European metropolis was draining back across the Atlantic.

Far from the bloodbath in Europe, Rio was taking on a festive air. At great expense, Dom João sponsored a succession of lavish carnivals of empire. The *Campo de Santana*, a parade ground built especially for the processions, was lit up by thousands of coloured lamps, its staging area scattered with flowers, and

aromatic plants with hundreds of palms lining its perimeter. In
Rio's sultry night air, crowds filled wooden stands to sample a
series of medieval tournaments.

The first major festivities were held in 1810, in commemora-
tion of the marriage between the Infanta Dona Maria Teresa and
Dom Pedro Carlos, Dona Carlota's cousin. John Luccock, the
Yorkshire clothier, had a ringside seat at this strange event and
described the floats and costumes which had been transformed in
their new context:

> 'The genius of Brazil made his appearance, represented by an
> Indian on horseback, whose courser spouted vapour. The long
> past glory of Portugal was shown by the models of some forts in
> the East Indies, taken by her victorious troops almost 300 years
> before. And the present power of the sovereign was displayed by
> an assemblage of every class of human beings, who live under his
> sway; of Europeans in their full dress, Asiatics in their regular
> costume, South American Indians in their gaudy plumage, and
> Africans dressed like baboons, with moss instead of hair . . .
> Every country brought forward its peculiar diversions, and all
> joined to render homage to their Prince.'

Luccock left unimpressed, amused by the fact that the bullfights
staged especially for the occasion were a farce. Mounted picadors
lapped the arena, but whether 'from nature or climate, the bulls
could not be enraged'.

The Brazilian priest, Luís Gonçalves dos Santos, was more
generous, relishing the decadence of the ceremony's opening:

> ' . . . a large and excellent orchestra erupted as the first float
> entered the square, artificially composed and intricately deco-
> rated: it was a mock-up of a mountain on which stood "Amer-
> ica" with a quiver over her shoulder and a bow in her hand,
> wearing a headdress of variously coloured feathers and a loin-
> cloth similarly decorated. Several animals roamed the mountain
> and native birds fed in amongst the foliage and flowers. This
> beautiful float was used to water the square, and for this reason

water spouted from various fountains positioned between the
flowers, which were all artificial.'

In front of this elaborate prop danced a troop of natives who
were also fakes – Europeans, got up in feathers and loincloths
performing 'extremely difficult' ritual dances. The tournament
lasted for days, with processions, imitation fifteenth-century
caravels, staged fights between 'Moors' and the Portuguese,
fireworks and equestrian events. Many such festivals would
punctuate the court's stay in Rio, staged on the pretext of royal
events – births, marriages, birthdays, anniversaries.

They were somehow unconvincing. The aromatic plants
momentarily sweetened the air, but were soon smothered by
the more familiar odours of a city whose population had soared
overnight but had seen few improvements in sanitation. Hastily
painted allegoric panels were used as hoardings, closing off
unsightly vistas, and heavy use of ephemeral architecture –
wooden arches, hollow obelisks and pyramids – gave the
proceedings a stagy, insubstantial feel. Almost in spite of themselves, the processions hinted at the deeper fragility of the exiles'
position in Rio.

SEVEN

A British Invasion

Dona Carlota's political failures affected her profoundly. The years that followed were ones of frustration and unhappiness, characterised by a flamboyance by now expected of the princess regent. She was restless, moving between the royal palace, a villa on a nearby hillside in Laranjeiras and her house on the beach in Botafogo. Accompanied by her guards, she ranged around the city on horseback, galloping between her various residences, often riding through Botafogo and Laranjeiras where many of the foreign diplomats lived.

On her journeys, the royal protocol of forcing passersby to stop, dismount or leave their carriages and pay deference was enforced with a ruthlessness that sullied her reputation. The British navy officer Commodore Bowles was set upon by Dona Carlota's guards when he ignored the protocol, prompting an official complaint to the palace. Even Lord Strangford was not spared from attack. Strangford, who was short-sighted, may not have even seen her horsemen approaching, but ended up being struck several times by the crop of one of Dona Carlota's guards for not kneeling in the street before the princess. One Russian diplomat found the situation so intolerable that he moved out of the neighbourhood altogether.

Not everyone complied. Thomas Sumter, the United States envoy to Rio de Janeiro, was stopped by Dona Carlota's guards and told to remove his hat and get down on his knees. The son of Gamecock Sumter of South Carolina, a hero in the revolutionary war against Britain, he had little respect for royalty, and was not about to grovel in the street in front of the princess regent. Challenged by Dona Carlota's guards, he pulled a pair of pistols and threatened to shoot. Dona Carlota urged her men on, but after a tense stand-off they retreated. Over time the complaints about Dona Carlota piled up, and eventually Dom João exempted foreigners from the protocol.

When Dom João moved out to São Cristóvão, Dona Carlota's life was complicated by the fact that court etiquette required her presence for morning mass and the early evening meal. Many days involved two, six-mile round trips for Dona Carlota and the younger daughters, who continued living with her throughout her time in Rio. There were more rows, the first over the marriage in 1810 of Dona Maria Teresa and Dom Pedro Carlos. The union was a part of Sousa Coutinho's strategy of strenghtening Pedro Carlos's claims to the Spanish throne. Preparations were made in secret and when Dona Carlota found out, she was furious, branding her husband 'a pimp' and saying that she would rather her daughter was thrown down a well than marry her cousin.

While Dona Carlota railed against her situation in Brazil, Dom João was slipping into an easy routine. He would rise early, at around six, and make his way to his private chapel for morning prayers and mass. He would then be shaven by his valet, before exchanging pleasantries with his palace workers. After breakfasting with his family, Dom João would be in session with his advisers, often Paulo Fernandes Viana, with whom he would discuss the running of the city. Early lunch (around midday) was a major event. Any staff in the palace at the time – his titled attendants, his wardrobe assistants, palace officials and his physicians – would assemble to be present at the prince regent's table. By all accounts Dom João was a phenomenal chicken eater, a characterisation borne out by surviving records of court expenses in which pigeon and turkey also figure prominently. He ate with his hands – three chickens at a single sitting, according to some accounts – accompanied by lightly toasted bread. In Rio, he added a further element to this huge meal – four or five Bahian mangoes. All this was washed down with water (Dom João rarely drank wine). The lunches were ceremonial events, held at a large oval table, with a white tablecloth reaching the floor, and always concluding with the hand washing ritual. Pedro would hold out a silver basin into which Miguel poured a pitcher of water over their father's greasy hands.

The prince regent would then sleep, dozing off in the thirty-five-degree afternoons to the sound of the children taunting caged monkeys or playing with the parrots and cockatoos in the palace aviary. After his nap he would attend to business or tour the city in his carriage. He tried to visit his mother every day, travelling into the centre, or having her brought out from the royal palace to São Cristóvão, but on lazy days he would simply don a wide-brimmed straw hat, take his walking stick and stroll around his new estate. The evenings, after vespers, would be taken up with meetings with ministers and advisers or paper-work after which he would turn in at around eleven.

Business at the palace, though, was as stressful as ever for Dom João, who remained caught between his own ministers' desires and Strangford's overbearing presence. Although at first em-broiled in the court's Spanish regency intrigues, Strangford's real reason for being in Rio was to broker a trade treaty drawn up by Canning in London, the aim of which was to transfer the privileges Britain had enjoyed in Portugal to Brazil. By 1810, the document was being finalised. Strangford had one crucial ally, Sousa Coutinho, but otherwise faced fierce opposition.

'Your brother is alone in this court,' Strangford wrote to Dom Domingos in London, 'He has hardly any friends, or support. The Prince likes him, it's true, but those around His Majesty detest him, and make a profession out of eternal enmity. You know the generosity of the Prince, but perhaps you do not have a good idea of his extreme impressionability, and the enthusiasm with which he receives all kinds of ideas.' Dom João was, indeed, wavering in his support for the British. Opponents like Antônio de Araújo had the regent's ear and they were horrified when they heard of the terms on offer.

Even before the passage of the treaty, Rio had been struggling to adapt to the new, aggressive presence of British traders. With the opening of the ports a deluge of British goods which had been locked out of Europe by Napoleon's blockade hit the Brazilian markets. British merchants flooded into Rio, buying up all available space in the city's warehouses, renting shops in the centre and snapping up the most sought after properties on the surrounding hillsides. Rents rose steeply, and soon Brazilian traders were being priced out of their own city. The influx caught Rio unprepared. There was chaos in the customs house, rudimentary port facilities struggled to land the cargo, warehouse space was soon filled up. Goods started piling up, left exposed to the sun and tropical rain storms on the beaches around the bay – 'one mingled mass of cashmeres, muslins, lace, butter, fish, and oil' according to the Yorkshire trader, John Luccock – pilfered by anyone who could bribe those guarding the stock to look the other way.

It was a speculative boom, and the market – small by European standards, given that up to a third of the population was enslaved – soon became saturated with British merchandise. Anything and everything was shipped out, including goods that were completely unsuitable for the Brazilian culture and climate. Ice skates and bed warmers were, not surprisingly, non-starters; women's stays and coffins, neither of which were used in Brazil, began stacking up; and luxury items – fine woollen cloth and expensive saddles – were well beyond the range of ordinary Brazilians. Outdated ideas that mining equipment might still be in demand left crates of pickaxes unsold in the port. Soon, skating blades began appearing as improvised door handles; bed warmers were perforated and used in the plantations to skim vats of cane syrup.

John Luccock was typical of the traders who were then pouring into Brazil. An apprentice in the textile industry, he had married into a successful merchant family with business interests in Portugal. After the French invasion, he was sent out to Brazil to try and make good their losses in Europe. He arrived in July 1808 with twenty pounds, some bales of cloth, two sets of weights and measures, counting house books, and some reading material: *Dubois on Commerce*, Moseley's *The Climate of the West Indies*, and Bonnycastle's *Arithmetic*.

The early years, a roller coaster of glut and scarcity, were difficult. Luccock found the amount of fine cloth that had been rushed to Rio was 'sufficient for several years'. He ended up spending three weeks trying to hawk two ends of cloth, before, in exasperation, putting them up for public auction. He dealt in wools, but soon realised that the climate was too hot to compete with the cottons that were being shipped directly from Asia. Overcoats, prized in England, were used only *in extremis* in Rio – 'a man wants a greatcoat here not to keep warm,' wrote Luccock to his suppliers, 'but to make him decent when he has no other garment on whatever.' Even the English colour schemes went down badly. 'We live in a lively climate, and with people who love to laugh,' Luccock wrote back to Leeds, 'let us have no drabs – we have no Quakers here. We want no dismal colours suitable for an English November.'

International trade in the early nineteenth century was a hit and miss affair. By the time a request was sent to England, the order filled, the goods shipped across the Atlantic, unloaded and cleared by customs in Brazil, six months or more may have elapsed. There was little the trader could do to hurry the process along. It was partly to do with the speed of the ship – 'when you hear of a vessel named *Rapid* or *Active*, always suspect their quickness of sailing' was Luccock's advice on the matter – and partly a question of the cargo's position in the hold. If it was buried at the bottom, it might mean a wait of weeks in port for it to be unloaded, while a rival's more accessible cargo captured the market.

But mostly it was to do with timing – extremely difficult to get right with the uncertainties and the long delays in getting goods to market. When, in the early days of the renovations in Rio, Moorish latticework verandas were outlawed, Luccock saw an opening for iron balconies. By the time his shipment arrived, though, the market was swamped and he was left with a large cargo of unwanted ironwork. Luccock had difficulties even giving his stock away, but at one point 'prevailed upon a Gent to accept two as a gift'. Years later, Luccock was still lumbered with the rusty remnants of his iron balconies and had concluded that the only way of offloading them was by 'selling beat iron by the quintal'. On another occasion, noticing a scarcity of soap, Luccock put in a sizeable order, but by the time his forty boxes had arrived Rio was piled high. Soap that had once sold at a premium was now virtually worthless. Despite these disasters, Luccock ended up with a successful operation in Rio. His business grew to $100,000 worth of imports annually; he employed a Lancashire clerk, an office boy from Leeds and several slaves.

As the trade in Rio settled, many goods found their mark: bottled porter, Cheshire cheese and Irish butter sold in quantity, wiping out indigenous produce. 'Cheese was made in the district of Minas-Geraes [Minas Gerais]', noted Luccock, 'but against the rivalry of English Cheshire it stood no chance.' Even traditional goods like hammocks and ponchos began to be undercut by British imitations. And British penetration did not stop there. In a voyage to the interior, Luccock came across 'civilised Indians' wearing 'all the finery which the cheapness of British goods had introduced among them'.

Brazilian houses of the well-to-do were soon decked out in British-made furniture, crockery and cutlery; advertisements for British products filled out the *Gazeta do Rio de Janeiro*. Industrial goods – watches, telescopes and pianos – spread through the upper echelons of Brazilian society. Glass, until then a rarity, was very popular, making an appearance in all its various forms – as windowpanes, fine cut crystal, chandeliers and lenses. Behind the scenes, the British were ensuring that the trade would continue unabated. In June 1809, Luccock was pleased to report that 'the English have become masters of the Customs House, that they regulate everything and that orders are given for the officers to pay particular attention to the directions of the British consul.' This was not the only area in which they would dominate. The British soon became the major creditors of the continuing slave trade which their government was trying hard to put an end to.

Strangford's treaty would press home the advantage. The final draft was at the extreme end of the type of agreement which formed the backbone of Britain's informal empire around the world. The British re-established the right, which they had enjoyed in Portugal, to their own judicial representation. An English judge, who could only be removed by appeal to the British authorities, would preside in Rio over litigation involving British subjects. British warships had unlimited access to Brazilian waters and were to be victualled by the court should they be used in its defence; wood from Brazilian forests could be used for shipbuilding; the British could trade and own property without restriction; they were exempt from the powers of the Inquisition and were free to worship as they pleased – a sticking point in a devoutly Catholic culture. Most outrageous of all were tariff levels set for British traders – at 15 per cent, they were marginally lower than those of the Portuguese and Brazilians themselves. Although the treaty was cast in the language of fairness and exchange, the Brazilians and the Portuguese were granted no reciprocal rights in Britain, quite the reverse. They could not own property, they could not be naturalised if they were not Protestant. Entry into and travel within Britain was restricted. Land ownership was illegal for Brazilians in Britain, at the same time as Dom João was giving out free land grants to the British. The treaty was to apply for 'an unlimited time of duration', its conditions 'perpetual and immutable'.

A battle erupted within the court over whether to block the treaty's passage. Dom João dithered, never 'being in the same mind during two Successive Days'; but pressured by Sousa Coutinho and with Strangford making veiled threats about the future of Anglo-Portuguese relations, the prince regent finally committed himself. Strangford was jubilant. 'We have won everything, the Inquisition and everything else,' he wrote to Dom Domingos in London, '. . . the onslaught was furious against your brother and me. Never has victory been more complete, nor more difficult.' Sousa Coutinho was also happy, and in the fullness of time would be repaid handsomely for his support, receiving, on one occasion, a 'portrait of His Majesty [George III] enriched with diamonds' and on another, a diamond box, courtesy of a grateful foreign office.

The court had, however, resisted Strangford in one crucial area covered by the treaty: the vexed issue of the slave trade. A week before the court had disembarked in Rio, Britain had followed Denmark and the United States in prohibiting the importation of slaves into her colonies. For a variety of reasons – moral, economic, strategic – Britain was now pushing to ban the trade altogether, and had the naval might to back up any agreements she could broker. With the abolitionist cause gathering pace in Europe, enquiries into the conditions and treatment of the trade's victims were well publicised, and slavery was seen as scandalous by anyone without a direct financial interest in it. The Portuguese were emerging as one of the most culpable nations and the most resistant to a self-evidently humane cause, Brazil being, in the words of the abolitionist William Wilberforce, 'the very child and champion of the slave trade, nay the slave trade personified'.

Portuguese slaving ports stretched down the African coast; the Brazilian plantations were totally dependent on the thousands of slaves who arrived, exhausted, off the freighters. Whatever Dom João's personal opinion on the matter (his statements were diplomatic and deliberately vague), prohibition was not an option if he wished to continue his reign from Brazil. The Brazilian elite, on whose goodwill his court depended, was deeply implicated in the trade, and would oppose any measure to curtail it. At first Dom João was unwilling to make any concessions to the British; but finally, after much debate, he agreed to restrict the trade to between Portuguese Crown territories, shutting off exports into Spanish America. And in a nebulous formula that would become Dom João's trademark on the issue, he promised a gradual winding down of slave trafficking without specifying any timescale.

On other matters, though, Strangford had indeed won

through. In the end, the prince regent had had little choice but to sign. Apart from his complete reliance on British military protection, his court was bankrupt. The treasures loaded on to the convoy in Lisbon had soon been exhausted in setting up the new court in Rio and paying the running costs of its outsize bureaucracy. By the time Strangford began negotiating the treaty, Dom João had already been forced to arrange a £600,000 loan from London to keep his administration afloat, pledging revenue from Madeira and the Crown monopoly on brazilwood – the founding sources of income for the empire – as guarantees of repayment.

Strangford's treaty was the culmination of a long history of contacts between Portugal and Britain. From the mid-seventeenth century onwards, Britain had given military protection to Portugal and her empire in exchange for preferential trade relations. With the move of the court and government to Rio, this age-old understanding had been transplanted to Brazil, as the centre of Portugal's empire moved from Europe to South America. But the Peninsular Wars had unbalanced a relationship which was already heavily tilted towards Britain. Britain now had a stranglehold over not just Portugal, but the rest of the Portuguese Empire. Against the court's wishes, the British had garrisoned Madeira, Goa and Macao to prevent them falling to the French. Of their remaining colonies, the African slave trading centres of Angola, Mozambique, São Tomé and Príncipe and Upper Guinea (now Guinea Bissau), were under threat from the British drive for prohibition.

Realising the vulnerability of his position, the prince regent went out of his way to protect the interests of British residents in Rio. In one incident, Dom João ordered his royal carriage to stop so that he could enquire whether 'anything unpleasant had occurred among the British' who were attending a Brazilian child's funeral. In another, a British malcontent outside the royal palace was tolerated instead of being ousted by guards. More seriously, in a case that caused consternation within the court, Sousa Coutinho intervened personally to prosecute a Portuguese merchant for trying to defend his slave girl against the advances of two Englishmen.

The number of British traders in Rio grew steadily throughout Dom João's years in Brazil. By 1819 there were sixty British
firms operating in the city. An Anglican church was built, along
with a special cemetery on a hill overlooking the bay with its
own docks for ferrying in the dead. A hospital, shops, a
circulating library and a newspaper followed. Maria Graham,
a high-society visitor to early-nineteenth-century Rio, was
surprised to find numerous British taverns and pubs 'whose
Union Jacks, Red Lions, Jolly Tars, with their English inscriptions,
vie with those of Greenwich and Deptford . . . Most of the
streets are lined with British goods. At every door the words
London superfine meet the eye. Printed cottons, broad cloths,
crockery, but above all, hardware from Birmingham, are to be
had little dearer than at home . . .'

Strangford's successes brought him great unpopularity in Rio.
He came to symbolise British imperial power and the impotence
of the prince regent, who seemed more and more to operate as a
mere figurehead under British control.

Local merchants were already turning against Strangford, as
the effects of the treaty began to bite. 'The Brazilians are in
general jealous and discontented,' he wrote in a foreign office
dispatch, 'they look upon the English as Usurpers of their
Commerce; they are offended with the haughty language and
proceedings of our Consuls, and with the heavy charges which
are levied in their Departments.' A petition, signed by over 100
merchants in Rio, set down their complaints to the Crown.
British traders were using 'all sorts of exchange rates and
algorithms' to dominate the market, the merchants protested,
and the time had come to rid the city of these 'usurious intrigues
and swindles'. And the complaints were not just economic. The
drunken sprees of British sailors, the casual disregard for Brazilian
cultural sensitivities, the 'insults daily offered to their Prejudices,
Customs, and Religion, by the English Settlers in this Country'
rankled with the local population. A mutual antagonism developed, summed up with a nationalistic twist of his own by a
French traveller, Jacques Arago: 'It is customary for the English

to ridicule the Brazilians, and for the Brazilians to hate the English. Both nations are right.'

Strangford's unpopularity within the court was reinforced by his heavy-handed interventions in the ongoing fight for the Banda Oriental. By the middle of 1810, the region had degenerated into a complex three-way battle between irregulars led by a local cattle-rancher, José Gervasio Artigas; revolutionaries from Buenos Aires; and forces loyal to Spain. Brazilian troops were massing on the border, Sousa Coutinho eager to send them in. Besides believing that the River Plate formed Brazil's natural border, the court was anxious to prevent a revolutionary government from setting up on Brazil's doorstep. Strangford was ordered to hold the line, London being wary of the Rio court's vision of a greater Brazil in South America.

When an insurrection broke out in early 1811, Luso-Brazilian troops crossed the border in defence of the Spanish loyalists. Strangford pulled his diplomatic weight, and by October 1811 had managed to broker a truce between the combatants. The following year he sent British army officer Lieutenant Colonel John Rademaker to Buenos Aires, and secured an agreement, accepted with great reluctance in Rio, for both the Luso-Brazilian and the rebel Spanish armies to withdraw.

Again Strangford had won through, but the tide was about to turn. Early in 1812, Sousa Coutinho fell ill. He had been carrying a heart condition for a while, as Strangford noted in one of his earlier letters back to Dom Domingos in London: 'Your brother will hardly have time to write to you by this Packet. He still complains of those terrible *vertiges* to which he is so subject, and which really make me uneasy.' Sousa Coutinho died suddenly, on 26 January 1812, after collapsing at the palace in the midst of a row with Dom João. His death was a disaster for Strangford. Despite their differences over the Banda Oriental, Sousa Coutinho was a staunch defender of the Anglo-Portuguese alliance, Strangford's one and only ally within a hostile court. It was the beginning of a steady decline in Strangford's influence in Rio that would, in the end, lead to his recall to London.

Sousa Coutinho's replacement was Dom Fernando José de Portugal, the Marquis of Aguiar, one of the few within the administration who knew Brazil well. He had served as viceroy of Brazil from 1801 to 1806 before returning to Lisbon, only to have to flee back to Rio a year later. By this stage an ageing nobleman, Aguiar, like Dom João, lacked in any clear vision; and after the energy of the Sousa Coutinho years the court drifted on a tide of inchoate anti-British rhetoric. With poor leadership at the top, Araújo began to play a progressively more influential role from the wings. Strangford was scathing about the new arrangements, writing back to London:

'The situation in this court is truly singular . . . Every department exhibits the most scandalous neglect and mismanagement, or the most disgraceful Corruption and there does not seem to be the least hope of a change for the better. It is in truth lamentable to witness the declining prosperity of this Empire, which had made rapid advances until the Death of Conde de Linhares [i.e. Sousa Coutinho] . . .'

By 1813, Strangford's position was being eroded by another factor: the war in Europe was turning decisively against Napoleon. When the allies crossed the Bidassoa at the Spanish frontier on 7 October 1813, Wellesley's soldiers trod French soil for the first time. Meanwhile, in the east, Napoleon was fighting and losing the battle of Leipzig. March 1814 saw Fernando VII released to resume rule over a country that had been destroyed by the French army's five-year occupation. With Napoleon all but beaten, maintenance of the Anglo-Portuguese alliance became less urgent. No longer the court's military guarantor, its protector from Napoleon's rampant armies, Strangford's grip over both the Rio administration and affairs in the rest of Spanish America began to fail. In 1814, the truce that he had imposed in the Banda Oriental fell apart, leaving the renegade Artigas besieging Montevideo. In Rio and Madrid there was dismay at the way Strangford had mishandled the affair, and rising frustration at the British envoy's machinations.

Strangford himself vividly described the anti-British feelings that had festered in the years following the trade treaty. 'The hatred of the Natives of Brazil towards England is more violent than I can describe,' he wrote in 1814. 'It pervades every class of Persons in this Country, except perhaps the Planters in the neighbourhood of the Northern Ports, whose Interests have certainly been benefited by direct Trade with England . . . The merchants of Rio de Janeiro . . . have suffered severely from the opening of Free Trade between this Country and Europe . . . [which] has generated an almost irreconcilable animosity against the British Name and Nation.' Britain's animus towards the slave trade was also isolating Strangford. In Bahia, slave houses were being ruined by the restrictions contained in the treaty; elsewhere there were fears of what a total ban might mean for Brazil. Strangford tried to promote the prohibition movement by requesting the publication of debates in the Houses of Commons and Lords on the subject. In response, the court threatened to prosecute him for inciting slave rebellions.

Movements within the court would seal the British envoy's fate. After years working behind the scenes, Antônio de Araújo re-entered the ministry in early 1814. Dom João's government finally had a man of substance to prosecute the anti-British line, the chief tenet of his views, according to Strangford, being 'that connection with England has become oppressive and degrading to Portugal'. Strangford remonstrated with Dom João, fighting Araújo's appointment hard, but this time he did not prevail. Araújo's return to the government was celebrated in Rio with three nights of illuminations as the city rejoiced at the court's anti-British coup.

In London there was unease about Strangford, and a re-evaluation of the strange situation that had developed in Brazil. Thanks to Strangford, the *raison d'être* behind the transfer of the court had been fulfilled – Rio's port was now full to overflowing with British goods. Britain, through Beresford, controlled Portugal, but as Strangford began losing his sway over the court, Dom João's residence in the Americas was becoming problematic. Strangford himself was advising a change of policy,

writing to foreign secretary Viscount Robert Steward Castlereagh: 'My Lord, I should fail in my Duty, did I not earnestly
recommend to the Consideration of His Royal Highness's
Government, the speedy return to Europe of the Portuguese
Royal Family, as the only effectual Remedy for the shock which
the Alliance with Great Britain is likely to receive in consequence of the order of things now established at this Court.' By
Dom João's return, Strangford went on, 'we should also get rid
of the serious Evil arising from the contradiction and conflicts of
Two Governments [i.e. Rio and Lisbon], placed at so great a
distance from each other, that one of them can scarcely take any
measure without being exposed to the chance of its having been
counteracted by the other, before any Communication of it can
have been made.'

Following Strangford's advice, Britain resolved to put an end
to the court's sojourn in the tropics. In May 1814, Strangford
read out a letter from the prince regent of Britain (the future
George IV) to Dom João, stating Britain's desire to complete
what she had started in Lisbon years before and return the royal
family to Portugal. At the same time, a British squadron was sent
to Rio to escort the court back to Europe, and Strangford
suggested that Dom João should prepare his own ships as
transports for the voyage.

The moves left Dom João in a quandary, and not for the first
time torn between Strangford and his court advisers. Strangford
claimed that Dom João was in favour of returning to Portugal,
that he was 'impatient to visit His Native Country, but this desire
is increasingly counteracted by His Two Ministers [Araújo and
Aguiar], who have succeeded (absolutely in opposition to the
Prince's own Feelings and better judgement) in persuading His
Royal Highness that His Return to Europe would only serve to
place Him entirely and irrevocably under the Control of Great
Britain.' Strangford needed to 'break through the spell which it
is endeavoured to cast around Him [Dom João], and, by
removing Him at once to Portugal . . . to place before His
eyes, an actual exhibition of the great and striking advantages
which He has derived from British Connection and Support.'

At first, the court did appear to be preparing for their long-awaited return to Europe, readying the fleet in Rio and recalling Portuguese mariners and shipping from abroad. London, too, was taking diplomatic steps, sending former foreign secretary George Canning to Lisbon, ready to meet Dom João off the boat and take over from Strangford as British envoy to the returned court. But while British escorts were at sea, plans for the royal family's departure were scrapped. Canning would wait in Portugal for almost a year, before giving up and moving on to take up a position in France. The escorts arrived on 28 December 1814 to a muted reception. Strangford faced an awkward situation all round, left to explain to the foreign office why, after an expensive two-month voyage, three British ships were at anchor in Rio's Guanabara Bay to no apparent end. He said that he had previously received assurances from Dom João that he would return to Lisbon if the British sent out escorts, a claim that was vehemently denied by the court in Rio. Defending himself to Castlereagh, Strangford wrote that although he was not in a position to accuse Dom João of lying 'all the world knew the sovereign's word was false'.

In a limp dispatch, Strangford suggested that the British ships could try to take back some of the less important members of the royal family which 'would serve in the eyes of the Portuguese Nation Dom João's intention to return' and perhaps more importantly for his own, faltering career, 'would do away with the unpleasant appearance of Rear Admiral Beresford's Voyage to this country having been altogether fruitless.' In the end, it was Strangford himself who would sail with the escorts back to Britain, cruising past the Sugar Loaf Mountain, and pulling into the open sea on 8 April 1815. He had been instrumental at all stages of the court's flight from Lisbon and its establishment in Rio, but had begun to personify Britain's imperial agenda. In the final move, the government in Rio had blocked Strangford's access to Dom João, rendering his position as envoy untenable. He left Rio refusing the customary gift of twelve bars of gold but, much to the annoyance of staff, in the possession of two song books which he had borrowed from the royal library and never returned.

It was a sour end to a difficult relationship. The prince regent was so angry with Strangford that he retired to one of his island residences in the bay rather than see off the British squadron. Dom João was even moved to write a letter of protest about Strangford's conduct in Rio to the British prince regent:

'. . . At times he abused my confidence, whether it be with indecent and scandalous talk that he indulged in about his influence over the government, or taking the liberty of using injurious phrases against some of my most valued magistrates and other employees, or, lastly, excusing himself on occasion from the court on the most celebrated days under the pretext of feeling ill, while at the same time turning up in the city, making a show of his disrespect. Nothing beats, however, the expressions that Lord Strangford dared to use in front of me because of the nomination of a minister of state [i.e. Araújo] that I had just made.'

Strangford's loss of influence in Rio was due in part to a change in mood in Europe. The long war, whose opening salvos had sounded over two decades earlier, was finally over. Napoleon's abdication was celebrated in parades throughout Europe. In the summer of 1814, London's Hyde Park was decked out in oriental temples, pagodas and bridges; a mock naval battle was staged on the Serpentine while hot-air balloons hovered overhead. With the celebrations, there was a sense that a continent, shattered by revolution and war, was at last returning to normal. Royal families and their courts had weathered the revolutionary era, exiles throughout Europe were making their way home. France was now back under a Bourbon king, Louis XVIII (the brother of the guillotined Louis XVI), resuming the throne after decades of anti-monarchist violence. In Spain, Fernando VII was installed in Madrid, and the country, after the radicalism of the patriot governments, chafing under the stifling absolutism of old.

Later that year, sovereigns from around Europe gathered for the Congress of Vienna – a meeting to discuss the post-war settlement. There was an Old World feel to the proceedings, accompanied by some suitably Old World entertainment. Woods around Vienna reverberated with the reports of shooting parties and a medieval joust was staged by the imperial riding school. There were balls, light operas and heavy banquets. After a performance of *Cinderella*, a procession of sledges, under the regal glow of torchlight, carved its way through the snow to the palace of Schönbrunn. It was a showcase of aristocratic wealth and power, a conservative riposte to Europe's revolutionary years.

Business at the Congress strengthened the feeling that the clocks were being turned back. The great powers – Britain, Austria, Prussia and Russia – tried not only to create a Europe of agreed borders, but to shore up the sovereignty of the monarchs who ruled within them. There was a revived sense of solidarity between Europe's courts at the Congress after the years of manipulation by Napoleon; as well as a fresh confidence – a feeling that royal houses could no longer be pushed around by military commanders and diplomats as they had been through the wars. While their lavish entourages amused themselves in Vienna, the representatives of the old order, once more relevant and powerful, strode the stage of a liberated Europe.

It was in this atmosphere of chummy aristocracy, of port, cigars and political horse-trading, that the position of Dom João's court in Brazil was informally discussed. With the renewed sympathy for the Portuguese royal family's plight, the machiavellian Charles Maurice de Talleyrand, who had served as foreign minister under Napoleon, came up with a solution to the unseemly appearance of a European court resident in one of its own colonies. In conversation with one of the Portuguese delegates to the Congress, he suggested the elevation of Brazil to the status of a kingdom – a kind of tropical extension to Portugal. Talleyrand's idea was sent on to Rio where it was adopted by royal order. In December 1815, The United Kingdom of Portugal, Brazil and the Algarves was born. Across Brazil's borders in Spanish America there would be violence, colonies torn apart by the coming wars of independence. Brazil, for a time, would cleave a different path, becoming a realm in its own right, a co-kingdom, the senior partner in a transatlantic union.

Celebrations broke out around Brazil at the official recognition of their formal equality with their imperial overlords, and 'addresses of exultation and gratitude to the Sovereign poured in, by one simultaneous movement, from every part of the country,' wrote Luccock, as even 'the most remote and obscure township felt proud of the privilege which admitted it to address its own Sovereign under a Brazilian title, on Brazilian ground.' But across the Atlantic, the reaction was very different. Lisbon's historic position at the centre of Europe's oldest extant empire had been dislodged; the prospect of any return to the *status quo ante* dashed.

On the more substantive issues discussed at the Vienna Congress, though, there was some hard negotiating for the Portuguese delegates. Portugal would receive paltry restitution for her suffering through the peninsular campaigns, with claims to Olivença, a border town seized by Spain in 1801, upheld but never honoured by the Spanish (a dispute which remains unresolved to this day). More important was the question of slavery. Dom João's representatives, including the ubiquitous Palmela, found themselves isolated on the issue. Russia and Austria, staunch Portuguese allies, sided with Britain, which was pushing for prohibition. Under enormous international pressure, Portugal escaped this time with a ban north of the equator, and an agreement to hold talks at a future date on phasing out the trade altogether.

Overall, though, the Congress of Vienna strengthened the prince regent's position in Rio. Dom João's old-fashioned court, his love of ceremony and hereditary privileges, was back in vogue. Warming relations with the conservative courts of Austria and Russia offered a counterweight to Britain's overweening influence, Strangford's departure being merely the outward sign of the shifts in the Continent's political alignment that the conclusion of the wars had brought. The Brazilian court no longer needed Britain's naval patrols to ensure their safety in

Rio; Britain, for her part, had achieved her aims in South America, with the exception of the ongoing battle to put an end to the slave trade.

With the creation of The United Kingdom of Portugal, Brazil and the Algarves, the years of doubt were over, the tedious politicking within the court at an end, and the British delegation silenced. Dom João could finally begin to settle in to a country that he had already fallen for. Over the years, his residences had grown and aside from the main palaces, he had taken over a series of beautiful villas located on various palm-fringed islands inside Rio's harbour. Royal barges, their slave oarsmen stroking evenly across the bay, would ferry the prince regent out to the island of his choice. Once installed, Dom João could look back across to Rio and the mountain ranges which backed it, without the uneasy sensation that his time in Brazil might soon be coming to an end.

What, perhaps, he could not appreciate from his tropical outpost, was the vulnerability of the new order in Europe. The Ancient Regime was back in control, but over lands that had been seeded with France's revolutionary ideas. During the wars, Napoleon's rhetoric was often dismissed as propaganda; after them it would provide radicals with a blueprint for a new, more democratic Europe.

EIGHT

The Archivist

With the relocation of the court to Brazil, a whole class of people in Lisbon faced ruin. Anyone connected to the court or government or any institution sponsored by them was left without income or career. Over the years there was a steady exodus of priests, librarians, bureaucrats, noblemen and women who boarded ships bound for Rio. While some were driven through poverty to try their luck in Brazil, others were personally summoned by the prince regent – more evidence, if any were needed, that Dom João was settling in for the long term.

One such courtier was the archivist to the royal library, Luiz Marrocos, who looms large in the story of the court in Brazil because he left behind him a thick sheaf of letters, written to his family back in Lisbon. Together, these letters offer one of the clearest views of the complex and forever-evolving psychological state of those living in exile in Rio. Intimate, candid, certainly never meant to be widely disseminated, they unveil Marrocos's most private thoughts as he grappled with his new life in Brazil. He left a Lisbon besieged, Wellesley's Torres Vedras defences keeping the French army at bay. Arriving in the early years of the court's exile, he would live through the exhilaration, but eventual disappointment, that Napoleon's defeat brought those stranded in Brazil, and stay on to experience the flourishing of Rio as an imperial city.

He unburdened himself to his father, a philosophy professor, who had put in many years of loyal service to the Crown in the manuscript section of the royal library in Lisbon. Following in his father's footsteps, Marrocos had become an archivist and translator. Before he left for Brazil he had translated three volumes of a monumental French medical treatise – 2,500 pages in all – by royal order, under the pressure of a tight deadline, but after all his efforts the work was never published. Indeed, Marrocos seems to have been jinxed in some way – a unique exemplar of another of his epic translations was lost somewhere on the docks during the royal family's scramble out of Lisbon. Marrocos's correspondence with his father would be regular and intense, but would end abruptly a decade after the archivist's first anxious letter, written on the high seas.

Marrocos boarded the *Princeza Carlota* for the transatlantic passage in 1811. On the first days out from Lisbon, nausea spread through the decks of the frigate. Passengers hung their heads over the sides or lay immobile on the decks, trying to ignore the slow, rhythmic movements beneath them. As the *Princeza Carlota* approached the Cape Verde islands Marrocos took up his pen.

'My father . . . I am writing this between the heavens and the ocean, under the strain of a thousand afflictions, sorrows and travails of a kind that I never imagined I would suffer . . . On the eighth day of the voyage our water rations were already infested and putrid and in the morning we had to remove mites in order to drink them. Many barrels of salt meat went off and had to be thrown overboard . . . all the ropes of the frigate are rotten, except for the mainstay; all the sails are in poor condition and will probably tear with the slightest manoeuvre. The crew is helpless and as things are we will be lost if by misfortune we are hit by heavy weather.'

As the ship sailed on his concern turned to his fellow passengers. 'I felt great compassion seeing how poorly those on board were, because out of 550 people here, few were spared from sickness.' Maroccos feared not just for his life, but for the safety of his charge: sixty-seven boxes of books and manuscripts that he had been ordered to take with him, fresh additions to the expanding royal library in Rio. 'If I had known the state of the frigate *Princeza Carlota*,' Marrocos wrote, 'I would have refused point blank to travel in her with the library, and in doing so I would have done a great service to His Majesty.' The collection had been rescued from the French after it had been left behind on the dockside, a casualty of the court's hurried exit from Lisbon. It had been a close run thing. Orders had been given that, in the event of invasion, certain elements of the collection should be burnt, but the instruction had been ignored. Junot's occupation had left behind substantial damage and his men had taken large amounts of loot out of the city in the wake of the Convention of Sintra. At the end of 1808, though, word came through that the library was still in Lisbon: 'The royal palaces suffered extensive damage,' wrote officials, 'but the royal library of the Ajuda Palace with all its papers, even the most secret, survived intact.' With further French invasions expected, it was decided to ship the library's contents out to Rio in three dispatches, the second of which was Marrocos's.

After the early jitters, fine weather aided the crossing, and ten weeks after Marrocos's first despairing letter, the clapped out frigate entered the heads of Rio's harbour. Marrocos was thirty years old. He arrived in a tropical city, thousands of miles from the turmoil in Europe. His academic background, and perhaps some string-pulling from his father, had landed him a job in the inner sanctum of the court. He would work on Crown manuscripts in a room above Dom João's in the royal palace. Each morning at seven, he later boasted to his father, he would have the honour of kissing the prince regent's hand. It was a privileged position but Marrocos, like many of his countrymen, would have considerable difficulties coming to terms with his new life in Rio.

The first years were hard for those who travelled out to work within the court. They had left behind families, close relatives and friends, and were coming to what they saw as a colonial backwater, far from home. Back in Portugal, many had never ranged far from the palaces in Lisbon in which they had won royal patronage, working the dynamics of court life to their advantage and securing pensions for ill-defined services. In Rio they found themselves exposed. A smallish city was now awash with extras – royal dependants, footmen, messengers, lawyers and archivists – an enormous bureaucratic structure grafted on to a modest colonial base. Some managed to adapt as the years went by, but most responded to their new circumstances with prejudice, fear and a longing for Europe – however dire the circumstances they had left behind.

Marrocos was no exception – on arrival he fell into a great depression and his early letters are an unrestrained outpouring of negativity. He was scathing about Rio, its climate, the people and their behaviour. For Marrocos, Rio was like Lisbon's worst neighbourhood, the Alfama, a warren of low-arched passageways, stone stairwells and blind alleys which housed Lisbon's poorest. Or, being generous, Marrocos stretched his comparison to the filthiest parts of a hillside district in the capital's centre, the Bairro Alto. Brazil's climate was more pestilent than Mozambique – then an outpost of the Portuguese Empire notorious for its unhealthiness (probably due to malaria) – the air, a rank mix of noxious vapours rising off the city's swamplands.

Some of Marrocos's fears may have been justified. In one letter he wrote of the constant pealing of funeral bells, adding, 'in one year alone just in the church of *Misericórdia* they buried over 300 natives of Lisbon.' At another point, he spoke of an epidemic which was carrying away so many people in the city that Dom João was forced to suspend his usual daily outing, and confine himself to São Cristóvão. Nor was the royal family spared from Brazil's new diseases. Dom Pedro Carlos, husband of Dom João's oldest daughter, Maria Teresa, was an early victim of the move to Rio. He would enjoy only two years of married life. Always in poor health, he died of a 'violent nervous fever' in May 1812. Dom João, who was very close to him, was devastated. A year later, Marrocos was recording another royal illness, that of the queen's sister, Dona Maria Anna – 'The Infanta D. Maria Anna has been sick for many days with a stomach spasm,' wrote Marrocos to his father, 'vomiting everything, not being able to hold anything down.' She died soon after, although she was by this stage well into her seventies. Marrocos himself seems to have suffered from a variety of illnesses: references to nose bleeds, persistent coughs, haemorrhoids, weight loss and head-aches crop up again and again. During one serious bout he spent twelve days in bed, ten of which he subsisted on soup.

There was, however, a moral undercurrent to Marrocos's complaints against the climate. Tapping into popular images of degeneration in the tropics, he turned on the *cariocas*. Brazil was a 'land of savages', its people 'immoral, indigent, hedonistic, vain and arrogant'. Marrocos felt threatened, unsure of whether he was strong enough to resist the temptations Rio would throw in his path. Many Portuguese women in Rio, he confided to his father, had already earned the loose reputation that Brazilian women had gained back in Lisbon.

Then there were the slaves, whose malign influence, accord-ing to Marrocos, pervaded the city. Aside from encouraging laziness and spreading exotic diseases, Marrocos argued, the institution created a hothouse atmosphere of violence and retaliation. Harsh discipline was necessary: 'You have to punish them to get their respect,' wrote Marrocos, adding a cautionary tale: 'They recently sent a black to the gallows who murdered his master, his mistress and their son and raped their niece, killing her afterwards. These cases happen often; slave women also poison their masters.' Marrocos himself employed a slave who was compliant and respectful, but at times needed attention: '. . . he has been given a dozen *palmatoadas* [beatings with a wooden paddle] for being obstinate but I have broken this vice.' Even-tually a sort of warped intimacy existed between them. 'He has the curious habit of standing watch over me while I take my nap,' wrote Marrocos, 'just to swat flies so I don't wake up.'

As the early letters progress it seems, if anything, that Marro-cos's hatred for Rio intensifies. At times he appears lost for words to describe the visceral repulsion that he feels for Brazil: 'My father, when I think about the negative aspects of Brazil, it provokes in me such hatred and anger – going beyond any reasonable limits. I think that I even curse this country in my

sleep.' Even his prestigious job seemed to offer him no comfort:
'I sincerely confess that I would much rather live in our house [in
Lisbon] in great poverty than here [in Rio] with abundant
wealth, and I would leave without hesitation if, throwing in
my job here at the library, I could get another job in Lisbon . . .
Everyone here says the same thing and those who don't are
telling barefaced lies.' Most damning of all, in November 1812,
clearly a low point, he wrote: 'I am so scandalised by this
country, that I want nothing from it, and when I leave here
I will not forget to wipe my boots on the edge of the docks so
that I do not take back even the smallest vestige of this land.'

With each day in Rio, his yearning for home and family
increased. Letter writing was therapy for Marrocos, especially in
the first years, and he lived for those few private moments in
which he felt some psychological release from his loneliness and
isolation. It was through these imaginary conversations that he
was able to purge himself and emerge reborn. Like many of his
compatriots, he was in denial. His mind remained in Europe
long after his body had reached Brazil. He simply could not
believe that the court was choosing to stay on in Rio. And in this
state of half presence, he hung on every word that arrived from
abroad.

Marrocos consoled himself by following the progress of the
wars in Europe, which, as they climaxed, seemed to point
towards a possible release from his purgatorial existence in Brazil.
Colourful accounts reached Rio of Joseph Napoleon's lucky
escape from the allied advance on Vitoria, and the ransacking of
his caravan still containing the army payroll, military equipment,
and large quantities of wine. There was talk of the ignominious
demise of Junot, whom many blamed for their exile. Junot had
disgraced himself on the battlefield in the middle of the disastrous Russian campaign, descended into madness and thrown
himself out of a window to his death. As Bonaparte's empire
collapsed around him, everyone was on tenterhooks. For the
exiles in Rio who had left Europe at Napoleon's peak, news of
his abdication seemed incredible. Many believed that they
would soon be back in Lisbon, their days of exile behind them.

There was a flurry of letters from Marrocos during this period, asking for clarification from his father of the rumours that were doing the rounds.

But the end of the war resolved nothing for those in Rio. When news came through of the surreal coda to the Napoleonic era – Bonaparte's miraculous 100 day return, and his subsequent demise at Waterloo – hope of return to Portugal had already dwindled. As Napoleon headed for his own South Atlantic exile on the island of St Helena, the Portuguese in Rio were left in limbo. Talk of the departure of the court for Europe came and went. Although no official announcements were made, work on Dom João's residence, São Cristóvão, and his summer palace at Santa Cruz went on apace. There seemed no end in sight for those who, like Marrocos, were attached to the court but yearned for Europe. They were trapped financially, dependent on royal patronage in an absolutist bureaucracy that had incongruously set down its roots in the New World.

The issue of when or even whether the Portuguese court would return to Portugal is thematic in Marrocos's letters home. His correspondence bears witness to the court's chronic indecision throughout their time in Rio, his exchange with his father at times resembling a comparing of notes, a search for signs in Europe or Brazil of the court's current thinking.

On leaving Portugal, the prince regent had said publicly that he would return once it was safe to do so. As it turned out, Lisbon had been liberated from the French less than a year after the exodus. Masséna's army had been driven out of Portugal altogether in 1811 and by the middle of 1812, as the Peninsular Wars swung in Wellesley's favour, the court's return was a real possibility. With the end of the war in Europe (1814–1815) the pressure for some decision, one way or the other, mounted.

It was not just homesick *émigrés* like Marrocos who were hanging on every word from the court. Traders were monitoring the situation with trepidation. 'Should they return, by far the best of our trade will cease or at least be greatly curtailed,' warned Luccock at the close of hostilities in Europe, 'therefore,

while the uncertainty lasts, ship no more superfines, nor superior
toilettes nor Hats, nor any articles adapted to the consumption of
higher classes of society.' 'Only plain common goods until the
mind of the Prince Regent is known,' he jotted down in another
note to his suppliers.

Marrocos was at first sceptical of the British plan to bring the
court back to Portugal. On telling his father about the letter
from the prince regent of Britain that Strangford had read out to
the court, he concluded: 'I don't know what His Highness's
reply to all this was . . . Nothing is certain . . . everything is in a
state of lethargy . . . which suggests that we will stay here for
three or four more years.' Just five months later, though, in
November 1814, his tone had changed. Hardly able to contain
his excitement, he wrote that preparations for the return were
under way. Doubts still lingered. No public announcement had
been made, although Marrocos had heard that there would be an
official statement sometime in December with a projected date
of departure the following March. Marrocos's hopes evaporated
soon after. 'The current assembling of our warships has got many
people talking,' he wrote to his father, 'taking this as proof that
the royal family will soon be leaving these lands. How I wish to
God that this was true!'

Whatever promising signals Marrocos managed to pick up
through his working day – eavesdropped comments, loose talk
in palace corridors – he could see with his own eyes that the
prospects for a speedy return were not good. As he sat writing
to his father, buildings were going up all over the city. Top
officials in the government were investing heavily in long-term
projects. Carpenters, stonemasons and labourers were in heavy
demand.

'Antônio de Araújo is undertaking major works in his houses
that will take several months,' wrote Marrocos to his father,
'otherwise, all is quiet which suggests a very long stay in this
country. Talk of going to Lisbon is virtually prohibited – God
knows when it will come to pass.' Joaquim José de Azevedo, the
courtier who, years before, had worked day and night from his
dockside stall to embark the royal family, was now the Baron of

Rio Sêcco. He had become extremely rich since arriving in Brazil (accusations of corruption were never far from him) and was another who was spending freely: 'the Baron of Rio Sêcco is building a superb palace in the Largo dos Ciganos,' wrote Marrocos, '. . . and others are setting down deep roots in this country.'

Marrocos also noted other, less concrete signs of the court's intentions. Officials were sent on long and complicated round trips. An ex-governor of Angola and Maranhão had been told to go on a diplomatic mission to England, France and Italy, after which he was to return to Rio – a voyage of a year or more. The secretary of the Nuncio – the Pope's representative in Rio – was setting out on another epic journey. He was to call at Lisbon then travel via the Mediterranean to Naples and Rome before returning to Brazil.

It was, though, the extensive building works for the housing of the royal family itself that sealed the argument for Marrocos. In 1815, he was again dampening down his father's expectations:

'. . . you say that there [in Lisbon] they are readying the palace of Ajuda for the royal family. I can also tell you that here they are preparing the palace of São Cristóvão, enlarging it by more than a half so that it can accommodate all the royal family, and once finished, they are going to do the same type of work on the palace of Santa Cruz, fourteen leagues from here, so that all the family can stay there on their annual trips in February, June and November.'

Far from any return to Lisbon, there was even some suggestion that the royal family might move on to another location in Brazil: '. . . it is said that orders have been given to examine the roads from here to the city of São Paulo,' wrote Marrocos, 'since there is talk of going and establishing the court there, because of the good airs which are similar to those in Portugal.' Difficulty with the climate was a recurrent theme in the royal family's experiences in Rio – Dona Carlota's continuing illnesses were attributed to the unhealthiness of the tropics. São Paulo would

have been preferable, but the costs of the move were pro-
hibitive.

Instead, the court tried to replicate in Rio the network of
palaces and country houses – Ajuda, Queluz and Mafra – that the
royal family had lived in and moved between in Lisbon. São
Cristóvão was Dom João's main residence, the royal palace in the
centre reverting more to an administrative base, with Santa Cruz as
the country retreat. The work was effectively doubled, since Dona
Carlota needed separate quarters: 'We are continuing to see large-
scale works and huge expenditure,' wrote Marrocos, 'in the
Andrahry [Andaraí] country house (two-and-a-half leagues from
the city) they are preparing a substantial palace, using fifty workers,
for Dona Carlota to live in when she leaves her residence in
Botafogo. At the library construction work continues with the
same enthusiasm.' And it was not just the library that was being
renovated. At enormous expense, artisans were at work gilding
the whole of the inside of the royal chapel and yet another palace
was being planned near Ponta do Cajú.

As the wars in Europe wound down, the tone of Marrocos's
letters back home subtly shifted. Two-and-a-half years after he
had arrived in Rio, Marrocos married. He chose a Brazilian, the
twenty-two-year-old Dona Anna. 'I am living with a *carioca*,' he
wrote to his sister, adding one of his characteristic backhanded
compliments, 'whose only shortcoming is that she is a *carioca*.' It
was a major turning point in his life in Rio, something he himself
realised and commented on:

> 'After reaching the age of thirty-two-and-a-half and having
> adopted a life of celibacy, I came to this court, and changing
> climate, I changed my mind . . . having tried out many different
> paths in my life, suffering many outrages . . . I have at last realised
> that it is not right to continue living in this way, like a
> misanthrope . . .'

On the eve of his wedding, a weary resignation had taken hold:
'. . . after all the dangers and privations that I have suffered,' he

wrote, 'Brazil has opened my eyes and taught me things not found in books.' Marrocos had been worn down. He was finally giving up his fight as an outraged expatriate and trying to build a life in the new country in which he found himself.

His transformation was hurried along by an explosive falling out with his father over his marriage to the Brazilian. Perhaps a crucial letter had gone astray, maybe the time lags involved in transatlantic correspondence had produced some misunderstanding, but Marrocos's father claimed that his son had not asked his permission to marry. Since we only have one side of the story, it is impossible to know exactly what happened, but harsh words were exchanged, culminating in a lengthy letter written in November 1815 in which Marrocos responded to his father's outrage in no uncertain terms, saying that he had spoken rashly 'and in no way in keeping with your previous expressions of affection and warm friendship . . . characterising me as vile, uncivil, lacking respect . . .' As the letter progressed, Marrocos took on his father methodically, at one point, asking, incredulous: 'Was it hatred, jealousy, or some other passion that sometimes blinds us, that moved you to make me continue to endure my past sufferings and to afflict me with still new ones?' And in the only indication of what Marrocos was actually responding to, he quoted back some of his father's words in disgust: 'I was also unhappy with the ironic expressions which you used in your letter of 3 July, ones like: "your wife, Senhora Dona Anna, object of love and veneration, first in exuberant virtues, propagator of numerous offspring etc." – expressions that are more appropriate to a Panegyric than a letter, making the lack of sincerity with which you treat me all too obvious.'

From this point on, communication was difficult between father and son, leaving Marrocos seething in Rio. He continued to write, but apparently received little in return, prompting him to fire off a wounded letter in which he wrote: 'I find it incredible that you have worked out a way to treat me with this type of indifference and abandon, not wanting to waste any time thinking about writing to me.' There could well have been reasons other than personal hostility for this trailing off of letters from Portugal. Marrocos's family had fallen on hard times in post-war Lisbon. At one point, Marrocos wrote of his shock on receiving a letter from his father describing the terrible poverty to which his family back home had succumbed.

In contrast, things seem to have gradually improved for Marrocos in Rio. By 1817 he had left the library and secured a position in the government. Marrocos's paltry salary rose to a substantial income and he moved house, from the filth of the centre of town into one of the more pleasant and sought after hills nearby. Anna Maria bore him three children – a son who died tragically just days after he was baptised and two daughters.

And with the improvements, Marrocos began to adapt to life in Brazil. After the birth of his first daughter, he refused to have her breastfed by a slave wet-nurse: 'I don't want her brought up by a black woman which is the custom here,' he wrote, adding, 'I firmly believe this, because it seems more natural and decent that the breastfeeding should be done by the mother rather than the blacks, a practice I find nauseating and disgusting.' By the time Anna was about to give birth to their second daughter, Marrocos's position had changed completely, and he had started, unconsciously, to adopt the Brazilian customs that he had once so abhorred. 'I have bought a black wet-nurse to breastfeed for the price of 179$200 *réis*,' he explained to his sister, 'and I ordered an abandoned child to be brought from the orphanage to my house so as to conserve the black woman's milk until Anna gives birth.'

He began to settle down; his criticisms of Rio dried up. He had changed, but so too had Rio. In the crucial decade that Marrocos's letters span, Rio had been transformed from a closed, provincial town, into a relatively sophisticated city. With the court's presence, the population had rocketed. Foreigners who were once treated with the utmost suspicion now lived and traded freely in the city's centre. Amenities that were sorely missed by Marrocos on his arrival – bookshops, restaurants and boutiques – proliferated.

The wheel had come full circle for Marrocos, and he wrote to his father urging him to come and join him in Brazil. He

Dom João VI was a man of simple, courtly tastes. He enjoyed long banquets in which he consumed prodigious quantities of venison and game fowl, as the ballooning belly on this late portrait demonstrates.

Dona Carlota, princess regent and queen of Portugal, was a flamboyant, difficult-to-read personality. Here, she holds open a locket with a portrait of her husband Dom João, but in real life their relationship was famously fraught.

Crown prince Dom Pedro had just turned nine when the ships set sail for Brazil. He spent his adolescent years in Rio's sultry climate, growing up to be a libidinous, passionate young man. He is immortalised in Brazilian history for his *Grito do Ipiranga* (cry of Ipiranga) in which he proclaimed independence from Portugal in 1822.

Lord Strangford, amateur poet and translator of *Camões*, was Britain's envoy to Portugal in the run up to the French invasion, before following the court to Brazil in 1808. He was the archetypal diplomat of the Napoleonic era, defending British interest with whatever means necessary.

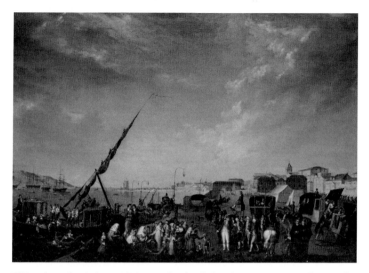

This sedate oil painting, with its air of melancholy calm, gives a sanitised view of the evacuation from Lisbon. Numerous eyewitness accounts describe the turmoil and desperation of the embarkation, as the Portuguese raced to clear the port before Napoleon's troops reached the city.

This allegory features the classical allusions favoured by the Portuguese court. In the murky background are scenes from peninsular campaigns. The idealised figures in the foreground, bathed in warm colours, gesture in adoration at Dom João's ethereal seat in the heavens.

As the fleet passed through the heads of Rio's famous harbour, to the left was the *Pão de Açúcar* (the Sugar Loaf Mountain), which the German artist Rugendas described as "a strange rock pyramid".

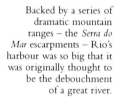

Backed by a series of dramatic mountain ranges – the *Serra do Mar* escarpments – Rio's harbour was so big that it was originally thought to be the debouchment of a great river.

Off in the distance, the *Pão de Açúcar,* shrouded in low cloud, tilts gracefully away from the bay; in the foreground are a miscellaneous collection of *cariocas* – military men, friars, slaves, street sellers and bourgeois men and women.

A slave is whipped by another slave at the *pelourinho* (whipping post), as an appreciative audience looks on. Repulsed by the spectacle, the court put a stop to this practice, confining punishment to prison yards, administered by Crown officials.

This is Debret's detailed typology of the African nations and the slave women's occupations in Rio including: "No. 10, Girl: head slave of a European businessman (a favourite target of the whip)."

This typical Brazilian house scene has an ambience of cosy domesticity, but note the handily positioned whip sticking out of the basket, used constantly, according to Debret, to threaten the slaves.

The husband eats in silence while the wife amuses herself by giving leftovers to a slave child. Children were spoilt until the age of five or six, explains Debret, before ending up as slaves of other slaves – abused, beaten and forced to live off stolen fruit or animal feed from the garden.

Maria Leopoldina Josephina Carolina of Habsburg travelled 5,000 miles for her wedding to crown prince Dom Pedro in Brazil. In Europe she fantasised about the purity and innocence she believed she would find in the New World, but she was soon disillusioned by court life in Rio.

Dona Leopoldina arrived in Rio to great pomp and ceremony. The tiny figures of Dona Leopoldina and Dom Pedro can just be made out ascending the ramp, followed by Dona Carlota and Dom João.

The Queen embarks with her daughters and chamberlain, ending an unhappy thirteen-year period of exile in the tropics. As she left, she delivered a cutting parting shot, according to Debret, shouting deliriously: "Finally, I am going to a land inhabited by real men."

After over a decade in Brazil, the court was finally forced to return to Europe by a constitutionalist revolt which swept through Portugal. When Dom João stepped ashore he had lost many of his ancient powers, reduced from an absolute monarch to a parliamentary figurehead.

described life in the tropics enthusiastically. Everything could be found in abundance in Rio; his house was ample and well situated, cooled by the ocean breezes; the climate that he had once despaired of he now recommended to his father as ideal for the elderly. With the library set up, his father could even continue pursuing his philosophical studies in Rio. It had been an idea that Marrocos had 'been thinking about for some time', ever since the 'melancholy scene' of his family's suffering in Lisbon had been described to him. His entreaties were ignored, leading to one last, and rather brutal appeal to his father to bring the family out to Brazil:

> 'My father, this is the moment to decide . . . Throw off the disgraceful lethargy that you have lived in and moaned about for so many years; leave the land in which you have not prospered and that has set back your career; come and enjoy more relaxed and happy days, savouring all your spirit desires.'

His father never came out to Rio and Marrocos never returned to Lisbon. Like so many whose lives were changed when the court left Lisbon for Rio, their family had been permanently split between Old World and New. Separated by historical accident, their relations ruptured under the strain. Heartfelt words had crossed and recrossed the Atlantic for years, but at some point the conversation had stopped, dropping off into an obscurity as imposing as the ocean that divided them.

NINE

The Vicissitudes of Exile

With Strangford's departure the court could at last start prose-cuting its own foreign policy, freed from British interference. For the next four years, Britain would not even field a replace-ment for Strangford, working instead through consul general Henry Chamberlain as she continued to press for the court's return to Europe. First on Dom João's agenda was the Banda Oriental. Early in 1816, three squadrons of cavalry and a battery of artillery were dispatched from Portugal, sailing directly for staging areas in the south. Dom João also requested Beresford in Lisbon to send 5,000 Portuguese troops, veterans of the Penin-sular Wars, to the battlefields of southern Brazil.

The request came at a delicate moment for Beresford. It was now five years since Marshal Masséna's army had withdrawn from Portugal, and two years since Napoleon's abdication, yet Beresford was still in charge of the Portuguese armed forces, with a modified form of the council of governors running day-to-day affairs. The emergency measures hurriedly put in place during the evacuation from Lisbon were still in operation in the expectation that the royal family would soon be returning from Rio. The relationship between the council of governors and Marshal Beresford had been poor during the Peninsular Wars, but had deteriorated further since, and was fast becoming unworkable. The council saw the British as a colonial presence and were humiliated by their continuing control over the

Portuguese military in peacetime; Beresford complained of corruption within the council and their general un-cooperativeness. In exasperation, the council of governors protested to Dom João about the size of Beresford's army budget, which consumed three-quarters of Portugal's public revenues and was ruining any attempts at post-war reconstruction. They argued that the money was being squandered on Beresford himself, his staff and unnecessary tiers of officers and generals, rather than on front-line equipment.

Beresford decided to accompany the battalions to Rio, and speak with Dom João in person about the worsening state of Portugal. He was heading for 'the fountain head' as he wrote to Castlereagh in London, in the hope that 'the stream will be clearer there'. In private letters, Beresford told of his own misgivings about the future of Portugal. 'The state of affairs here is indeed very critical,' he wrote on the eve of his trip to Brazil, 'and no one sees that better than I do . . . there is no prospect whatever of any attempt to rectify the abuses, that are really weighing down the State itself, and which must in the end destroy it, and that end is not far off.' He was understandably fearful of leaving Portugal at such a sensitive and unstable time – 'I see much danger of some ebullition of public discontent' – but decided in the end that he could not make the changes necessary without negotiating directly with Dom João.

While Beresford was on the Atlantic, other problems were vexing the court in Rio. The royal family was now an ocean away from Europe's court circuits, where favour was sought and dynastic alliances sealed through marriage. Dom João's two middle daughters had arrived in Rio as children, but by 1816 were of marriageable age. Feelers were sent out from Rio to members of the recently liberated Spanish court and a double union of the type not uncommon in the Iberian peninsula was agreed on: the two daughters would marry their Spanish uncles, Dona Maria Isabel being joined with Fernando VII (and becoming queen of Spain), and Dona Maria Francisca with Don Carlos. For Dona Carlota, the wedding would be doubly significant. Her daughters, to whom she was very close, would be marrying her brothers.

The weddings would take place in Madrid, leaving the court in Rio with one of a growing number of diplomatic difficulties arising from its lengthy stay in the tropics. The normally prosaic notion that Dom João and Dona Carlota would accompany their daughters to Spain for their wedding ceremonies was charged with uncertainty. Once in Europe, it was unclear what effect their presence would have and whether they could return to Rio without destabilising an already tense situation in Portugal.

Faced with this dilemma, Dom João lapsed into one of his characteristic bouts of indecision. At first it seemed as if both he and Dona Carlota would travel to Madrid, but after several sessions with his advisers, Dom João ruled this out. It was then proposed that Dona Carlota would sail alone. With negotiations ongoing in Madrid, a bizarre scheme was put forward whereby Dona Carlota would travel incognito as the Duchess of Olivença and slip into Europe unnoticed. The idea was ostensibly driven by concerns over expense – neither the Spanish nor Portuguese courts wanted to pay the additional costs of Dona Carlota travelling as princess regent. Dona Carlota's doctors weighed in with their own, unambiguous advice, declaring that 'If she stays any longer in America, there will not be any cure for her illness.' By this stage, rumours were flying in both Portugal and Spain. There was talk that the whole of the royal family were finally returning, some saying that the fleet was already on the Atlantic.

Within the court, there was a flurry of diplomatic activity aimed at burying the idea of Dona Carlota's return, with Dom João's advisers coming up with reason after reason as to why her trip to Europe could prejudice the Crown's interests. Her health problems were used against her, Paulo Fernandes Viana arguing that the return could aggravate her condition 'because of the inevitable travails of a long journey'. There could be 'a thousand and one contingencies' wrote the minister Tomás António de Vilanova Portugal to Dom João. She could be snubbed by the

Spanish court, jeopardising Portugal's relations with her neighbour; she could be trapped by events in a still unstable Portugal.
Or, wrote Vilanova Portugal, in a moment of rare honesty, she
might simply stay on of her own free will. He advised Dom João
to make some excuse, to rule out the trip on health grounds.
Others in the court agreed, citing the huge additional expense if
Dona Carlota travelled as herself and the indecency of her
travelling in disguise. But these were merely polite covers for
deeper worries. By this stage Dona Carlota was feared, her
behaviour deemed erratic and inherently unpredictable. In
Europe, alone, she would be impossible to control.

Dom João wavered, and then, against the wishes of his
advisers, gave his consent to Dona Carlota's trip to Spain. By
February 1816, preparations were already well advanced, as the
archivist Marrocos wrote to his father in Lisbon:

> 'There is now no doubt about the departure of Her Royal
> Highness [Dona Carlota] for Spain or Lisbon. The preparations
> are decisive in every respect: all the family, along with their
> servants, are ready . . . The departure date has been set for 20
> March [1816] . . . I cannot tell you, my father, the fervour and
> urgency with which they are embarking the belongings of those
> who are leaving; I have seen great chests which require twenty
> blacks to carry; the *Sebastião* is very beautiful, having been
> repaired and painted, as is the frigate *Espanhola*. Their Royal
> Highnesses have dined on board many times . . .'

After the years of frustration and suffering in Rio, it seemed as if
Dona Carlota would finally return to her homeland. If she had
left at this point it is difficult to imagine what would have
become of the court in Rio. Her appearance in Portugal would
have been incendiary. On past performance, she might well have
attempted some form of royal coup, forcing the hand of Dom
João.

But as Dona Carlota made final preparations, the trip was
suddenly put on hold. Queen Maria had been taken seriously ill,
and fears were growing over her worsening condition. She was

eighty-two years old and those close to the court sensed that she was entering her last days – hours, for her, of pain and discomfort. She was racked by dysentery and fever. She soon lost all sensation below the waist, her feet and hands swelled up. 'There have been moments of relief,' wrote Marrocos, 'but, once over, the symptoms return stronger than ever.' As her illness continued, a team of doctors tried to alleviate her suffering. Every day she was lifted from her bed and wheeled around the palace as a substitute for the carriage rides she used to take through Rio before she had fallen ill. Towards the end, there was talk of moving her out of the centre of the city into a villa in nearby hills where she could take the airs.

She died in March. She had spent her declining years in Brazil, but it is uncertain whether she had fully comprehended where she was or why the court had left Lisbon so abruptly eight years before. An extended period of mourning paralysed the city. Slow processions moved through its streets, crucifixes upraised. For over a week the royal chapel hosted lengthy masses, orations and remembrances in what was the biggest event in Rio since the arrival of the royal family. Rio's churches were decked out in deep tones of purple. There was the usual array of religious decoration, with eccentric Gothic touches: Corinthian columns, fashioned in wood and plaster, velvet domes, an obelisk topped by an angel holding a skull. The corpse was dressed in black and covered with a crimson cloak. It was placed in an open casket, strewn with aromatic plants for a posthumous performance of royal duty. Crowds, weeping at the sight of their dead queen, queued for one last *beija-mão* ceremony.

News of the queen's death reverberated throughout the empire. It spread slowly along the oceanic sea routes which still loosely bound Portugal's scattered possessions. It swept up the Brazilian coast on trade vessels, and into the interior along mule trails. Packet boats soon reached Lisbon, and the city descended into grief. Months after the event, the news was still being disseminated by commercial ships docking in Mozambique, Goa and Macao. Memorials took place across four continents, as Portugal and Brazil were joined by a collection of trade ports in Africa, India and Asia mourning the passing of their queen.

The death of the queen fundamentally changed the situation in Rio. The formal succession of Dona Carlota and Dom João was now imminent. When preparations for the royal brides' journey to Spain were recommenced later that year there was no berth for Dona Carlota. Dom João's long regency was over. Dona Carlota was now queen – albeit in a court thousands of miles adrift from its traditional seat – and her presence in Rio was required.

Beresford arrived with his huge consignment of troops for the war in the south to a city in mourning. Four battalions of light infantry disembarked and began their training with Brazilian regiments. Amid subdued pomp and ceremony he inspected the troops with Dom João, and in private meetings renegotiated his position in Portugal. He would return with his powers greatly strengthened, being made Marshal General of all the king's armies and given the right to recruit fresh troops. His job done in Rio, Beresford would sail with Dom João's daughters back to Europe.

The day before the departure of the royal brides, the bishop went on board to bless the boats for the long voyage ahead. The next morning, crowds gathered to see off the flotilla. The ships left on a fair breeze to salutes from the forts which ringed the bay. 'The departure was spectacular,' wrote Marrocos, 'but emotional.' Dom João, already distraught because of the death of his mother, left the ship in tears. Dona Carlota stayed on board until the very end, accompanying her daughters past the Sugar Loaf Mountain and out through the heads. For a brief moment she was where she had striven so hard to be in the years since she had come to Rio – in the open sea, on a convoy heading towards Europe. But after she had bid farewell to her daughters, a brig ferried her back to Praia Vermelha, a small beach on the ocean-facing side of the Sugar Loaf, from where she watched as the convoy disappeared over the horizon. A few days later, letters from the fleet arrived back in Rio, the opening words of a correspondence that would bridge the coming years of separation.

It was the last time Dona Carlota would see her daughter Dona Maria Isabel. Two years later she died in Madrid in a botched childbirth. As it was first thought that she had already passed away from a seizure suffered in the course of a marathon labour, a rough Caesarean section was performed in which arteries and vital organs were sliced through in a frantic effort to save the baby, the heir to the Spanish throne. The child was stillborn, but the mother revived, only to register, briefly, the scene of butchery in which she figured before dying of her multiple wounds.

Trapped in Rio, Dona Carlota's life became insufferable, the prospect of an indefinite stay in Brazil bringing on bouts of depression. She wrote to her brother Fernando VII, pleading that he arrange some way of taking her away from Rio, a city that she found repugnant. Its slave population disgusted her, its lack of European sophistication grated on a woman for whom even Lisbon had seemed like a cultural backwater. She felt imprisoned in a country that she dismissed as 'a land of monkeys and blacks'. The tropical downpours and airless humidity were also taking their toll – each summer, Dona Carlota wilted in the heat, and her health deteriorated. She was now forty. With her brother back on the throne in Spain, her court intrigues were at a definitive end, her life wasting away in exile.

It was in these dead years that the contradictions in her complex character were most evident. Her restlessness continued – she still moved house regularly, enjoying some of the most spectacularly situated villas in the hills around Rio, and in the process upsetting a string of owners whose properties she sequestered. She took a liking to a house in Laranjeiras belonging to the Baron of Tuyll, plenipotentiary minister of Russia. He was forced, unwillingly, to move out after he had spent a fortune renovating it. Another unhappy property owner was the French diplomat Colonel Maler. Dona Carlota claimed she needed his villa for health reasons and after much protest, he too was forced to sell. From these mansions she ran a quasi-court, similar to that which she had operated from Ramalhão in

Lisbon, but it was hardly a satisfactory arrangement. Excluded by Dom João from any real power, Dona Carlota smouldered with frustration.

The great bane of her life was her financial dependence on Dom João, and by all accounts she fell into some difficulties in Rio. The French botanist Auguste de Saint-Hilaire, who visited Rio after the end of the Napoleonic Wars, described an incident that suggests corners were being cut in Dona Carlota's household. One evening the chaplain on a ship from Europe, Father Renaud, went to pay her a visit. On leaving, he was accompanied back to the port by Dona Carlota carrying a candle, since there were no attendants available to escort him to his ship.

If she was in penury, her acts of generosity are all the more remarkable. The archivist Marrocos wrote of an episode that seems to run against the usual portrayals of Dona Carlota as a woman who used her powers irresponsibly. The wife of one of the servants at the royal library had been accused of adultery, and as a result had been abandoned by her husband, and left in a poor house in failing health. Hearing of her situation, Dona Carlota sent out a carriage to bring her to the palace, where the woman was granted an audience and invited to kiss the princess's hand. What followed was an outpouring of generosity that went well beyond what could have been expected. Dona Carlota provided fresh clothes and ordered her personal physician to treat the woman. 'Her Royal Highness was so attentive on this point,' wrote Marrocos, 'that she reminded the sick woman each time during the day when she had to take her medicine, administering to her on these occasions. Finding out later that the woman had two young daughters who were destitute, she ordered them to be fetched, dressed them up with an exquisite wardrobe of clothes, and placed them in a girls' school, paying monthly for their education . . .'

And for all her hatred of Rio's African population, on one occasion at least, she was not blinded by prejudice. While touring the city, Dona Carlota came across a master dealing out lashes to his slave girl for stealing half a pound of sugar. She stopped to investigate, and seeing the brutality of the punishment, ordered him to desist. Continuing on her way, she sent a guard back to check up on the master, who was caught wielding the whip once more. Dona Carlota returned to the scene and after reprimanding the man, granted his slave girl her freedom. It seemed that in Rio Dona Carlota treated the vulnerable with considerably more respect than those of her own class.

Dom João was now travelling regularly between his royal residences, spending longer and longer away from the city. Visits to the farm retreat at Santa Cruz grew from weeks into months at a stretch. He also spent time on the islands in the bay and on occasion went to Praia Grande (modern-day Niterói) on the other side of the harbour. The palace at São Cristóvão had been completely refitted. The court had employed a British architect, Peter Johnson, who had carried out a series of works to give the former planter's mansion an air of royalty. Thanks to a donation from the Duke of Northumberland, the entrance to its grounds was now graced by a new portal, an exact replica of the gate at London's Sion House. Johnson had sketched out plans for a series of pavilions at each corner of the palace, only one of which ended up being built. A Gothic façade was also being designed to give what was a plain classical mansion house a more elevated feel. Inside, there had been renovations to accommodate the royal family, with a special apartment for Dom João, a throne room and servants' quarters.

Come early evening, the gardens were lit up by small lamps, and in the fading light the chirrup of insects started up around the grounds. When in residence, Dom João would stroll about the palace grounds, unwinding after his day, making his way between the flower beds, orange groves and coffee bushes that had been laid out in the fields. Banana leaves stirred in the warm air, while off in the distance fireflies scribbled luminous patterns against the night sky.

There was something profoundly dysfunctional about the Portuguese royal family which their long stay in Brazil only accentuated. As the years passed, the familial rifts took on new dimensions, the Braganças becoming more and more

Brazilian from their youngest members up. The stolid, ritualistic life promoted by Dom João would never be reproduced by his offspring. His medieval tastes and patriarchal demeanour were already dated by the time he left Lisbon; life in Rio had, if anything, frozen his reign in time, as if the remnants of court life in the Napoleonic era were slowly fossilising in the tropics.

For the royal children, life in Rio would be a continuation of a troubled upbringing that had begun at the nadir of the Lisbon court. Their grandmother's madness (none of the children would have remembered her sane), their parents' early separation and the royal household's split between Queluz and Mafra had already destabilised the family. In Rio, they were divided once more, this time between São Cristóvão and Dona Carlota's various residences, with Pedro, Miguel and the eldest daughter, Maria Teresa, staying with their father, and the younger girls with Dona Carlota.

The royal children's education was neglected in Brazil. The younger girls were practically illiterate and after years of instruction Miguel still had problems writing his own name, repeatedly misspelling it 'Migel'. Pedro also wrote poorly, making frequent grammatical and spelling mistakes. His letters to his mother were often brief, and to the point: 'My Mother and my Senhora, I hope that Your Majesty has been well and will continue to be. From this, your humble son who kisses your hand, Pedro.' But perhaps his brevity was intentional – he never got on with his mother, always siding with his father in the constant disputes in which the family was embroiled. Much later, Dom Pedro would try to make amends for his lamentable upbringing, ordering his own children to follow a strict educational routine, in an effort to ensure that 'my brother Miguel and I will be the last ignoramuses of the Bragança family'.

As heir to the throne, Dom Pedro had, in fact, undergone some instruction in Latin, English and music. He learnt to play several musical instruments, including the clarinet, flute, bassoon and harpsichord, and would later take to composing music. He had also dabbled in woodwork, carving a figurehead for the frigate *Príncipe Dom Pedro* out of tropical hardwoods. Academically, though, he was not a diligent student. Like his mother, he developed a love of horse riding and long summers at the royal family's country estate, Santa Cruz, were spent galloping through cane fields and up into the forested hillsides. On hot afternoons, Pedro and Miguel would play war games at Santa Cruz, commanding armies of slave children against each other in skirmishes involving hails of sticks and stones.

There was something unrestrained, almost out of control about Pedro's childhood and early adolescence in Rio that would leave a mark on his personality. Impulsive, impatient, a libertine, Dom Pedro cared little for the niceties of court ceremony. Although destined to rule, he enjoyed mixing with commoners more than royalty, and as a young man toured Rio's taverns, disguised in the large cape and wide-brimmed hat of a *Paulista* horseman. Even when he became emperor of Brazil, he seemed more comfortable chatting to his servants than entertaining heads of state. He would also, following his mother's passions, turn into an inveterate womaniser.

He grew into a handsome young man, with an athletic build, thick, wavy brown hair and dark eyes. Sexually, he was as brazen and reckless as he had been in his childhood play. He would ride through the city on the lookout for women, stopping litters in the street, and propositioning any good-looking passengers he found. By his mid-teens he had become notorious in Rio, so notorious in fact that the head of one wealthy family barred him from his house. He had an eye for foreign women – 'Italians, French, Spanish Americans, something different each week', according to one contemporary – and would have his first serious relationship with the French ballerina, Noémi Thierry.

In early 1817, Noémi Thierry fell pregnant. It could not have happened at a worst time, as Portuguese envoys were then involved in delicate negotiations with the Austrian court. They were trying to match Dom Pedro with the Habsburg princess, Dona Leopoldina, and stories of the prince royal's loose behaviour filtering back from Rio were not helping their cause. In the end, Noémi Thierry was hurriedly removed from the city, paid off from the royal treasury and sent away to the north-east of Brazil where their child was stillborn.

Pedro's younger brother, Miguel, had also run wild in Rio. He was restricted only by intermittent health problems, which were by all accounts serious – Marrocos went as far as describing him as consumptive. Widely considered a bastard son, he was Dona Carlota's favourite, although 'tough love' was her approach to his upbringing – there are several accounts of her beating him mercilessly with her slipper. He would grow up in the same anarchic environment as his brother, but developed a more sinister personality in the process. He became an avid bullfighter, and hunted deer. Street sellers ran for cover when the adolescent Miguel would drive a six-horse carriage at a gallop through the city centre, scattering everything in its path. Later in life, he was lucky to survive when, in some kind of military accident, his hand was ripped apart in an explosion, damaging it so badly that it had to be pieced together by surgeons.

While their children were coming of age in Brazil, Dom João and Dona Carlota's relationship was reaching a new low. In 1817, an incident involving Dona Carlota mired her in fresh controversy. It concerned the murder of Gertudes Carneiro Leão, who, returning to her house one night with her daughters, was ambushed and shot dead. The assassin, the mulatto Joaquim Ignacio da Costa (known as *Orelhas* or 'Ears') was arrested and during the course of the trial, claimed that he had been operating under Dona Carlota's orders. Suspicion already hung over Dona Carlota, since at the time she was romantically linked with the murdered woman's husband, and she was also said to have coveted Gertudes Carneiro Leão's house. The details of the affair remain obscure, the official version of events lost for ever when, after a court enquiry, Dom João burnt all incriminating evidence, yet again covering up for his wife. Thereafter, Dona Carlota was confined to her residence under a loose form of house arrest.

Dom João himself was not free from scandal in his time in Rio. There were rumours from within the palace about his excessive affection for his chamberlain – one of the Lobato brothers, a family of palace favourites who had been the prince regent's confidants in Lisbon. Dom João had bestowed on this particular servant the title of 'Viscount of Vila Nova da Rainha', an honour unheard of for palace attendants. The rumours – going as far as accusations of homosexual activities – are suggestive, although they could have arisen from court jealousies. One priest, Father Miguel, who served at Santa Cruz, claimed that while he knelt praying in a darkened corner he actually witnessed acts of intimacy between Dom João and another man. Father Miguel was later exiled to the Bishopric of Angola for reasons that have never been clarified.

Incidents such as these did the court no favours in Rio. The royal couple were proving themselves to be mere mortals, and, to the devoutly Catholic *cariocas*, morally suspect ones at that. The use and abuse of power – at the root of criticisms of the absolutist system that were beginning to be voiced across the new Europe – was particularly marked in the way Dom João and his court dealt with accusations against them. The court's position was still solid in Rio, but the years of corruption and scandal were slowly chipping away at its legitimacy.

TEN

A Subtropical Rome

The air was thick with a fine powder, dust clouds that were held suspended over the city. Powerful explosions echoed across the bay. At the foot of the Corcovado Mountain, labourers blasted granite off the rock-face. There were other quarries in Glória and Catete, a twenty-minute walk from the centre, where the sides of mountains were reduced to rubble to be hauled back to construction sites across the city. Elsewhere, low hills were being raised. In biblical scenes, teams of slaves stripped to the waist carried hundreds of tons of earth, rock and foliage, dumping them into the swamplands which still surrounded the town. They laboured in forty-degree heat, their task literally one of moving mountains, as Rio's landscape began a process of monumental change that would extend well into the twentieth century.

A gradual levelling of the central area took shape, while on the outskirts chain-gangs cut trails through the mountains, opening up spectacular parklands and connecting the growing number of hillside villas to the city centre. More roads were paved, new routes constructed. In time, real improvements were made to Rio's sanitation through the organisation of a slave-run sewage system. Those unfortunate enough to be recruited had to carry barrels of human waste to the beach on their heads and dump them into the bay. Ribbons of pale skin formed on their shoulders and backs, bleached by acids which fell from their load. They became know as 'tigers', due to the streaky patterns

that were left as reminders of their status as Christian untouch-
ables.

Rio was changing rapidly, spurred on not just by court-
imposed city works, but by a deeper sense of its own importance
on the international stage. With the court's tacit decision to stay
on, more embassies were set up and foreigners poured into the
capital. Diplomats and their teams created new demands, bringing traders with their luxury goods from post-war Europe. Rich
travellers spent weeks, months, sometimes even years sampling
the delights of a city that was fast becoming one of the New
World's foremost attractions.

The end of the war and Britain's waning influence also
brought the French. They came in large numbers and were
at first not easily accepted. 'It is impossible to describe the
phenomenal quantities of French goods and trinkets which
are flooding this city . . .' wrote Marrocos to his sister, 'you
no longer see much English merchandise . . . everyone is dressed
up in French fashions, except me who is old-school Portuguese
. . . The port is packed with French ships – only in the last
month, twenty-nine have entered, loaded with goods.' It was a
state of affairs with which Marrocos was far from comfortable: 'I
still hate them [the French] so much that I cannot look them in
the eye – for me France is still an odious nation', a sentiment that
was widely shared. Stories of French atrocities were fresh in the
imagination and the anti-French propaganda that had been
produced during the war years still filled the shelves of Rio's
bookshops. But the French population grew steadily and soon
outnumbered the British. They took up the feminine side of the
city's trade. While the British continued to import heavy
building materials – iron, glass, copper – and manufactured
goods, the French established themselves as *coiffeurs*, milliners,
dressmakers and language teachers. As small traders they sold
fans, perfumes, jewellery, silk shoes, lace, plumes and assorted
decorations. They were favoured by the court, whose women
aped Parisian fashions and hair styles. This was the beginnings of
what would be an enduring influence on Brazilian tastes, habits
and intellectual life.

With the Francophile Antônio de Araújo back in office, France's cultural role was actively encouraged by the court. Pensions were paid to The French Artistic Mission (established in 1816) – a group of painters, sculptors and architects, led by Joachim Lebreton, who were brought out to found an academy of fine arts. Their presence in Rio involved several layers of irony. As former Bonapartists, they were themselves exiles, refugees from post-war Europe's resurgent monarchism. On the restoration of the Bourbons, the French ambassador to the Portuguese court even petitioned for Lebreton's arrest for his past association with Napoleon, but the appeals fell on deaf ears. The Rio court's goal of civilising its former colonial port overrode any residual bad feelings towards the regime that had forced it into flight. Long after Waterloo, Napoleon's influence would linger in Rio, as The French Artistic Mission brought neo-classical architecture to what had been a Baroque cityscape. Aside from its public buildings, graceful fountains, sculptures and pavilions spread through Rio, giving the city a subtle Gallic flavour.

Rio's population swelled, and not just from the influx of the British and French. Brazilians themselves migrated from all over the country in search of work; Germans, Irish, Spaniards, Italians, North Americans, even a handful of Angolan ex-slaves, travelled out to what was developing into a thriving South Atlantic port. Dom João helped the process along, setting up a formal immigration scheme to settle a group of Swiss recruits in a new colony just outside Rio called Nova Friburgo. The overwhelming majority of newcomers, though, were the Portuguese. Ship after ship disgorged thousands fleeing the poverty and uncertainties of postwar Portugal. There were so many that the city's administrators went so far as to propose a series of measures for stemming the tide. It was thought that Portuguese immigrant ships should be diverted to other ports in Brazil, and that Rio's excess Portuguese population could be dispatched as farmers to colonise Brazil's expanses of unproductive land. In the end they were absorbed in the capital, though many ended up living on the fringes of an already overburdened system of court patronage.

As Rio expanded, so too did the ambitions of the court. The duplication of the Lisbon bureaucracy was relatively straightforward, but recreating a court life rich in pageantry was a long, slow process. In Lisbon, ecclesiastical music, theatre and ballet had been focal points of the court's very public cultural life, with cycles of operas and plays attended by the royal family and the city's dignitaries. Little by little, Dom João brought this world back into being. At first he worked with what he had – a small group of talented but poorly equipped Brazilians – but they were gradually replaced by composers, musicians and singers who were brought out from Europe at huge expense.

In the early days, musical life centred around the royal chapel, where José Maurício, a mulatto priest, known as 'the Brazilian Mozart', led his orchestra through sung masses and orations. He composed his own sacred music and extended his repertoire from manuscripts that came with the royal family in order to cover the stream of festivals and holy days that filled the Portuguese religious calendar. After serving for three years, he was brushed aside by the arrival of Marcus Portugal, a favoured court composer who was sent out from Lisbon. An active collaborator during the war, in the not-too-distant past Marcus Portugal had been dedicating his operas to Napoleon, but now found himself back in the royal fold.

A lottery was created, the proceeds going into the building of a theatre of European metropolitan proportions. It had a capacity of over a thousand, and was ringed by 112 boxes. Full-scale Italian operas began to be performed along with French ballets; allegorical plays with names like *The Triumph of Brazil* were staged on special occasions, their plots stacked with characters from Greek and Roman mythology mouthing adulations to the king and Portuguese imperial achievement. They drew big crowds, watched over by the royal family and court dignitaries from the vantage points of their box seats. What they saw was a mix of the familiar and the unexpected. Slaves filled out the choruses in the operas; many of the ballet dancers were, as one observer delicately put it, 'not quite of European tint'.

Stagehands and set designers were drawn from Rio's large community of freedmen, and on ceremonial occasions, a slave orchestra and choir, schooled from an early age at a conservatorium at Santa Cruz, performed for the royal family and their courtiers.

Dom João also contracted the best musicians he could find in Europe. Sigismund von Neukomm, who came as a part of The French Artistic Mission, was his biggest draw in the later years. A student of Haydn's in Vienna and the musical director of the French delegation to the Congress of Vienna, Neukomm had also served as chapel master to the Tsar in St Petersburg as well as French foreign minister Talleyrand's personal pianist. His reputation as one of the most promising talents in Europe at the time had been established after a joint concert with António Salieri. Under his direction, the first ever performances of Haydn's *Creation* and Mozart's *Requiem* took place against the backdrop of Rio's sumptuous harbour.

A final extravagance was added to the court's growing entourage of musicians and singers: Italian *castrati* (eunuchs) were brought over at phenomenal cost. Their soaring vocals filled the royal chapel with an ethereal grace, their presence in the court elevating it, in at least one respect, to levels of refinement expected of European royalty. In a sense, the hiring of the *castrati* summed up Dom João's approach to Rio's cultural transformation. It was expensive – a wasteful indulgence for a court that was by this stage heavily indebted. It also harked back to another era. The *castrati* had been used throughout Europe from the sixteenth century onwards, first for church music and then for opera, but by the nineteenth century were beginning to look like survivors from another age. In Rio they met with a mixed reception. They performed at *soirées* for Brazilian high society, not always provoking favourable comment. They were 'disgusting', wrote an anonymous traveller who attended one of these evenings. 'Their whole gait announces effeminacy and their figures are remarkable for the narrowness of their shoulders, width of hip, and an extraordinary development of the femur and tibia.' They sang well, the commentator went on, but in conversation their voices were 'squeaky'.

Away from the royal chapel and the newly built theatre, different kinds of music that owed nothing to Europe's arias and polyphonies were coming into being. They could be heard in the heart of the city, as slave work gangs chanted to ease their burdens, filling the muggy air with African cadences taking root in a new continent. The songs were dismissed by the incumbent Portuguese as vulgar, perhaps even dangerously so. But it was this set of distinctive rhythms that would, in the fullness of time, develop into something far more important than the costly European imitations that the court brought with them. Long after the impact of Dom João and his civilising mission had faded, the city's cultural landscape would continue to bear the unmistakable imprint of its Afro-Brazilian soul.

After almost ten years in Brazil, the gulf between *carioca* and court society was more evident than ever, a separation that manifested itself in the more mundane aspects of day-to-day living. The different breads and European fruit, the wine, the hams, Italian salamis and liqueurs that were shipped out to supply the court distanced it from life on the streets. There, *cariocas* enjoyed a cuisine heavily influenced by their colonial heritage. Coarse manioc flour, beans and rice were dietary staples, often eaten with the hands. Varieties of pork and bean stews such as *feijoada*; corn-based dishes with the consistency of porridge and mixed with the simplest of ingredients, such as *canjica* (boiled with milk) and *jacuba* (boiled with brown sugar and water); and jerked beef, known as *carne de sol*, were local dishes that never reached the banquet halls of the court.

The lifestyles of Brazilians and Portuguese diverged in other, more intimate, respects. Standards of hygiene differed radically. The wealthy invalid Henry Koster, who travelled through the northeast, wrote that the Brazilians were 'notably fastidious in the cleanliness of their bodies', while another visitor observed: 'As a rule the Brazilians have one quality in common, even the very poor never leave their houses or huts without washing, and if they possess two shirts, the one next to their skin is clean.' The

Portuguese, on the other hand, had a more medieval approach. There is not a single reference to Dom João ever having washed himself all over with soap and water in more than a decade in Brazil, where temperatures regularly topped thirty-five degrees Celsius. By all accounts, not washing was a point of honour amongst upper-class Portuguese in Rio. One contemporary writer told the story of a recently contracted maid being berated for bringing a pitcher of water to her mistress in the morning. Refined women did not bathe, as they touched nothing dirty, explained her mistress; bathing, she went on, was a lower-class practice.

Long before the Portuguese arrived so unexpectedly on that clear, late-summer afternoon in 1808, a 'tropicalised' society had emerged, modern Brazil in embryo, with its eclectic mix of African, European and indigenous influences. Afro-Brazilians had created a parallel cultural universe of their own, one which had been formed out of centuries of contact between Portugal and Africa. It was not only Dom João's royal entourage that had washed up in Brazil – a Congolese court operated in Rio and was tolerated, to a large extent, by the colonial authorities. Each year, Afro-Brazilian freedmen and slaves elected a king who took on the trappings of European royalty, using robes, crowns, a throne and sceptres. To the onlooker this may have seemed like a sly parody of Portuguese ritual, but the court was a genuine Afro-Brazilian entity. It maintained relations with the Portuguese royal family, attending important feasts and festivals.

This was the carnivalesque world immortalised by Jean-Baptiste Debret, a pupil of David and a member of The French Artistic Mission, whose prints and engravings have become iconic representations of the era. His gaze was sophisticated, focusing on the minutiae of *carioca* life; domestic scenes, street life and intimate portraits of slaves, at that time often shorn of their individual features by racist caricature. Without the Debret engravings, descriptions of early-nineteenth-century Rio might have sounded like fanciful exotica; with them, a striking portrait of the unusual cultural juxtapositions that the Portuguse Empire had created in Rio was captured for posterity.

*   *   *

The court could clean out the city, set up new cultural institutions, encourage education, but no matter what gloss of refinement they brought to Rio, they could not escape the less savoury aspects of Portugal's imperial legacy. Even with its choirs, orchestras and theatres, Rio de Janeiro was still essentially an enormous slave market town – by far the biggest in the Americas. Slaves poured into the port to be sold on to plantation owners around Brazil or affluent *carioca* families in the city itself. Every aspect of life in Rio was touched by slavery, from the central districts filled by day with African labourers, to the massively serviced households of rich Brazilians. For the court, reminders of the trade were unavoidable – chain-gangs marched right past the royal palace, chanting as they went, led by an overseer who marked out the rhythm by rattling a pebble-filled gourd. Slaves milled around the palace at São Cristóvão, toiling in its fields, working as farmhands and gardeners.

Brazil had, after all, been built on the slave trade. Well before large-scale slaving had reached the Caribbean and North America, the Portuguese had been transporting Africans in numbers to work the plantations of the Brazilian northeast. Slavery had been the thread that bound her Atlantic empire together, the motor of virtually all economic activity in her South American colonies. By the end of the seventeenth century, more slaves had entered Brazil than would ever reach British North America from abroad. At the turn of the nineteenth century an elaborate organisation of colonial officials, financiers, African agents and slave 'freighters' was transporting up to 20,000 slaves a year to Rio alone. When the court arrived in Brazil, one third of Rio's population was enslaved. 'A stranger unacquainted with the slave trade,' wrote Charles Abel, an English botanist who visited Rio de Janeiro during the court's stay, 'might have imagined that the slaves were its proper inhabitants, and their masters its casual dwellers.' Rio *was* a kind of subtropical Rome, but in a way that was far from the court's aspirations of culture and nobility.

The busy port area had no cranes or pulleys; there were few wheeled vehicles; beasts of burden were scarce, water pipes almost nonexistent. Instead, a vast portage industry had grown up, with slaves hired out to carry everything that needed moving in the city, including people. Slave ships docked daily, their half-dead 'cargoes' often having to be carried ashore on the shoulders of other slaves to be 'warehoused' in the notorious Valongo district – the sleazy hub of operations, where the slave market, a cemetery and mansions built on the proceeds of the trade were grouped together in unholy union.

The well-to-do developed a horror of manual labour. It was an attitude that dated back to the earliest days of colonial expansion, a dream of living from the labour of others that spurred on migration from Portugal out into the empire. When a colonist arrived in Brazil of the sixteenth century, according to one contemporary, 'he acquired two pairs of slaves or maybe half-a-dozen . . . one slave fished. Another hunted. The others cultivated and tended their fields.' Transplanted into an urban setting, this ethos lived on in Rio. Upper-class Brazilians were waited on hand and foot by cleaners, cooks and childminders. In this respect, the archivist Marrocos became typical. Over his years in Rio, he and his *carioca* wife accumulated a team of household slaves: a wet-nurse, several cooks, a washerwoman, as well as two runaway girls who were employed to do the sewing and ironing. Like many households of means in Rio at the time, Marrocos's family was outnumbered by its slave workers.

Visitors to early-nineteenth-century Rio were shocked by the indolence of ordinary *cariocas*. Carpenters hired slaves to carry their tools; army officers, their weapons and ammunition. In well-heeled homes women sat idle, dealing out trivial requests to their numerous slave helpers, and when they went out they were carried short distances in sedan chairs. Slaves were even dispatched to perform religious duties, mouthing *Ave Marias* mechanically on their masters' behalf in front of the glass-cased Virgin Marys positioned around the city.

While idleness was frowned upon, foreigners idealised the African slave at work in descriptions that bordered on the homoerotic. James Henderson travelled out to Rio in 1819 hoping to secure a post in the British diplomatic corps, but

ended up writing a history of Brazil instead. He described the
bonded population in flattering, if suspect terms:

> 'Many of the negro slaves are remarkably well formed, parti-
> cularly some of those who labour at the customs house, and
> exhibit such muscular strength about their whole frames, com-
> bined with such symmetry of form, that the lineaments and
> swelling muscles of their naked bodies reminded me of some fine
> antique models.'

No less impressed was the French writer Fernand Denis, who
passed through a little later:

> 'One of the things that always excites the admiration of the
> foreigner who arrives in the street leading to the customs house
> which carries almost all the goods transported in the city, is the
> collection of blacks from all the races of Africa, a scene that is
> always disorientating at first glance: their semi-nudity, as they
> wear only linen loincloths; their strong limbs which bring to
> mind statues from antiquity, the exotic shapes of their bodies . . .
> all this forms a canvas that quickly turns quotidian, but that at first
> sight strikes one as a revelation of an unknown world.'

The Valongo slave market became just another attraction, like
the Sugar Loaf Mountain or Tijuca Park – a macabre stopoff on
the city's otherwise sumptuous circuit. Visitors strolled past the
rows of iron-barred warehouses where those waiting for the
auctioneer's hammer were slumped in depression. 'The smell
and heat in the room was very oppressive and offensive,' wrote
one traveller. 'Having my pocket thermometer with me, I
observed it stood at ninety-two degrees [Fahrenheit]. It was
then winter . . .' Tourists watched as recently arrived slaves were
subjected to the humiliation of being sold like cattle, sellers
parading their wares naked while potential buyers inspected
their teeth, checked their genitals, got them to run on the spot
and made to strike them in order to test their reactions. Bidders
were normally men, but Brazilian women could also be seen in

the market in search of domestic helpers or wet-nurses, spruced up for their day out shopping.

There is an uncomfortable voyeurism in some of the accounts of the market's workings. Those visiting the market betrayed a hint of nostalgia – the thought that they were witnessing the workings of a dying trade, remnants of another, more brutal era that would soon be at an end. But the institution was deeply rooted in Brazilian society, and it would take more than half a century to completely dislodge it. If anything, in the years to come the sense of impending abolition worsened conditions, as the rush of last-minute orders, the slave 'stockpiles' and the eagerness of the supplier to fulfil the booming demand took their effect.

Much later, a select committee hearing in London was told of the horrors of these last days:

> ' ". . . Expecting that the Slave trade was to have been stopped, everything was brought over that could be brought," said a former Brazilian trader being questioned by the committee, "the lame, the blind, the deaf and everything; princes, priests and patriarchs, everything that could swell the number was brought over then."
>
> "And were there more women then?" the committee's chairman probed.
>
> "Everything that could be bought, young and old; women with little babies, and women that were pregnant; everything was brought over then . . ." '

The court passed a series of measures to eliminate the most offensive practices associated with slavery. Some were cosmetic – blue cotton loincloths and red caps were issued to avoid unseemly nudity – but others were more substantive. Branding was, for a time, outlawed, only to be replaced by the even more uncomfortable metal bracelet or collar. The system proved unworkable, widespread fraud forcing a return to the permanency of the branding iron. New standards of hygiene were introduced at the Valongo market and its nearby cemetery, which over the years had turned into a mass grave with bodies lined up in trenches, buried head to foot to save much needed space. Attempts were also made to reduce the overcrowding and subsequent mortality rates on the Atlantic crossing, with limits put on the number of slaves per tonnage and a requirement for each ship to carry a surgeon. And in a law that exposed that terrible losses were still being suffered on the slave boats, cash rewards were given to captains who could keep their death rates below 3 per cent.

The policing of the slave population was given a good deal of thought. The slave uprising of Saint-Domingue (Haiti) in the 1790s was within living memory – a story with terrifying implications for Brazilian slave owners. Travelling by word of mouth, it had spread through the country, gaining legendary status in many of Brazil's slave communities. The court was acutely aware of the potential threat of rebellion, yet in Rio the authorities quickly realised that restricting slave gatherings was impractical. Slaves powered the city, their presence along every road and on every street corner an integral part of the urban infrastructure.

Dom João's chief adviser on the running of the city, Paulo Fernandes Viana, could, however, take action on one emotive front. Public flogging had long been a feature of colonial cities up and down the Brazilian coast, with crowds gathered to view marathon lashings, usually administered by other slaves, at *pelour-inhos* (whipping posts) prominently positioned in each town's main square. These remain stock images of Brazilian colonial life, just as similar scenes are to Australia's vision of its own convict society. Viana decreed that where possible whippings were to be carried out in the prison yard, administered, for a fee, by Crown officials. As with most of these measures, the motivating senti-ment was less humanitarian concern than a combination of pragmatism and the demands of courtly decorum. It was felt that 'whipping them in the streets and in the places of their infractions provokes uprisings' while at the same time that 'it was truly indecent within a court to have whippings in public squares'.

At heart, though, Rio de Janeiro remained a slave city. Its very existence depended on a crude system of exploitation in which masters, as property owners, were given *carte blanche* over the treatment of a captive population. Under these circumstances the slaves' plight was variable. At one end of the spectrum they lived a life that was no worse than the European working classes of the day, whom they effectively replaced, slotting into an urban economy that had grown up around the use of slaves in Rio. They were advertised in the papers, rented out by their masters, hired by the day, and trained up in specific areas – gem cutting, cobbling, midwifery and bloodletting – in order to increase their going rate. Such was their hold on the artisan trades that there was little legitimate work for those not enslaved, giving rise to a perhaps even more desperate category in Rio and elsewhere in Brazil: the poor whites. As neither slave nor master, they had no real role to play. Manual labour for the non-slave was socially unacceptable and in any case largely unavailable. They sank into terrible poverty, subsisting on the margins of colonial society.

At the other end of the spectrum was daily humiliation, overwork, and the threat of abandonment if they were no longer able to carry out their workloads. Such treatment was actively resisted. In a fascinating set of legal cases, some slaves even challenged their oppressors through the courts and won at least their liberty from abusive masters. Others chose more realistic options, fleeing to people the hills around Rio in small *quilombos* or runaway communities. By all accounts Rio was permanently ringed by these *quilombos* which, in contrast to some romanticised images, were in many cases no more than groups of frightened individuals living off stolen scraps and sleeping rough.

A few went one step further. Often, after the trauma of their journey and arrival in Brazil, slaves were subjected to a vicious 'breaking in' period. In their first months they were punished for the most minor indiscretions to ensure their future subservience. After sinking irretrievably into depression they disappeared without warning, their bodies later found washed up on the city's beaches or hanging from branches in nearby forests. They had become, in one contemporary's words, 'runaways who have reached the spirit land', renegades who chose oblivion over the lives that lay before them.

As memories of their former lives in Lisbon receded, the royal family and their retinue became more and more accustomed to this unfamiliar world. They became slave owners in their own right, and court life took on the flavour of a city state in antiquity. A dozen slaves dressed in red livery carried Dom João in his sedan chair around Rio. Royal barges glided across the bay, powered by rows of slave oarsman. On special occasions slave musicians provided court entertainment. The palace received gifts of slaves as tribute from wealthy planters. And all the while the public works went on, with chain-gangs cutting roads through forested hills that surrounded the city, sweating teams hauling granite blocks from nearby quarries and slave labourers laying the foundation stones for the new Rio.

ELEVEN

The Turning Point

A tick had burrowed into Dom João's leg. It was removed, but an infection spread out from the wound and the leg swelled up. Dom João's physician ordered what was, for Portuguese royalty of the time, radical action. The leg was to be regularly bathed in seawater. At Cajú beach, on the bay near São Cristóvão, a special mobile bathing house was built to assuage the king's fear of being bitten by crabs. In it was placed a wooden tub in which Dom João could sit and be lowered into the waters by his attendants. The treatment lasted months, but the infection was stubborn and the leg continued to fester. Dom João found himself confined to the palace, while the works that he had initiated in the city went on.

By 1817 the court had been in Rio for almost a decade, and the projects that had been instigated on its arrival were coming to fruition. The royal gardens had expanded since their inauguration – 'Several fine alleys of bread-fruit trees, from the South Sea (*Artocarpus incisa*), the shadowy ytó (*Guarea trichilioides*) and mango trees, lead through the plantation,' wrote the Bavarian naturalists Martius and Spix who arrived in Rio in 1817, 'in which the most important object of cultivation is the Chinese tea plant.' It was thought that this crop, which had been so profitably grown in other subtropical climates, might do well in Brazil, and 200 Chinese especially chosen for their skills in the cultivation of tea were recruited in Canton, and transported from

Macao to start trials. Six thousand trees were planted in rows, some at the botanical gardens, others in fields around Santa Cruz, where a Chinese colony was set up to tend the tea plantations. But the experiment failed. A hardy, coarse variety grew from the tropical soils, its bitter taste making it commercially worthless. The failure of tea gave way to the phenomenal success of coffee. Exploitation of the crop was in its infancy when Dom João reached Rio, but thanks to his encouragement plantations were now spreading through the city's outlying districts. Other plants were taking well to their new surroundings. Dom João's *palma mater* was now over thirty metres tall, given pride of place amongst the various botanical specimens. Each time it seeded a guard was posted to prevent the duplication of the king's inaugural palm.

The royal library had been open to the public for several years. It was originally lodged on the top floor of a hospital in the centre of the city, but had gradually expanded to take up the whole building. Nurses and patients were transferred to make way for the stream of crates arriving from Lisbon, and the entrance to the building was made over with allegoric panels depicting the history of the universe from the creation of the world until 1793. Brazil's first printing press was also transforming the intellectual life in the colony, albeit with works carefully vetted by Crown censors. One publication which captured the *carioca* imagination was Pero Vaz da Caminha's letter in which he described Portugal's first contact with the Brazilian littoral and its indigenous peoples. Published as a dedication to Dom João by the royal press in 1817, the letter was an instant success. After centuries hidden in the Lisbon archives, it was a document whose time had come. In the past Caminha's letter had been filed away with the many eyewitness accounts from Portugal's Age of Discoveries; but now, as the Portuguese court consolidated its rule from the tropics, it was transformed into the founding statement of a new empire.

From the outside, it seemed that the move to Rio was now permanent. Plans were already well advanced for two historic

events, the formal marriage of the heir to the throne, Dom
Pedro, to the Austrian Archduchess, Dona Leopoldina; and the
'acclamation' of Dom João as king, both of which would take
place in the New World.

Behind the scenes, though, the regime was faltering. Over the
years, Dom João had made as few changes as possible to his
government. He had relied almost exclusively on the men who
had seen him through the difficult years leading up to his exile –
every minister that Dom João had previously appointed had
been with him on the Atlantic during the flight of 1807–1808.
One of his most capable ministers, Dom Rodrigo de Sousa
Coutinho, was long dead. His rival, Antônio de Araújo, was into
his sixties and in poor health. In his final months, he was said to
need two assistants just to sign documents. When he died,
Strangford's replacement, consul-general Henry Chamberlain,
went to see his interim successor, João Paulo Bezerra, and found
him in bed suffering from palsy – a condition that Strangford had
first described in December 1813 as 'a violent Paralytic Affliction, which has reduced him to a state of the most deplorable
Imbecility'. 'It is in fact somewhat surprising,' wrote Chamberlain in 1817, 'how the government has gone on even till this
time with two such infirm ministers [Bezerra and Araújo] . . .
every branch of the administration is reported to be in almost
irretrievable confusion.' Maintenance of the *status quo* had been
taken to extremes; mountains of paperwork that had built up
during each minister's final convalescence were left untouched.
Those remaining took on ever greater responsibilities, with
remits covering two, three, sometimes four ministerial port-
folios.

After Araújo's death, the reins were taken over by the ageing
Tomás António de Vilanova Portugal, a man with conservative
instincts who would not just head the treasury, but also deal with
both interior and foreign affairs as well as the war ministry. He
was 'full of good intentions' according to Palmela, but 'did not
have the slightest idea of the state of play in Europe'. This was a
critical time for Dom João's administration to be working in the
dark. Problems relating to the court and government's reloca-

tion which had never really been faced were beginning to press and the small, clubby gerontocracy that the king gathered around him was unequal to the task. Ten years had passed since any of the king's advisers had been in Europe, a decade in which the Napoleonic Wars and their aftermath had fundamentally changed the dynamics of the Continent. In the early years, Strangford had kept officials up to date (even if it was with a British-biased version of events) but since his expulsion, the court found itself isolated.

More and more, Dom João focused on his pet project – the military campaigns to secure the Banda Oriental in the south – to the exclusion of European affairs. But this was a deeply un-popular war, as hated in Portugal as it was in Brazil. Taxes were levied on both sides of Atlantic and provincial troop regiments went unpaid while resources were poured into a distant conflict which was little understood. Veterans of the Napoleonic Wars were shipped out from Portugal, and agents swept through Brazil, press-ganging farmers and small traders into the army. From the tropical climate of Bahia, the recruits were transported to the far south, and froze in winter temperatures which could fall below zero at night.

The court's awakening would be sudden and violent, its world jolted by insubordination from an unexpected quarter. Life in Rio would continue as if nothing had happened, but events in the plantation heartlands of Pernambuco caught Dom João off guard, destroying the illusion that in Brazil he could be exempt from the problems that had plagued his reign in Europe.

In March 1817, more than 1,000 miles up the coast from Rio, the governor of Pernambuco was in closed session with officials in the captaincy's capital, Recife. The discussions revolved around rumours of a conspiracy led by army officers. There had been accusations which linked the conspirators to the shadowy activities of the Freemasons, an organisation that had gained footholds in both Portugal and Brazil and was fast becoming a conduit for anti-royalist sentiment. The governor opted to act quickly. He ordered the arrest of all key suspects and dispatched his guards to the army barracks. It was a move that he would live to regret. One of the guards was slain as he tried to apprehend an officer suspect and the army barracks broke into open revolt. The governor sent out more guards to quell the dissent. He heard shots fired against them and in the heat of the moment made a sudden, rash decision. He gathered his family together and fled.

News of the governor's flight had an explosive effect. On the streets of Recife there was confusion. Portuguese traders were running for their boats, troops switching sides, officials fleeing a city that, from one moment to the next, had awoken with a start from its colonial slumber. The captain of a French boat, the *Perle*, was witness to the initial bloodletting: 'The freedmen and the slaves, as well as the mulattos, armed themselves with pikes and axes, massacring all those who were trying to escape in the first moments, particularly the sailors, as the insurgents were aware that the son of the quartermaster went on board the Portuguese boats to call for help for the royalists.'

For those with any real power in the city, the turning of the tables was swift and complete. Formerly respected Portuguese officials were reduced to fugitives. Some, with varying success, fled into the interior; others headed for the port. A much-hated magistrate, José da Cruz Ferreira, commandeered a *jangada* (a small, raft-like fishing vessel) and tried to sail up the coast to Ceará, but after battling for a time against stiff headwinds, ended up disembarking on a nearby beach and seeking refuge in a fishing hut. He was later captured and imprisoned, along with a growing number of his associates.

The governor took refuge in the city's fortress with residual loyalist troops. He might even have had a chance to retake the city if he had held firm, but he soon capitulated. The 'Republic of Pernambuco' had come into being. Royal seals, coats of arms and ceremonial staffs were destroyed. A new government was formed, headed by one of the architects of the revolt, the merchant Domingos José Martins. A string of classic revolutionary acts followed: unpopular taxes were abolished, prisons were thrown open and old scores settled. Placards reading

'Death to aristocrats' began appearing in the streets as centuries of deference fell away. One upper-class resident, João Lopes Cardoso Machado, who survived the purge, wrote in horror to a friend that 'half-castes, mulattoes and Creoles had become so daring that they declared all men equal, and boasted that they themselves would marry only white women of the best stock.' Cardoso was refused a shave at the barbers, and affronted by the new equalitarian spirit in the town: 'Your Grace would not permit a half-caste to come up to you,' he wrote to his friend, 'hat on his head, and clapping you on the shoulder address you: "Hi there, patriot, how are you doing? How about giving me a smoke . . ."'

The revolutionaries sent envoys to Britain and the United States asking for help and recognition, and agents fanned out into the surrounding captaincies to forment dissent. One of the conspirators, Padre Roma, headed south for Bahia. He made his way to the coastal town of Maceió by land, preaching republican propaganda to appreciative audiences as he went. From Maceió he took a *jangada* and headed down towards the city of Salvador in Bahia, but as he neared the city, the loyalist response was already under way. Padre Roma landed his craft on the idyllic sweep of palm-lined beaches just up the coast from Salvador, only to be arrested and shot three days later.

Although Bahia held firm, the revolt spread from Pernambuco into the neighbouring states of Paraíba do Norte, Rio Grande do Norte and, for a time, Ceará, but there was little sense of the creation of a unified republican resistance. Each state set up its own, independent provisional government. Different flags were designed for each new republic on a common theme of an iris, a sun and a cross. The defining feature was the number of stars and it was thought that as each new state won its independence, an additional star would be added to make up its flag.

It was 'an astounding event', wrote a magistrate in Pernambuco to his brother in Lisbon, 'five or six men destroyed in an instant an established government, and all the authorities conformed to what had happened without hesitation'. It was a defining moment too for Brazil. As colonial authorities in other states rushed to impose their authority, the Portuguese presence began to resemble a besieged military occupation. From a European perspective, the image of Brazil as an oasis of calm within a continent otherwise racked by revolutionary uprisings was shattered.

In the capital, news of the revolt came in the most vivid form possible for those not privy to government intelligence. The new authorities in Pernambuco decided to dispatch the governor and his family back to the court in Rio. After tracking south from Recife down the Brazilian coast, the ship approached the heads of Rio's harbour. Hoisting a white flag it entered the bay, but was immediately fired on by one of the forts at the harbour's entrance and forced to drop anchor. Army officials rushed on board to prevent the rebels having any communication with those on land and the crew were imprisoned on one of the islands in the bay. But the story was impossible to suppress. Word of the governor's humiliating return as a prisoner on a rebel ship spread rapidly through the city.

The revolution also awakened fears on another front, in one of the more curious aspects of the uprising. On hearing of the revolt, a small fleet set out from Philadelphia. On board were a group of Bonapartist sympathisers, their plan to mount a rescue operation from Recife to free Napoleon, now imprisoned on the South Atlantic island of St Helena. On being questioned later, they claimed they were working under the orders of Napoleon's brother, Joseph.

Brazil could have broken apart at this point. At the time of the Pernambucan revolt, Spanish America's wars of independence, which would see Spain's former possessions fragment into more than a dozen separate countries, were already under way. In Brazil, a similar process could have produced four giant states; with the Amazon, the northeast and the far south splitting off from the core districts around Rio. Even today, Brazil could easily be divided in this way, and in the time of Dom João, these regions were so remote that they were often seen as virtually separate countries. Distances were immense, overland routes often unfeasible and many regions of Brazil had closer contacts with Europe than with each other. Brazil could have fragmented further. Around Rio, the Minas and São Paulo districts were economic successes in their own right and already saw themselves as distinct, culturally different entities. Remarkably, however, this vast conglomerate of different interests and geographies would survive, hanging together through the turmoil of the following years.

The court responded to events in the northeast in the only way they knew: with overwhelming military force. Recife was blockaded. Thousands of troops from Rio and Salvador were loaded on to convoys and set sail for Pernambuco. There was consternation in republican areas as news came through of the impending attack. The movement itself had ended up as a conservative tax revolt and support was draining away, particularly from slaves who had began to realise that the revolutionary talk of 'equality' was, in their case, trumped by their masters' 'property rights'.

The new republic did not even hold together long enough for the convoys to reach the northeast. While Dom João's troops were still at sea and a loyalist army closed in on Recife by land, the fledgling republic was descending into civil war. The rebels were faced by an unlikely collection of patriots: 'natives with their bows and arrows, farmhands and locals grouped together unarmed and virtually naked'. When the legitimate forces arrived, they found Recife deserted and the rebels on the run. In the weeks that followed most were tracked down. Several committed suicide, twenty were executed. The revolt had lasted just seventy-five days, but its impact on both Portugal and Brazil would be felt for years to come.

Tension in Rio was eased by victory celebrations – the usual parade of fireworks, processions and floats – while behind closed doors repressive measures were being hurried into place. Court agents followed up denunciations, Masonic lodges around the country came under renewed scrutiny and were eventually banned. More importantly, preparations for Dom João's much anticipated acclamation as king were put on hold. Covert activity was accompanied by very public military measures. Portugal would lose four more troop regiments for the defence of Brazil, two stationed in Rio with one each in Salvador and Recife. It was meant as a show of force but instead betrayed panic. A decade earlier, the court had arrived in Brazil to an outpouring of celebrations and goodwill; now, they were reduced to deploying troops to enforce the loyalty of their own vassals.

The Pernambucan rebellion, short-lived as it was, struck a chord with many in Brazil, particularly in regions far from Rio. Stories of an extravagant, free-spending court with its numerous palaces and villas did not sit well with rising taxation in captaincies thousands of miles away. Complaints of injustice, corruption and bureaucratic interference echoed around the country. While it lasted, the relocation of the court was seen by some as a kind of internal colonialism in which Rio imposed its will over the Brazilian provinces.

Beyond the expansionist moves in the south, the court appeared uninterested in the rest of Brazil. Dom João never travelled out of Rio (he had, in fact, rarely ranged beyond his royal residences in and around Lisbon in his years there as prince regent) and many within the court seemed ignorant about the country they had found themselves in. They arrived in the New World as government functionaries, educated for narrow bureaucratic roles in Lisbon. Continuing their work in colonial mode, they focused on how revenues from the provinces could be best spent on their growing metropolis. Other Brazilian cities retained their run-down colonial façades, while Rio was undergoing full-scale reconstruction.

Rio had the most to gain from the Portuguese court's relocation, but even there discontent was growing. Houses which had been requisitioned on the arrival of the court, given up for what was thought to be temporary, emergency accommodation, were never returned. Some were even rented out by the Portuguese after they had moved on, rather than devolved to their rightful owners. The court cultivated an air of limitless wealth but was always behind in its payments for the prodigious

amount of produce and labour that was required to keep it
afloat. The money that it did spend seemed to go on imports of
goods and personnel from Europe. Local artists, architects and
musicians were used but then passed over as Europeans on large
salaries were shipped in to take their places. The arrival of The
French Artistic Mission and the composer Marcus Portugal were
seen in this light. There was resentment too over the funding of
the Nova Friburgo colonisation scheme. Grants of land and
housing went to a group of Swiss farmhands while their Brazilian
counterparts struggled to make ends meet. Indeed, farms around
Santa Cruz were regularly ordered to supply goods but were
inadequately compensated. And within the court itself there
were ongoing tensions between *cariocas* and European exiles.
The Portuguese reserved 'undisguised hatred' for the few Brazilians who had managed to gain a foothold, according to
Marrocos; '. . . They were naturally competitors of the Portuguese,' explained the archivist, 'who thought themselves to have
exclusive rights to all the jobs and all the favours of the Crown.'

From afar, images of the king as the empire's moral guardian, a
figure of spiritual strength and the subject of religious adoration,
had been cultivated in allegories, songs and poems. In Rio these
images were tarnished by the dealings of a court that was forever
scrabbling for funds. The awarding of honours, treated at first
with reverence, degenerated into a money-making exercise.
Dom João found that not only could he create vital alliances
with the Brazilian elite through the honours system, he could
also generate significant income in the process. During his time
in Rio he created twenty-eight marquises, eight counts, sixteen
viscounts, twenty-one barons and over 4,000 knights. 'To
become a Count in Portugal required 500 years,' wrote historian
Pedro Calmon, 'in Brazil, 500 *contos*.' Financial scams were
institutionalised by the creation of the Bank of Brazil, which
was used by the royals as a source of limitless credit. The bank
quickly became overexposed to unsecured loans, a situation that
the court used various unscrupulous methods to remedy. Silver
coin was melted down and then re-minted in debased form;
large quantities of paper money were issued to pay off debts. As a

result, inflation spiralled – by the mid-1810s, the cost of rent, food and water were by all accounts comparable to those of London or Paris.

Despite rising dissatisfaction, Dom João still commanded great loyalty amongst the bulk of the population in Rio and through-out Brazil. Royalist sentiments ran deep, so much so that many in Rio volunteered to join the fight to retake Pernambuco. The king was immune from direct criticism. It was thought that Dom João did not know of the criminal acts that were committed in his name by his own court officials. There may have been some truth in this. As this extraordinary venture saw out its first decade with no end in sight, the structures of government that had been set up on arrival were beginning to creak.

There were signs of growing instability in Portugal, too. Just after the revolution in Pernambuco a similar conspiracy – military, but with Masonic connections – was unearthed in Lisbon. The revolt was small and poorly planned, but it was a foretaste of things to come – a light tremor that opened Portugal's prolonged era of civil strife. It was dealt with effec-tively by Beresford, who rounded up the conspirators in a pre-dawn raid on 26 May 1817. The captives were then tried in secret and twelve were later publicly executed without being given the customary right of appeal to the king. The chief conspirator, Freemason and ex-Bonapartist General Gomes Freire de Andrade, was hung, drawn and quartered, and, as if this were not enough, his dismembered body was burnt and his ashes thrown into the sea. Order had been restored but at a price. Freire was seen by many as a martyr to a just cause and in death his name would become a rallying point for the coming revolution. The sense of injustice, of impotence, of disgust at both foreign domination and local corruption was reaching its limits.

The strength of feeling at the time was graphically illustrated by a series of open letters to Dom João, published in the London-based expatriate press. The missives spoke of the depths that Portugal had plumbed since the departure of the court and

pleaded for the king's return. 'The suffering of our people breaks
my heart with bitterness and pain,' read one. 'Bands of tramps,
spectres of hunger, poverty ridden and dressed in rags, wander
through the streets . . . Pale, deformed and disfigured . . . dying
or close to death along with their homeland. This is the state of
the population of Lisbon, and almost all of Portugal!' Another
letter went further: 'Your Majesty should be well informed
about the poverty that is seen in Portugal . . . [which] is virtually
a cadaver, hardly showing any signs of life . . . The discontent-
ment in Portugal is so great . . . that only the armed forces are
preventing it from breaking out in rebellion.'

Even Dom João's advisers in Europe were beginning to come
clean about the true state of affairs back in Portugal. For H. J.
D'Araújo Carneiro, a government official working in London,
foreigners were now capitalising on the Crown's prolonged
absence:

> 'News has been put about in Portugal and throughout Europe
> that Your Majesty has abandoned them, and has transferred all
> the revenue and wealth from Portugal to Brazil . . . that Your
> Highness has invited all the best-known families and richest
> property owners to emigrate . . . If Your Majesty's residence in
> Brazil serves to guarantee the independence of Portugal, the
> people don't see this. What they see is a vacuum, and their
> transformation from metropolitans into colonials . . .'

An air of cynicism spread through Lisbon. There were rumours
that a territorial swap had already been drawn up, that the
government in Rio was poised to cede Portugal to Spain in
exchange for some equivalent territory in South America.
Although unfounded, the reports touched on very real fears
of a Spanish invasion of Portugal. Dom João's military adventures in the Banda Oriental had not only provoked fury from
Madrid, but also angered the British, who refused to guarantee
Portugal's territorial integrity in the event of a Spanish invasion.
Palmela had expended considerable diplomatic energies trying
to placate the court in Madrid, but Spain had responded by

carrying out provocative military manoeuvres near the Portuguese frontier.

For the British, who were now lumbered with the military protection of Portugal without any diplomatic leverage over its errant court, the situation was becoming acute. A cornerstone of their foreign policy was the abolition of the slave trade, and Portugal's reluctance to move forward on the issue was a major stumbling block. Dom João, as usual, was stalling, pleading special dispensation, arguing that the abolition of the slave trade 'goes against a habit formed by two centuries, would offend the opinion of the owners and perhaps fire the imagination of the slaves'. He proposed 'indirect means', substituting 'the black population with white colonists' so as not to risk unrest in Brazil. There was little support for abolition in Brazil, although a handful of Brazilian thinkers were beginning to question the trade. As in the American south, the argument was framed in more economic and racial terms than on the religious and humanitarian grounds expounded by abolitionists such as William Wilberforce in England. Slavery was seen by Brazilian liberals as retarding their country's development, the continuing importation of huge numbers of Africans threatening to 'bastardise' the Portuguese race, turning Brazil into a 'Negroland'.

The ban on trade north of the equator agreed at the Congress of Vienna had dealt a blow to Portugal's West African ports, but was more than compensated for by an acceleration of orders from Angola and Mozambique. In the circumstances, Dom João seemed content to hold out for as long as possible in Rio, where direct pressure could not be brought to bear on him. It was an approach that had been broadly successful since the expulsion of Strangford, but it was now clear to all involved that a complex and unpredictable endgame was already in play.

TWELVE

Dona Leopoldina

A fleet of carriages headed south from Vienna, flashing through the Austrian town of Klagenfurt before entering Italy and moving on to Florence, via Padua. In it travelled a team of attendants – ladies-in-waiting, a head butler, chaplains, a librarian, doctors and a six-strong royal guard – surrounding the twenty-year-old Maria Leopoldina Josephina Carolina of Habsburg, Archduchess of Austria and daughter of Emperor Francis I. It was the beginning of a journey beset by delays, storms and naval accidents. Five months after leaving Vienna, the entourage would finally reach the port of Rio de Janeiro on 5 November 1817.

The trip was the culmination of a year's efforts on the part of the Portuguese court to find a Habsburg bride for Dom João's son and heir to the throne, Dom Pedro, as part of a strategy to ally Rio with one of Europe's most powerful courts. It had been down to the former French collaborator, the Marquis of Marialva, to convince the Habsburg emperor of the wisdom of the match. Now one of the Rio court's representatives in Europe, Marialva had coaxed the Austrians with a lavish display of New World riches, distributing gold bars, diamonds and jewellery to the Austrian elite, playing on an out-dated image of Brazil as a country of untold mineral wealth. He had also visited Dona Leopoldina, feeding her with lies about her prospective husband – talking at length about Dom Pedro's supposed interest in science and natural history and of his perfect health (in fact he suffered from disturbing epileptic fits). Marialva had left her to contemplate a diamond-encrusted locket with a flattering portrait of the eighteen-year-old prince, which Dona Leopoldina found 'pleasing'. 'He is not extraordinarily handsome', she wrote to her aunt, although 'he has magnificent eyes and a beautiful nose and his lips overall, are thicker than mine.' She seemed more impressed by the diamonds around the portrait which were 'the size of a solitaire on the button of father's Tuscan hat'.

At first Dom Pedro was to travel to Lisbon for the wedding, but the plan ran into the usual political problems. In an unprecedented move, it was decided that Dona Leopoldina would travel out to Rio. Doubts about the wisdom of the voyage were assuaged by Dom João's assurances that the court would be returning to Europe within two years. It was to be another first for the Americas – the wedding of an heir to a European throne would take place on Brazilian soil.

The wedding was not the only reason behind the 5,000 mile voyage. A team of diplomats, scientists and artists would accompany Dona Leopoldina in what would be a large-scale Austrian mission. Two boats – the *Augusta* and the *Austria* – had already gone on ahead, packed with scientific equipment, a reference library, easels and pigments, on the first stage of a journey that would take some of those on board out into the remotest corners of Brazil. On their return their transports would be loaded down with mounted insects, live animals – marmosets, parrots and strange, boar-like tapirs – seeds, rock and soil samples, along with volumes of observations and records. Artist Thomas Ender would arrive with over 700 watercolour impressions of Rio and São Paulo, many of which remain in the Academy of Fine Arts in Vienna to this day. Several *Botocudo* tribesmen would also make the journey back to Europe as live anthropological exhibits for the Austrian court. Like the many indigenous Brazilians who had crossed the Atlantic under similar circumstances before them, they would experience extreme disorientation, their subsequent lives as objects of European curiosity tragic and short.

The advance party's journey started badly, laying down a template for the convoy's trip as a whole. They immediately hit storms off the Italian coast and almost lost contact with each other, the *Augusta* later being forced into Chióggia for repairs. Meanwhile, Dona Leopoldina and her party waited in Florence for the arrival of the Portuguese escorts which had been sent out from Rio to collect them, but news arrived overland of delays – the Portuguese ships had cleared Lisbon but were now waiting for supplies in Livorno. Prince Metternich, charged with delivering Dona Leopoldina to her ship, was exasperated: '. . . the Portuguese are the slowest people in the world. The ships need a thousand things that the authorities have not had time to procure, because they have only had eight months to get ready.' It had, in fact, been British obstructions that had delayed the ships' passage from Lisbon. While they were in port, news of the Pernambucan uprising had come through and the British argued that the ships might be needed to put down the revolt.

From the outset, the omens were not good. Dona Leopoldina learnt of trouble in Pernambuco while she waited in Florence, and there were signs of more prosaic difficulties ahead. In Italy, Dona Leopoldina baked in the thirty-degree heat, writing of the unpleasantness of temperatures that she would soon be enduring year round. To compound matters, Metternich and Dona Leopoldina did not get on during their brief time in Italy together, the prince complaining in one letter to his wife, 'I have never seen a more spoilt and foolish child,' and in another, 'My little Archduchess is, between you and me, a child, and were I her father I would beat her.'

The Portuguese ships finally arrived – the *Dom João VI* on her maiden voyage and the *São Sebastião*, which had been involved in the first transatlantic wedding, the marriage of the king's daughters in Madrid. The *Dom João VI* was a ninety-six-cannon ship of the line, but sixty cannons had been removed to make way for the quarters of Dona Leopoldina's entourage. The crew had erected a marquee on the deck, in which an orchestra, brought out from Brazil, serenaded the Archduchess on her first visit to the ship. Dona Leopoldina would be travelling in luxury

– 'She has a very large and handsome dining room,' wrote
Metternich, 'a fine saloon, a bedroom, a dressing room and a
bath.' Johann Baptist Emanuel Pohl, a geographer who would
be travelling out to Brazil in the *São Sebastião*, also had a chance
to look around Dona Leopoldina's cabins before departure and
he was equally impressed. He described entering through a
crimson curtain embroidered with the Portuguese royal insignia
and making his way into an eighteen by twenty-one foot living
and dining room flooded with natural light from a roof window.
Through another curtain he found her sleeping quarters and
described her bed, made out of Brazilian hardwoods and decorated with red and white silk cords. All around the apartment
were gold-plated pitchers and basins.

The *Dom João VI*s decks were spacious, but the vessel itself
was slow and difficult to manoeuvre. It was also weighed down
with produce and passengers. There were large quantities of
provisions on board including 'a considerable number of cows,
calves, hogs, sheep, 4,000 chickens, several ducks, at least four or
five canaries and great and little birds from Brazil'. Its berths were
filled to capacity with officials from Lisbon, many of whom were
accompanied by their families – the king's commissioner, for
instance, would be travelling out to Brazil with five children in
tow. The Austrians found the boat overcrowded and dirty. They
complained about the animal stench that wafted up from the
holds, a smell they would have to endure for almost three
months. In last-minute changes, the Portuguese chef was replaced by an Austrian one, after complaints that the food 'looked
terrible and tasted worse', although, according to Metternich,
the change of personnel made little difference. Dona Leopoldina
was, however, pleased by her luxurious suite replete with a
piano, a sofa and several armchairs. Half refugee carrier, half
royal launch, the *Dom João VI* pulled uncertainly out into the
Mediterranean.

The convoy made slow progress until Lisbon, where they
faced further delays. With the Pernambucan uprising ongoing, it
was unclear whether it was safe to proceed to Brazil. The British
lobbied vigorously for Dona Leopoldina to stay in Portugal in an

attempt to secure the return to Europe of at least Dom Pedro, but in Lisbon too, in the aftermath of the Gomes Freire conspiracy, the situation seemed unstable. Dona Carlota had also voiced her objections, writing to Fernando VII, urging him to press the Austrian court to stage the wedding in Portugal. But on the morning of 15 August 1817, the fleet made its way down the Tagus and headed out into the Atlantic. Dona Leopoldina sensed that she was embarking on a journey from which she would never return, charging her farewells with a particular intensity. From this point on, her links to the Old World would be tenuous but vital, as letters travelled back and forth across the Atlantic in a disjointed exchange of six-month-old news and emotion.

It was a momentous move, but one which Dona Leopoldina had convinced herself was somehow fated. At the age of eighteen she had her first brushes with the New World when she had met an Afro-Brazilian maid – the servant of a Portuguese diplomat – and her two young children in Baden. 'I found them very kind and spiritual and talked with them at length [in French],' she wrote in a letter to her father, 'they were Brazilian and they also spoke their strange-sounding mother tongue well.' This may have been her first encounter with a black person outside of the stuffed exemplars in the court's anthropological collection and it left a deep impression on her. Even earlier there had been something that drew her to the New World: 'I have always had a particular affinity to America,' she wrote at one point, 'and even as a child I said many times that I wanted to go there.'

Born during the early campaigns in Italy, Dona Leopoldina had grown up under the shadow of Napoleon. By the time she was four, Austria had been forced to sign the humiliating Treaty of Lunéville (1801), ceding control over large parts of Italy, Belgium and the Rhineland. In 1805, the French had marched on and occupied Vienna and, as if to rub salt into the wounds, Napoleon had taken an Austrian lover. Two years later he returned, after Austrian forces had suffered another series of devastating defeats at the hands of the *Grande Armée*. While the

Portuguese court headed across the Atlantic, the Austrian royals were fleeing east, some ending up in Ofen (Budapest), but Leopoldina going with her mother to Brünn, in Moravia. Not surprisingly, she would grow up with a passionate hatred of Napoleon and all things French – in exile, the children played a game in which an ugly doll representing Napoleon was insulted and had pins stuck into it.

Yet the Habsburg dynasty's humiliation at the hands of Napoleon was far from complete. Backed into a corner in 1809, Francis I was forced to give up Leopoldina's sister, Marie-Louise, for marriage to Napoleon, who, after divorcing Josephine, was looking for a woman to produce him an heir. It is hard to imagine Dona Leopoldina's feelings on hearing about this disastrous turn of events. She was very close to Marie-Louise, and the thought of her having to marry the man whom she had grown up to despise would have been overwhelming. The sisters remained on intimate terms during the tragedy and its aftermath (Marie-Louise abandoned Napoleon at the end of the war) and it is largely through their candid exchange of letters that we can trace the emotional turmoil of Leopoldina's difficult marriage to Dom Pedro.

In the Austrian court, there was great sympathy for the plight of Dona Leopoldina, destined as she was to leave Europe for reasons of state, but courtiers soon found that the young Archduchess had no such regrets: 'When news of the wedding of Emperor Dom Pedro came out in Vienna,' wrote Baroness Montet, 'everyone felt sorry for the young princess, condemned to so great a separation from her family and her homeland; but people closest to her soon knew that she was enchanted.' Leopoldina was sustained by her romantic visions of Brazil. In her mind she contrasted the exhaustion of post-war Europe and the decadence she had witnessed first hand when the great powers had met at the Congress of Vienna, with the sense of freshness, youth and innocence that she thought the Americas promised. 'Europe has now become unbearable,' she wrote in her last months there; even Brazil's 'savages' were superior to the Europeans of her age, as they were 'children of nature . . . not

yet corrupted by luxury and its terrible consequences . . . I hope
that I will find more probity and less corruption in this New
World.'

In the months before she left, Dona Leopoldina read everything she could lay her hands on about Brazil. She pored over
maps, read the journals left by Alexander von Humboldt of his
famous scientific expeditions in the Amazon. She was particularly interested in natural history and made notes on Brazil's
unique flora and fauna, at that time scarcely documented. Her
library also contained travel books and histories, including Jean
de Léry's sixteenth-century classic, *Histoire d'un voyage fait en la
terre du Brésil*. Part narrative of the abortive colony, 'Antarctic
France', part utopian ethnography, Léry's book was in the 'noble
savage' tradition that chimed so well with Dona Leopoldina's
own New World fantasies. All the while she applied herself to
Portuguese, impatient to master a language she said she found
difficult because of its many Arab words. 'The ambassador
assures me that I am making enormous progress,' she wrote
to her aunt, 'but in spite of this, I am not satisfied and I want to
be able to speak already.'

Her preparations included moral fortification. Before Dona
Leopoldina left Vienna she had set out a series of resolutions that
would govern her behaviour in the New World. 'I will conduct
myself with all possible modesty,' she wrote. 'My heart will hold
firm against the perverse spirit of the world,' never being 'alone
with a man in a secluded place, however virtuous he might
appear.' She would avoid 'long and scandalous toilette' as well as
'any literature that excited sensuality or passion'. 'The only thing
that frightens me' wrote Dona Leopoldina, 'is my future
mother-in-law [Dona Carlota], who, according to what my
dear father says, is "unruly" and "intriguing". They say, however, that the king has an excellent character that holds her in
check, keeping her away from the children as much as possible.'
On the eve of her departure she had come to an almost religious
sense of duty: 'the voyage doesn't scare me,' she wrote. 'I believe
that it is predestined.'

It was, nevertheless, a terrifying journey that took twice as long as expected. The convoy spent a week pounded by storms off Madeira before being able to land. It was there that Dona Leopoldina got her first taste of the Portuguese pomp and ceremony that awaited her in Brazil. She attended a *Te Deum* mass, was carried around the island on a palanquin and would leave Madeira with a substantial collection of plants and animals. After Madeira they headed south, and into the path of several more raging storms. 'At one moment the ship lay on one side,' wrote Wilhelm von Grandjean, an Austrian bureaucrat, 'at the next, it swung over to the other so as to let a mountain of water pass over her . . . the wind buffeted everything in its path. The air was enveloped with thick clouds which periodically emptied themselves . . . the movement of the sea was so violent that we pushed on at eleven-and-a-half [sic] leagues per hour . . .' Five-course meals descended into a farce of upended chairs, spilt wine, broken plates and glasses. Towards the end of the crossing two boats almost collided, but after more than eighty days at sea, the convoy entered waters outside Rio's heads.

In Rio, the preparations for the wedding had been feverish. Dom João had ordered further renovations to the palace at São Cristóvão and his workers fitted a new pavilion with a cast-iron veranda looking out across the bay. The city itself had been made over for what was by far the largest reception of foreign dignitaries that the court would stage in Rio. Everything was ready when the Austrian fleet was sighted through the heads on Tuesday, 4 November 1817. Royal attendants stood to attention in the midday heat, cannons were primed to sound the salute, fireworks set to go off. But the ships could not make it through the heads, and were forced to drop anchor in sight of their destination, waiting for a favourable current to bear them into the bay.

When they entered the harbour the following day, they saw crowds gathered on the hills around them and were deafened by salutes from all sides. Large numbers of small craft gathered in the bay, crewed by scantily-clad Afro-Brazilian boys hawking fresh fruits and water. Austrian flags were raised alongside those of The United Kingdom of Brazil, Portugal and the Algarves and fireworks exploded out into the harbour. A golden barge bearing the royal family glided out to meet them. It was on this unsteady platform that Dona Leopoldina would catch her first glimpse of her husband. 'He [Pedro] was sitting in front of our princess,' wrote one of the Austrian party, the Countess of Künburg, 'eyes lowered, looking up at her furtively from time to time and she was doing the same.' What he saw was unexpected – Dona Leopoldina's blue eyes, curly blonde hair and heavy-set Germanic frame were unusual to the Latin eye. After the introductions, the royal family was invited back to inspect the *Dom João VI*, although Dom João, incapacitated by his leg, stayed behind on the barge.

The following day, the party disembarked to a parade through the city's streets. The procession was over ninety carriages long, leading off with three state carriages containing the royal family. In the first were the king and queen – Dom João and Dona Carlota – who would have to spend one of their longest periods together in many years. Behind them rode Miguel and the older daughters, and in the final carriage was Dom João's sister-in-law, Dona Maria Francisca Benedita, along with the younger children. This time the ephemeral architecture was more elaborate and better executed than on previous occasions. A series of triumphal arches were decorated by an eclectic set of motifs – references to Rio, Vienna and Rome mixed in with imperial allusions to Portugal's far-flung possessions. They had been designed and painted by members of The French Artistic Mission, whose expertise had turned the flimsy props into plausible monuments. The French artists had created a fantasy European metropolis, a stage set designed to stamp an Old World authority on to a tropical landscape. Incense burned, houses overlooking the street hung colourful embroidered spreads from Portuguese India over their balconies. Two boys dressed as Hymen and Love were hoisted on to pedestals on the top of one of the arch's Doric columns, from where they sprinkled flower petals and perfumes on the procession passing beneath them.

★   ★   ★

The first encounter between the Portuguese and the Austrians – the arrival of boats loaded with scientific equipment and their reception in a city decked out with mock Roman decorations – summed up the difference in style and orientation of the two courts. The Austrians were cerebral and serious. All branches of science had been cultivated within their court, with members of the royal family becoming professional scientists in their own right. Their approach to the world was primarily secular, and even in the spiritual realm they were inward looking, their sensitivities inflected with a mid-European romanticism.

In the ten years that the Portuguese court had been based in the tropics, something entirely different had evolved. Diplomats posted to Rio found themselves operating in a court that, in spite of Dom João's efforts to put on 'civilised' airs, had begun evolving away from its sister courts in Europe. The German envoy, Count von Flemming, wrote of his impressions in a report back to Berlin:

> 'Apart from the semi-Asian court of Constantinople there probably does not exist another in Europe characterised by an originality as strange as this one. Even though it has only recently been established in America it should be considered completely alien to European customs and entirely exotic . . . No other courts have such a large number of attendants, wardrobe assistants, and especially uniformed servants, coachmen . . . Such a tendency towards orientalism . . . in no way corresponds to its luxury.'

The cast of thousands was certainly one aspect that immediately caught the attention of foreigners. The large numbers of courtiers who had travelled from Lisbon had been swelled by teams of slaves, employed in the palace's gardens, its laundries and kitchens. Inside the palace, corridors were crowded with extras, although, according to the Austrian party, service was still poor. There was a great emphasis on conspicuous consumption as a means of giving a good impression to other courts in Europe. The staggering costs of the Marquis of Marialva's mission to Austria, Leopoldina's trip and her reception were designed to show off the Rio court as a metropolitan presence in the Americas. Yet in spite of all the expense lavished on the wedding, the palace at São Cristóvão disappointed – 'any provincial German noble would have a more beautiful house', wrote one of the Austrian party. The Austrians found it dirty and smelly, complaining about the dung heap kept in the palace's grounds and the clouds of insects that it attracted. Standards of hygiene were, indeed, low in the palace. Apart from the fact that Dom João never washed, he is said to have kept half-full chamber pots in a room where he received guests. All this was a part of medieval attitudes to the body and cleanliness, now being eroded in the palaces of Europe, but still very much in evidence in the Rio court.

The climate also posed problems for aristocratic guests to the Brazilian court. The heat made indoor events difficult, while there were other things to contend with for those staged outside. A Prussian diplomat described one farcical ball, hosted by the German physician and diplomat Baron Georg Heinrich von Langsdorff:

> '. . . the arms, shoulders and backs of the women, who were wearing fashionable low cut dresses, had been bitten by mosquitoes . . . so red were the women, that they looked like soldiers after they had been whipped . . . Even I, who didn't dance, stayed constantly on the move, jumping up and down like a grasshopper, trying to remove the mosquitoes from my silk stockings.'

But it was the ritualistic nature of the Portuguese court that was most uncomfortable for the Austrians. They sat through interminable religious services and attended the curiously old-fashioned *beija-mão* ceremonies, a regular occurrence at the palace. Visitors were forced to remain standing (or, exceptionally, for the frail or elderly, kneeling) when visiting Dom João during his mealtimes, events which could last many hours. Dona Leopoldina was subjected to other, more intimate court etiquette. On her wedding night, wrote a shocked Countess of Künburg,

Dona Leopoldina was joined by Dona Carlota and the princesses: 'The queen and all the princesses assisted in her night "toilette". I was obliged to undress her, lay her in bed and wait for the prince to lie by her side. Only then, mercifully, were they allowed to leave.'

Beneath the surface of religious observance and ritual niceties, there was a vulgarity to the Portuguese court, an earthiness that Dona Leopoldina would face at close quarters in her new life with her husband. Dom Pedro would never quite master the formality that was expected of him as crown prince and later Emperor of Brazil. European officers admired his military prowess, but were horrified by the fact that he defecated in full view of his troops during beach exercises on Praia Vermelha. In another instance he is said to have urinated off the veranda of São Cristóvão on to a palace guard down below. Apart from his many sexual indiscretions, he also affronted high society women by swimming naked in the surf. Among his papers survive bawdy verses, illustrated by pornographic doodles. He was frequently overheard calling his mother a 'bitch' and after Dom Miguel had returned to Portugal, Dom Pedro wrote, urging him to come back to Rio, 'There'll be no shortage of people telling you not to leave. Tell them to eat shit.'

For the men of science who had travelled out with Dona Leopoldina, Brazil was virgin territory. The court's work at the botanical gardens was mainly aimed at the cultivation of new crops – many not native to Brazil – for strictly commercial purposes. As for what lay beyond, in Brazil's vast wetlands, the arid planes of the interior and the Amazon's endless tropical forests, the exiles were none the wiser and could offer little advice to the Austrian explorers. Botanist Carl Fredrick Philipp von Martius and his zoologist partner Johann Baptist von Spix would instead be guided by the work of a late-eighteenth-century, Bahian-born naturalist, Dr Alexandre Rodrigues Ferreira – the 'Brazilian Humboldt' – as they headed into the jungles of Brazil.

In the eighteenth century, the Portuguese had come to the realisation that scientific knowledge was vital, and had made attempts at surveying the territories under their control. Following British successes at Kew, they established a botanical clearing house in Lisbon. They sent field researchers on poetically entitled *Viagens Filosóficas* (Philosophical Journeys) which took them deep into the backlands of Brazil, Angola and Mozambique.

In the late eighteenth century, Dr Alexandre Rodrigues Ferreira was sent from Lisbon, where he was cataloguing specimens at the Ajuda Museum, on one such journey. He was to have travelled with a team of scientists, but at the last moment his party was reduced to a gardener, Cabo, and two artists, Freire and Codina. They recruited a further two 'Christianised Indians' in Belém, at the mouth of the Amazon, and set off up the river carrying a field kitchen, hunting and fishing gear, a medicine chest and an eleven-book library. It was thought that the expedition would last three or four years, but it would be almost a decade before the surviving members emerged from the forest.

They worked their way up the Amazon and into the Rio Negro, collecting and sending crates of samples back to Lisbon as they went. Their brief was all-encompassing, and Ferreira's detailed descriptions ranged from new species of plants and animals and geological observations to meticulous hut plans of the native villages he passed through. As they travelled, the artists Freire and Codina took a visual record of their finds, producing a series of vivid watercolours of new orchids, fruits and seeds.

After years of travelling and collecting, the party had trawled the length of the Amazon and explored a number of its tributaries. Along the way they had suffered the usual array of skin disorders, parasitic infections and gastro-intestinal problems. They were more than three years out of Portugal, and they were tiring. Ferreira had virtually lost contact with Lisbon on his travels, his regular reports and updates prompting few replies. Encamped on the banks of the Rio Negro with his team of weary collectors he wrote asking for permission to return to Lisbon. This time, a letter came back as quickly as could be expected under the circumstances, but its contents broke the morale of the party. The authorities wrote that they were displeased with Ferreira's work and that he had not sent back sufficient samples. They ordered him to continue south down the tortuous Rio Madeira to Vila Bela, the remote capital of Mato Grosso.

The thirteen-month voyage took its toll on a party which had already suffered several bouts of ill health on the Rio Negro. Within reach of Vila Bela, Cabo, the gardener, died. The small, close-knit group, who had been travelling for years in difficult circumstances, was devastated. Mourning the passing of their companion, they made an inventory of the dead man's belongings for future restitution to his family. The list is curious. Some items are jungle gear – hammocks, mosquito nets and pistols – but others seem out of place in the depths of a tropical forest. Velvet breeches, lace shirts, silver forks and cheeses, along with a bulky Portuguese dictionary, had travelled the thousands of miles into the centre of Brazil.

Twenty years later, during the French occupation of Portugal, Etienne Geoffroy Saint-Hilaire was sent out from the *Musée d'Histoire Naturelle* in Paris to view the collections held in Lisbon. His mission was originally couched in terms of exchange, but ended up as straight theft. He went through the display cabinets of Lisbon's Natural History Museum, picking out the most interesting specimens to be sent back to Paris. He then asked to view what was stored in the museum's vaults. There he found Ferreira's specimens, still crated. 'All are untouched,' commented Saint-Hilaire, 'nobody has taken the trouble to work on them.' Some of the collection had disintegrated, still wrapped in the coarse cloth that Ferreira had improvised with in his rainforest field stations. Of what remained, Saint-Hilaire took the choicest specimens with him back to Paris. Caymen, huge manatees, stuffed parrots, Ferreira's Amazon herbarium, invaluable manuscripts and journals; all were loaded on to the French boats as the spoils of war in the wake of the 1808 Convention of Sintra. The British tried to stop him, retrieving three cases which contained minerals and sea turtles, but the cream of Ferreira's life work was secured for Paris.

The Portuguese could never quite fulfil their imperial role. Their plans were grandiose, but were rarely seen through to the end. When gold and diamonds were discovered in the interior at the end of the seventeenth century, they closed off Brazil from outside exploration, but found it difficult to launch adequately funded researches of their own, their policy of prohibiting the establishment of universities in Brazil disastrous for serious work in the region. Local enthusiasts who could not afford the trip to Portugal's famous Coimbra University worked with what they had; often producing, against the odds, detailed documentary records of their findings, while the fruits of research organised from Portugal rotted away in storage. The nineteenth century would be a period of intensive European exploration in South America but, for the most part, it would be foreigners who would retrace the steps of Ferreira's epic 'Philosophical Journey'.

With the court's arrival in Rio and the opening of the ports to foreign shipping, a new era began. After years of resistance, foreign exploration was encouraged by Dom João, heralding an epoch that has been termed 'the rediscovery of Brazil'. At the close of hostilities in Europe, scientists from France, Germany, Russia and Britain arrived to carry out research on a continent that had been much written about but little observed. Rio itself, with its verdant surrounds, was soon teeming with collectors. Some arrived raw and inexperienced – Allan Cunningham and James Bowie, both in their early twenties, were dispatched to Rio by Sir Joseph Banks to collect specimens for Kew Gardens. Others were seasoned campaigners who lit out into the roadless interior. In the early years, British mineralogist John Mawe was one of the first to survey the exhausted mining districts and diamond fields, so long protected from foreign eyes. Later, the French botanist Auguste de Saint-Hilaire travelled extensively in south and central Brazil, while Martius and Spix would follow Ferreira's route in reverse, in a four-year voyage through central Brazil and down the Amazon to Belém.

Dona Leopoldina's relationship with Dom Pedro was no meeting of minds, but they found some common ground in their first months together. Communication was at first difficult – Dona Leopoldina's Portuguese was faltering; they tried in French, but Dom Pedro could not keep up. They went on long horse rides up into Rio's stunning parklands of Tijuca which had been opened up and remodelled since the arrival of the court. In the subtropical forests which overlooked the city, Dona Leopoldina indulged her passion, collecting the plants and animals that she had read about in Vienna. On other days, she would accompany her husband on court business to the arsenal, after which they would ride out to the botanical gardens where they lunched on roast chicken and rice.

In letters to her aunt in Vienna she painted an idyllic portrait of life in Brazil, with some reservations:

'The country is entrancing, full of delicious spots, of high mountains, green fields, the rarest forest with trees of superb height and entwined with flowers upon which incomparable birds of exquisite plumage disport themselves. It must be said that Portuguese America would be paradise on earth, were it not for the insufferable heat of eighty-eight degrees [Fahrenheit] and the many mosquitoes which are a veritable torment . . . I spend my days writing, reading and making music with my husband, who plays almost every instrument quite well; I accompany him on the piano and thus have the satisfaction of being always close to this dear person.'

To her sister, Marie-Louise, she was more candid. Six months after her arrival in Brazil, she felt compelled to write 'a few completely frank words [about Pedro], confident that this letter will not reach any hands other than yours, my dear. In all honesty he speaks his mind, and this with a certain brutality; he is accustomed to do exactly what he wants, everyone has to accommodate him . . . In spite of all his violence and his own manner, I am convinced that he loves me tenderly.' In a later letter, doubts were growing and the germ of a depression that would later overwhelm Dona Leopoldina was in evidence – 'You are indeed right, true happiness does not exist in this world,' she wrote to her sister, 'and I constantly fear being disillusioned and upset . . . I cannot know for certain whether I have a friend in my husband, and if I am really loved.'

The differences between them were many – in temperament, upbringing and intellectual orientation. Pedro could be impatient with people to the point of hostility; Leopoldina was humane and concerned, even in her treatment of the most vulnerable. 'She was very kind when she passed by us slaves,' remembered an ageing slave worker at São Cristóvão, 'she used to stop and say to us words of comfort.' But 'her husband was arrogant,' the slave worker went on, 'he always walked around with a silver-handled whip with which he beat us on the slightest pretext.'

At first Dona Leopoldina had the support of her compatriots, but native companionship was stripped away with the steady stream of departures from the original Austrian party. Her ladies-in-waiting returned to Europe early, the scientists and explorers left after completing their research, and, most painfully for Dona Leopoldina, her doctor also went back to Europe after suffering heart problems. Through her many pregnancies in Brazil she would develop a loathing for Portuguese doctors, whom she branded 'barbarians'.

As time passed, she became more and more lonely; her Brazilian fantasies began to crumble, and her letters back home turned sour. She became desperate for news from Austria which was, however, very irregular: 'I only receive letters from Italian boats,' she wrote, 'and these, to my great anguish only once a year.' Soon after arriving in the New World she had longed for, she was yearning for Europe. The unbearable heat and violent thunderstorms brought out a melancholy that she found difficult to shake. She reminisced about snow falling over Vienna, and even eulogised a lone cloud which had strayed over Rio's normally azure skies. 'There is nothing that I desire with more ardour,' she wrote to her father, 'than to tread Europe's beloved soil once more.'

Dona Leopoldina developed a close relationship with Dom João – 'he had the kindness to tell me that he would be very content to see me always near him' – and also got on with Dom Pedro's older sister, Maria Teresa, but she struggled to come to terms with the culture of the court. The Portuguese women reacted badly to her; she was seen as an intruder – an unwanted foreigner – and treated with suspicion. From the salons of Vienna, Dona Leopoldina entered the closed world of the female courtiers, filled with what she saw as trivia and petty intrigue. She was shocked by their 'moral laxity' – perhaps a reference to sexual indiscretions or maybe merely disapproval of the extravagant way they dressed, with their bulky diamond necklaces and hair pieces decorated with jewellery and feathers. Many of the women were only barely literate, their skills extending little beyond prayer books learnt by rote. Dona Leopoldina, in contrast, was well educated and spoke several languages fluently. Marrocos, who met her soon after her arrival, was taken by her erudition and general comportment. Dona Leopoldina 'has pleased everyone in the extreme,' he wrote, 'she is very discreet, relaxed and communicative; she speaks, besides her native language, French, English and Italian; she has some knowledge of fine arts, and no less of botany, as well as those skills that are now appropriate for a distinguished woman; she is a fertile conversationalist, and gives very sharp replies . . .'

But as a woman, Dona Leopoldina was barred from the world of Marrocos, cut off from the intellectual life of the city. She was kept secluded in the palace, not allowed to travel into Rio on her own. For a time, she was not even allowed out walking – one of her great pleasures in Vienna – and forced instead inside the stuffy cabins of the slave-borne litters, hidden behind heavy velvet curtains in temperatures of over thirty degrees Celsius. Boredom took hold – 'the life style, in which people never go to the theatre, never have get-togethers, or pay daily visits is . . . dispiriting for a person who is accustomed to amusements . . . The climate and the laziness which it brings on, make reading and writing impossible.'

It seems that Dona Leopoldina suffered some kind of mental breakdown in Brazil. Certainly, there was a character change, which she admitted to and others commented on. 'Those who don't know her,' wrote her uncle in Austria, 'and only read her letters, would imagine a completely different Leopoldina.' She developed an obsessive attachment to her sister, Marie-Louise, writing a stream of letters of such pain and longing that they make excruciating reading. She modelled herself on Marie-Louise, thought of her as a guardian angel and felt that she could only half experience anything because of their separation. 'I think of you all the time,' she wrote, 'not a day goes by when I don't remember you one hundred times.'

Soon after her arrival in Rio, Dona Leopoldina began the first of an almost continual string of pregnancies. She was by now eating compulsively and starting to put on weight. Less than a year into her stay, she was writing of the resurgence of problems she had experienced in her adolescence. 'I must confess with total honesty that I have a marked tendency for melancholic thoughts,' she admitted as her psychological state deteriorated, '. . . my personality, which before was cheerful,' was now 'completely melancholic . . . I never laugh like I used to.' Problems in her marriage pushed her deeper into despair. Dom Pedro reverted to type and began a series of affairs that would become more and more open as the years went by. Abandoned and humiliated, Dona Leopoldina filled out her time on brooding field trips, augmenting her amateur collections of insects, flowers and rocks. From time to time she would pack up a crate with her finds and have it loaded on to a Europe-bound ship, sending something of her being back to Austria on the journey that she herself would never make.

THIRTEEN

Danger Signals

With Dona Leopoldina now in Brazil, preparations for the acclamation of Dom João as king were accelerated. The court's lengthy stay in Rio was about to reach its apogee; an official seal would be placed on a new colonial experiment. But there was a sense of unease in the air as carpenters, under the instruction of The French Artistic Mission, put the finishing touches to the latest set of ephemeral architecture – arches, pyramids and hoardings – being constructed for the ceremony.

Back in Portugal, the court's decade-long absence had created a power vacuum which radicals were rushing to fill. Anti-clerical, constitutionalist ideas had been toyed with during the brief period of French occupation. Through the war years, the Spanish constitutional experiments in Cadiz had been drawn on as an inspiring model for Portugal's future, once both the British and the system of absolute monarchy were dispatched. Discontent had boiled over with the Gomes Freire conspiracy, its suppression only hardening the resolve of the liberals. The longer the court stayed on in Brazil, the more insistent the calls for change became.

There was trouble across Brazil's borders as well. Fernando VII's return to the Spanish throne had seen a royalist backlash sweep through both Spain and her South American colonies. The constitutional government set up in Cadiz had been abolished, the country returned to the pre-war absolutism.

The moves had settled the situation in Spanish America, clearing up the ambiguities that had existed during the war years. Unrest in Mexico had been quashed, New Granada had fallen back into the loyalist camp, even the Buenos Aires *junta* had failed in its efforts to extend its authority over the Río de La Plata provinces. Yet appearances were deceptive. By the beginning of 1817, José de San Martín, a soldier who had served in Spain during the peninsular campaigns, had organised a liberation force – the 'Army of the Andes' – and was marching up the River Plate into Chile. After taking Chile and installing his commander, Bernardo O'Higgins, at the head of a government, he would prepare himself for an assault at the heart of Spanish power in the Americas: Peru. Meanwhile, the republican Simon Bolívar was continuing his campaigns in Venezuela, moving west into Angostura, on the Orinoco.

With the exception of the Pernambucan revolt, the Portuguese court's presence appeared to have stymied the development of a republican movement in Brazil. The disaffected were wrong-footed by the events of 1807–1808; their long list of grievances – trade restrictions, prohibitions on the manufacture of certain goods, enforced cultural and intellectual isolation – were eliminated at a stroke with the arrival of Dom João. It was as if they had been pushing at an open door; chains were not broken but fell away, their links fatigued and rusted. The old regime was still in place, but in an unforeseen development, it had come to rest on colonial soil. For those who pondered on the matter, the move seemed like the ultimate imperial finesse.

But it was flawed by what was, with the benefit of hindsight, an obvious tactical error. Portugal had been effectively abandoned by Dom João and his advisers, but the mother country's ability to strike back was everywhere apparent. During the Peninsular Wars and Beresford's subsequent control, Portugal had become an impoverished, but militarised state. More ominously, thanks to the Pernambucan revolt, Portuguese troops were now stationed at every strategic port up and down the coast of Brazil.

*   *   *

A specially designed colonnaded veranda spanned the frontage of the royal palace overlooking Rio's main square. Two sets of nine arches flanked a central balcony from where the royal family could wave to the crowds below. Heavy velvet curtains were tied open around the balcony, giving it the appearance of a stage at the head of an enormous open-air theatre. By February 1818, almost two years after Queen Maria's death, the city was finally ready for the long awaited 'acclamation' – the formal recognition of Dom João VI's accession to the throne. Various excuses had been given for the delays – that the ceremony could not take place until the priesthood had declared that Queen Maria had officially left purgatory; that ritual attendants had to be brought out from Lisbon; and that the event had been put on hold until the arrival of Dona Leopoldina. But it was undoubtedly the Pernambucan coup and the atmosphere that it generated in Rio and around Brazil that lay behind the postponement. On the day itself, uncertainties lingered. Troops had been issued with live ammunition, and in a measure that exposed the paranoia that was beginning to affect the court, talk in foreign languages in the crowd was banned.

People had travelled from all over Brazil for the event. The city was decked out with the classical features that were becoming almost commonplace in the later years of the court's stay in Rio. An obelisk, painted over to give off a solid granite effect, was positioned in the main square along with a mock Greek temple, and triumphal arches adorned the city's streets. For Dom João, the event was an important affirmation of his commitment to Brazil, an answer to the rumours of the court's departure for Lisbon which could still be heard in the city. For the first time, he was presenting himself to his Brazilian vassals in the ritual garb of a monarch – a gold-embroidered scarlet robe, stamped with the royal insignia. Dom João was on the point of becoming, in the words of Luís Gonçalves dos Santos, who watched the event, 'the first sovereign to be crowned in the New World'.

During the ceremony Dom João seated himself on the throne, took up his sceptre and recited a solemn oath to God. Kneeling before him were his sons, Dom Pedro and Dom Miguel, who

swore fealty to their father. On his right was the queen, Dona
Carlota, close behind the princess royal Dona Leopoldina, her
headpiece decorated with white feathers, in contrast to the other
princesses, who wore red. It was meant to be a day of celebration, of confirmation, a symbolic underlining of the enduring
power of the Portuguese Crown, but Dom João struck a note of
uncertainty as he walked along the veranda to receive his vassals.
John Luccock was well positioned in the crowd:

> 'The hesitation at the first and second arches, where I was quite
> close to him, appeared to arise from some vague suspicions
> generated by the evil reports, which have been continually
> poured into his ear. I had a similar opportunity of observing
> him within half an hour before the time when the ceremony
> began. He was then dressed in a plain blue coat, with a black
> handkerchief about his neck, was quite alone, and his counte-
> nance expressed marks of deep solicitude.'

In official versions, the event was a resounding success. A Debret
engraving shows the monarch being received by an enthusiastic
crowd of well-wishers. In the *Gazeta do Rio de Janeiro*, the
ceremony was described in glowing terms, Dom João's performance as assured and fitting of the great occasion. Its propagandist slant was picked up by Marrocos. 'I have to warn that the
news in the Gazettes was very inaccurate,' he cautioned his
father back in Lisbon, 'including many lies which cannot be
excused', with the writer 'reporting things that did not exist, or
giving great emphasis to trivial matters.' Yet these were the kinds
of descriptions that filtered back to Lisbon. Just as had been the
case in Brazil before the emigration of the royal family, an image,
distorted by time and distance, had been built up in the minds of
those back in Europe. Rio had started to take on a sheen of
wealth and splendour, in stark contrast to the poverty which
gripped the mother country.

Recent additions to the growing metropolis included a
bullring which had been built near the *Campo de Santana* as a
part of Dona Leopoldina's birthday celebrations. Portuguese-

style bullfights were staged, with mounted picadors manoeuvring hapless bulls around the arena. (This was one influence that would not last in Rio. The locals were horrified by the tournaments, which they found needlessly cruel, and bullfighting never set down roots in Brazilian culture.) On the biggest island in Guanabara Bay, Dom João had set up a hunting range where deer now roamed and, less successfully, a lone bear, courtesy of the Tsar Alexander of Russia, sweltered in the tropical heat. The king could now replicate almost every aspect of his former Lisbon lifestyle. He could listen to the choirs and orchestras that had been built up over the years, attend operas, visit his country residences and hunt – all this, untrammelled by the constant aggravations that life in Europe had brought him.

After the acclamation ceremony, the crowds dispersed into the parade grounds of the *Campo de Santana*, where four illuminated towers had been constructed, each containing an orchestra playing classical music. In the middle of the park were a Chinese pavilion, sixteen statues, and a waterfall cascading into a large tank filled with exotic shells. As night fell, refreshments and sweets were distributed to the crowds milling around and for the privileged, dessert was served on sumptuous gold and silver platters in a hall decked out in damask. The acclamation was confirmed by a *Te Deum* mass with specially composed music, and on the following nights, Rio erupted in celebrations in honour of its new king. The city was covered with subtle illuminations; overhead, fireworks rained down. A New World monarchy had been consecrated, its miraculous presence in the tropics no longer a temporary anomaly but an established fact, one which now was fixed in the consciousness of its Brazilian vassals.

*   *   *

On New Year's Day, 1820, near the port city of Cadiz in southern Spain, a small battalion of troops led by Lieutenant-Colonel Rafael del Riego mutinied. He thought he had chosen his moment well, since Cadiz was at that time crammed with potential sympathisers – soldiers waiting to leave on an unpopular tour of duty to fight the revolutionaries in Spanish

America. What he did not know was that yellow fever had taken hold within the city walls, sapping any appetite for revolt. Receiving no support from Cadiz, the small column set off inland. One by one, Riego's soldiers deserted. He was down to just 100 men when the movement broke up altogether, the rebels fleeing for their lives into the countryside. Riego also went on the run, heading back towards the coast across fields in the hope of escaping Spain by boat. When he emerged on the Mediterranean he found that he was not the fugitive he had imagined himself to be. He was a hero. Barracks all around Spain had risen up in sympathy; a liberal revolution was under way.

From Lisbon, Beresford watched events across the border with consternation. By April, Riego's unpromising revolt had spread right across Spain and forced Fernando VII to back down. The constitution that the Cadiz government had adopted at the height of the Peninsular Wars was reactivated, and the king ceded power to a reconvened parliament – the *cortes*. Soon after Fernando VII's capitulation, Beresford boarded a ship for Rio in a desperate attempt to secure the return of at least one member of the royal family to Portugal and stave off the coming unrest. He left behind him a country on the brink of revolt. 'Ideas of revolution were widespread,' wrote one observer, 'young and old, religious and secular, everyone was in favour . . . and everyone wanted the court in Lisbon because they despised the idea of being a colony of a colony.'

Beresford arrived in Rio in May. In sessions with Dom João, he tried to impress on him the seriousness of the situation back in Portugal, but found the king evasive and unconcerned. Instead, Dom João discussed military matters with the marshal. He sent Beresford on a lengthy inspection tour of the Brazilian army, its hospitals and supply centres, prolonging his absence from an increasingly unstable Portugal. The battle in the south had been going well. By early 1820 Artigas was imprisoned in Paraguay, the Luso-Brazilian forces in full control of the Banda Oriental. But as Dom João would soon realise, the real conflict was much closer to home.

The British were incensed by Beresford's delay in Rio and

eventually managed to have him recalled. He sailed in August, armed with a few minor concessions to the Portuguese: Dom João had agreed to clear the arrears in soldiers' wages and decreed that Lisbon no longer had to foot the bill for Portuguese troops stationed in Brazil. Beresford was ten days out to sea when revolution broke out in Oporto on 24 August 1820. It was, for all practical purposes, an anti-colonial revolt, taking place not in some far-flung outpost of empire, but on European soil; the fight for independence had started in Portugal, not Brazil. 'The idea of the status of a colony to which Portugal in effect is reduced,' read the Oporto manifesto, 'afflicts deeply all those citizens who still conserve a sentiment of national dignity. Justice is administered from Brazil to the loyal people of Europe . . . at vast distance . . . with excessive expense and delay . . .' By the time Beresford was halfway across the Atlantic, the revolt had spread to Lisbon. The council of governors was overthrown by the military, the new regime calling for the reconvening of the Portuguese *cortes* – a parliament which had last met in 1697. As in Spain, the *cortes* would exercise legislative power, as well as petition for the return of the royal family. Cries went up for the adoption of the Cadiz constitution while the rebel government worked on Portugal's own version.

As Beresford approached Lisbon, his vessel was boarded and he was informed that he was not permitted to land. '. . . Things will never return to how they were before', Beresford wrote on being barred from Portugal, '. . . the constitution should be adopted. It is now very clear that the king or the crown prince has to return.' On the question of Brazil he was even more pessimistic: 'The king is totally deluded about the Brazilian opinions and sentiments which are a thousand times more democratic than those of the Portuguese now . . . there is no doubt that all the provinces of the North, including Bahia, will be induced to revolt . . . if the king does not return or send the prince.'

The revolution as experienced in Rio would have a muffled, dreamlike quality to it, dulled by distance. The first that the court knew of developments in Portugal was when the Portu-

guese warship *Providência* arrived in mid-October. Although the
revolt had by that time spread throughout Portugal, dispatches
unloaded from the *Providência* told only of events in Oporto.
Dom João cut short his stay on one of his island villas and hurried
back to the palace at São Cristóvão. There were endless meetings, but few concrete ideas. The court was still uncertain as to
how to respond to the Oporto revolt when one month later
reports of the Lisbon coup came through. This time, there was a
panicked response from the palace – the news was embargoed,
but the operation botched. Letters arriving on the packet boat
were released and soon Rio was awash with talk of the dramatic
turnaround in Portugal.

Strangford's successor, Edward Thornton, who had only
arrived in Rio to take up his post the year before, rushed to
see Dom João at the palace. He was told to come back the
following day and it was only then that he had a chance to speak
to the king in private. He asked Dom João how he planned to
respond to events in Europe. 'The King answered with an
appearance of great Anxiety,' he wrote back to Castlereagh
in London, 'that he was reflecting Day and Night on what ought
to be done.' Thornton warned Dom João that Britain would not
intervene against the rebels in Portugal; nor would the British
army defend the country against Spain. He also cautioned Dom
João against believing that The Holy Alliance – a loose union
between Europe's conservative courts established at the Congress of Vienna – would come to his aid. In conclusion, he
advised that crown prince Dom Pedro be sent back to Portugal
to negotiate with the rebels, but told London that Dom João
would 'take no steady or quick decision, or perhaps none but
under the Impetus of some new and violent Emergency, for
which any decision may perhaps be too late.' 'Delay is the radical
fault of this government,' wrote Thornton in another dispatch,
'– I ought perhaps to say complete inaction.' The court was
indeed disorientated by the pace and decisiveness of events in
Portugal. Dom João began a hopelessly slow consultation
process, receiving thirteen written responses from his advisers
as to what the best course of action should be. A clear majority

opted for Thornton's suggestion, that of sending Dom Pedro back to face the constitutionalists in Lisbon.

In the midst of the deliberations, an anonymous pamphlet, descriptively entitled 'Should the King and the Royal Family in the Present Circumstances Return to Portugal or Instead Stay in Brazil?' hit the streets of Rio, causing a sensation first in Brazil and then in Portugal. The pamphlet was a vehicle for the ideas of the conservative minister, Tomás António de Vilanova Portugal who, although he did not write it, probably had a hand in its production. Vilanova Portugal maintained the absolutist line, arguing that the king should oppose the *cortes* and declare it illegal. In the pamphlet, the argument was taken to its logical conclusion: Brazil should abandon Portugal, splitting away to become a separate kingdom, ruled by Dom João from Rio. Like those who had predicted the move of the court to Brazil, the pamphlet made the point that Portugal, stripped of its American empire, was nothing, and could be sloughed off with little or no impact on Brazil's growing prosperity. These sentiments were echoed by Vilanova Portugal in a letter to the king: 'If it [Brazil] separates and cuts off communication, Portugal will fall into decay . . . it [Portugal] should be regarded as Hanover is in relation to Britain.' (Hanover was a small state on the Elbe in north-west Germany, ruled from 1714 to 1837 by the British Crown.) It was thought that once rejected, Portugal would eventually fall back into line and 'normal' relations would be resumed.

The court greatly overestimated its ability to control the forces that had been unleashed in Portugal. The years of relative isolation in Rio had made the king's advisers unfit to negotiate the political rapids before them. The pamphlet backfired. It was understandably unpopular in Portugal, and in Brazil it was seen for what it was: an attempt on the part of the Crown to preserve its absolutist powers in the New World, whatever might transpire back in Europe. Such was the uproar on its publication that the whole edition was recalled.

In the end, the court opted for caution, responding that although the seizure of power in Portugal was illegal, the king recognised the importance of convening the *côrtes* and would

consider the outcome of its deliberations. The king pardoned
those who had engineered the coup and ended with the vague
assurance that 'his Royal Person or one of his sons' would return
to Portugal. Behind the scenes there was disarray. Dom João
baulked at sending Dom Pedro back to Lisbon, unwilling as he
was to give way to the rebels so easily, and frightened that Dom
Pedro might be declared king on his arrival in Portugal. There
was another complicating factor – Dona Leopoldina was seven
months pregnant. Her desire to accompany her husband back to
Europe was so great that she had agreed to give birth on the
Atlantic if necessary. The unborn child would play a potent role
in the coming months, as discussions within the court continued
inconclusively.

On 23 December 1820, Palmela arrived in Rio. As a young man,
more than a decade earlier, he had elected to stay in Lisbon, rather
than join the flight to Brazil. Since then, Palmela seemed to have
had an uncanny knack of attending every event of historical
significance in Europe. He had served alongside Wellesley in the
peninsular campaigns; had gone on to represent Portugal in Spain,
putting Dona Carlota's case for the regency; and helped negotiate
the post-war settlement at the Congress of Vienna. More recently, he had been based in London, smoothing over the
increasingly fraught relations between Britain and the Brazilian
court. He was someone who had wined and dined with all the
players in the political and cultural life of the Continent, and there
was relief in European diplomatic circles that he would be
advising the court in person during this complex crisis.

Palmela stepped into the searing temperatures of the Brazilian
summer decked out in Bond Street linens, the diamond buckles
on his fashionable boots gleaming in the tropical sun. He found
Rio to his liking, although lacking the sophistication that he was
accustomed to. 'There are beautiful villas very close to the city,'
he wrote back to his wife in Europe, 'the bay of Botafogo is
without exaggeration comparable to the most beautiful in Italy
or Switzerland. There is a scarcity of white people, luxury goods
and decent roads, many things that will come in time, but there

is no shortage, as there is in Lisbon, of water and greenery around the city, since even in this the worst season, everything is as green here as in England.' He was less impressed, though, with the state in which he found Dom João and his advisers, who even now appeared not to have grasped the gravity of the events that were unfolding around them.

Palmela brought more bad news which he hoped would bring them to their senses. He had been witness to the revolution in Portugal, but it was during his brief stopover in Salvador that he realised the peril of the court's position. The city was on the edge of revolt, the governor hanging on, praying for some decisive action from Rio. He was told that the situation in Pernambuco was even more tense, that news of the Lisbon revolt had electrified the entire Brazilian coast. A combustible mix of disgruntled Portuguese battalions, posted in Brazil following the Pernambucan revolution, and Brazilian provincial discontent was pushing the Crown's authority close to collapse.

The desire for change was understandable among intellectuals on both sides of the Atlantic. Portugal and Brazil, in their different ways, had suffered under the secretive, autocratic style of Dom João's absolute monarchy. In Brazil, there had been the indiscriminate seizure of people's houses that had opened the court's stay – an act that symbolised the Crown's dictatorial writ in the most intimate way. The ancient law which allowed it was revoked towards the end of the court's time in Rio, but its impact lingered as legal wrangling between courtiers and the original owners dragged on. Crown corruption and the impunity of its perpetrators meant that people felt powerless in the face of the court. With the influx of foreigners, Rio was undergoing a cultural renaissance, yet Dom João maintained a regime of tight censorship which seemed backward and mean-spirited in the circumstances.

In Portugal, on the other hand, absolutism was an even heavier burden in the peculiar circumstances that the relocation of the court had thrown up. The opening of Brazil's ports in 1808 had had a devastating effect on Portuguese post-war commerce. British freighters returned with the produce which had once been controlled by a Portuguese monopoly, while merchants from the mother country now faced stiff competition in the large Brazilian ports. For more than a decade, the Portuguese had been left with no influence over the government which ultimately ruled them. Their pleas for the court's return had been ignored, their country abandoned to the whims of politicians in London and Rio.

In a letter to Dom João, Palmela set down his concerns:

'the disgraceful events that I witnessed in Portugal, and the impression that I had of the state of public opinion in Madeira, Bahia, and in this very Capital, obliges me to say firmly to Your Majesty, that there is not an instant to lose to adopt resolute, decisive measures, in keeping with the spirit of the times . . . the worst of all courses, in my opinion, would be to take no decision at all.'

Palmela urged Dom João to accept the liberals' demands in both Bahia and Portugal, but his voice carried little weight in a court that had run aground through its own indecision. He was seen as a metropolitan dandy, and quickly found himself hemmed in, attracting, in his own words, 'the hatred and slanders of both the extreme parties: one of which considers me a satellite of despotism, the other an agent of the "revolutionaries"'. He was, in fact, trying to steer a middle path, aiming for a moderate, constitutional monarchy, modelled on a British system, with the king bound by a parliament.

In the midst of all the negotiations, Dona Leopoldina's fears of being left behind in Rio while her husband sailed back to Europe were intensifying. Like everyone else, she was sensing that time was running out. 'Unfortunately, he [Dom João] doesn't want to take a decision . . .' she wrote back to Austria, 'morale here is so bad that everything will be lost unless the most energetic measures are taken.' She became hysterical when she heard that the Austrian representative to the Portuguese court, Baron von Stürmer, was supporting the return of Dom Pedro, writing to him: '. . . if you do not succeed through your

influence or that of the Count of Palmela to postpone the
departure of my husband or arrange for me to accompany him,
you will be the focus of all my ire and hatred for which you will
have to pay sooner or later.'

Palmela dismissed her concerns, telling Stürmer: 'this is painful
for the princess royal, but wouldn't it be even more so if we lose
Portugal, only because she couldn't be separated from her
husband for a few months?' As her pregnancy proceeded, Dona
Leopoldina's anxieties deepened. 'I found her very agitated . . .'
wrote Stürmer, after visiting Leopoldina at the palace, 'she
complained that she would be left abandoned if the prince
consented to leave without her . . . she added that in the event
of the departure of the prince coming about, no force would
prevent her embarking on the most miserable boat which turned
up were she to be reunited with him and return to his mother
country . . . that once really abandoned here her situation would
turn unbearable, that she would not stop being the target of
intrigue and ill will . . . and finally that she was convinced that
they would never let her return to Europe and that she should
prepare for eternal exile in a country she had always loathed.'

Dom Pedro, in spite of his history of extra-marital affairs, was
supportive, suggesting that if he had to go back to Portugal she
could accompany him, giving birth on the Atlantic if necessary.
The idea was that after the shipboard birth, the baby could be
sent back to Rio on another boat. In the end, Dona Leopoldina
was preparing to go it alone, writing secretly to a German friend
to arrange a passage for her and six others, including a 'healthy
and competent' wet-nurse for the baby 'who will be born at sea,
and in this way, will be neither Brazilian, nor Portuguese'. Yet
Dona Leopoldina would never return to Europe, and nor, at this
stage, would her husband Dom Pedro.

With all his years of experience in Europe and the overview
his journey had given him, Palmela realised that change was
inevitable. But he knew, too, that the palpable dissatisfaction in
both Portugal and Brazil had to be channelled in a moderate
direction if radical ideologues were to be held at bay. To this
end, he proposed to the king a set of principles, including the

separation of powers between crown and parliament, equality of citizens before the law and freedom of the press. He suggested that after these measures were adopted, Dom Pedro should travel with four warships and a battalion of troops up to Salvador, and proclaim the new constitutional monarchy, before sailing on to Lisbon. It was the kind of bold move that Dom João would never take, and in any case, Dom Pedro was still not prepared to leave without the heavily-pregnant Dona Leopoldina by his side. The stalemate prompted Palmela's resignation, exposing the dissension within the court to public view.

While Dom João prevaricated, Portuguese soldiers stationed around Brazil responded to calls from the motherland. In Bahia, troops stormed the governor's residence, and proclaimed a constitutional revolution. Belated loyalist resistance was beaten back by volleys of musket shot and artillery fire, and the Brazilian general Felisberto Caldeira Brant leading the counter-attack was lucky to escape with his life after his horse was shot from under him. His cause hopeless, the governor of Bahia capitulated and boarded a ship for Rio. There were similar scenes in Belém, on the mouth of the Amazon (although news of the uprising would not reach Rio for another six weeks) as the revolt spread along the Brazilian littoral.

With agitators manoeuvring themselves into position in Rio, the court appeared paralysed, unable to respond as the ground shifted beneath them. Expectations of some kind of official pronouncement were met with total silence from the palace, an impasse reminiscent of the long months Dom João had spent incommunicado in the run-up to his flight to Brazil. On both occasions, under mounting pressure, he would wait it out until the last possible moment. In Rio, as in Lisbon, only the threat of imminent violence moved him to act.

When news came through of revolts across Brazil, Dom João finally broke his silence, issuing two decrees on 23 February 1821. The first stated that Dom Pedro would be sent to Lisbon immediately, the second that a separate *cortes* would be created in Rio, composed of representatives from Brazil and the Atlantic islands. This consultative assembly would debate the decisions which had been reached in Lisbon, with a view to adapting them to Brazil. It turned out to be another miscalculation. The issuing of the decrees, like the earlier publication of the pamphlet, was seen as a strategy to avoid a full ratification of the future Lisbon constitution. Soon after they were released, copies were left outside the palace, defaced with anti-monarchist propaganda.

FOURTEEN

The Return

In the early hours of 26 February 1821, Dom João was roused
from his sleep at the palace of São Cristóvão. His son Dom Pedro
was also woken by a palace guard who had ridden out from the
centre of Rio. He brought with him news of unauthorised troop
movements: three battalions had left their barracks and were
gathering in a square in front of the royal theatre. Heavy artillery,
powder and shot were positioned at barricades which had been
set up along Rio's principle roads and squares. The soldiers were
Portuguese, veterans from the peninsular campaigns, their
actions the end point of a constitutionalist ripple effect that
had spread from Cadiz to Oporto to Lisbon, before making its
way down the Brazilian coast to Rio. They were joined by
dissident liberal factions which had begun forming in the city.

The moves were not entirely unexpected. With news of
revolts in other parts of Brazil coming through, Rio was
mobilising. Treasonous pamphlets and satirical verses that only
months before would have been confiscated now circulated
freely through the city, the authorities powerless to stop their
distribution. People were now openly speculating on what the
future held for the capital. At one point, it was said that Dom
João had actually signed up to the constitution, but the rumour
soon fizzled out.

In an attempt to stem the tide, the court released another
decree. Armed with the new formula, Dom Pedro mounted his

horse, and accompanied by a servant rode the three miles from
the palace to the city centre at a gallop. He arrived at five o'clock
in the morning, stepped on to the podium of the royal theatre
and addressed the rebels. Silence enveloped the hall as he began
reading out the decree. Under the proposed arrangements, the
king would accept the constitution being prepared by Lisbon
'except for modifications that local circumstances might make
necessary', and would appoint a consultative body to discuss the
matter in due course. But as he spoke, Padre Macamboa, a
bulky, forty-year-old Portuguese lawyer and priest, interjected,
demanding the king dismiss his ministers and accept a twelve-
man government appointed by the military. Macamboa was
calling for a *coup d'état*, though a conservative one: on the list
were Portuguese-born moderates, all well known to the king
and court.

Pedro returned to the palace, where he found his father in
session with Vilanova Portugal. He apprised them of the situation and urged them to bow to the rebels' demands. Hemmed
in, his authority reduced to just Rio de Janeiro itself, and even
there under threat, Dom João was left with no option. With
great reluctance, a third decree was released and with it, the
climb down was complete. Dom João agreed not only to
honour the constitution to be drawn up in Lisbon, but also
to withdraw his ministers, replacing them with the list drawn up
by the rebels. Dom Pedro set off once more, arriving back in the
city at seven o'clock, to a by now packed city centre. Facing
euphoric crowds in the royal theatre, he took an oath to the as
yet unwritten Lisbon constitution from the stage that had once
carried propagandist plays and operas – classical odes to the court
and the kingdom.

The crowd had one further demand, that the king himself
appear before them. Hours later, the king's carriage was spotted,
swaying in the distance, a nervous Dom João nestled in its cabin.
To Dom João's horror, the crowds surged forward, unhitched
the horses and hauled the carriage the last few hundred metres
into the square. But the mood was one of jubilation, not
violence, the gesture more a celebration of Dom João's enduring

personal popularity and of the decision that he had made. He was joined by his children and Dona Carlota and appeared at the window of the royal palace, where, three years earlier, he had been acclaimed king of The United Kingdom of Portugal, Brazil and the Algarves. A bishop administered the oath which Dom João repeated, swearing 'to observe, protect and perpetually maintain the constitution, exactly as it shall be made in Portugal by the *cortes.*' Applause broke out in the square below, marking the end of an extraordinary era of absolute rule from the tropics. On the following day, Dom João announced his departure for Lisbon. He would leave behind Dom Pedro, who would rule as regent at the head of the new constitutional government. On past record, Dom João's return to Portugal could not be guaranteed, but it was difficult this time to see how he could renege on his promise.

For Dom João – without doubt one of the motivating forces behind the court's extended stay in the tropics – a personal odyssey was reaching its end. He was profoundly saddened by the turn of events. His time in Rio had been the only period of relative stability in his long reign, and his sole opportunity to adopt the traditional role of absolute monarch. It had involved a very public, yet intimate relationship with his vassals, embodied in the antiquated *beija-mão* ceremony and the constant round of religious processions, both of which the king had derived great pleasure from performing. For his wife, Dona Carlota, the contrast could not have been greater. Although no constitutionalist, she was delighted by what had happened. The end of a protracted purgatorial existence, one that had taken her from her early thirties into middle age, was finally at hand.

Dom João's last month in Rio would be unpleasant, tainted by a sense that he and his court had outstayed their welcome. He was now rarely seen in the open, venturing out only under heavy guard. Celebrations for the birth of Dona Leopoldina's son were muted, the regal festivities which had been so much a part of the city in the last years had become dangerous and somehow inappropriate. The court's grip over its population was loosening, as the last rites were performed on its thirteen-year rule.

Yet ordinary *cariocas* – those not caught up in the political upheaval – saw things differently. Many, especially small traders, artisans, even slaves, were devastated by the news of the court's departure. A strong monarchist ethos underlay Brazilian society and despite the recent events, Dom João still enjoyed substantial popular support. Devotion to monarchy was mixed with more practical considerations – the departure of the court would mean a sudden loss of prestige for Rio de Janeiro, as the centrepiece of the empire was downgraded to a provincial capital overnight. The presence of the court had ensured large volumes of trade and had drawn wealthy diplomats, scientists and travellers from around the world.

Hundreds signed petitions calling for the king to stay on. There were also formal requests from the chamber of commerce and the city council, urging the king to revoke or at least delay his decision to leave. *Cariocas* who had long complained about the corrupt and bullying presence of the court in their city looked to the future with trepidation. A political void was forming, and it was unclear exactly how the new order would work, or whether the welcome reforms introduced by Dom João and his government would be maintained.

As the royal family prepared to leave, opposition to its departure began to take on a more hostile tone. Large quantities of Brazilian gold were said to be stashed on board the royal convoy. There was talk of financial irregularities: the Bank of Brazil's entire capital holdings had been loaned out to just a dozen men of influence and further advances had been made to the court, whose debts were reaching unsustainable levels. To make matters worse, rumours that the crown jewels, pledged by Dom João to the Bank of Brazil as collateral for the court's debts, were somewhere in the holds of the fleet prompted a run on the bank, clearing out its paltry reserves.

More stories of misdeeds were exchanged in the streets – the Portuguese had been using doors, window frames and shutters to make wooden packing cases for their belongings. Brazilians who had lent out their homes returned to find their houses vandalised

by outgoing officials. In acts that harked back to the November
1807 flight from Lisbon, the court was seizing anything of value
that it could lay its hands on, leaving behind a slew of debt,
unpaid salaries and bills.

The British envoy to Rio, Edward Thornton, described the
city's darkening mood as the court prepared to leave:

> '. . . Reports were spread of the Discontent of the People with
> the State of Things, with the Honour and Pensions lavished in
> the last few days with a most prodigal Hand, with the great sums
> of money said to be on board the squadron; and it was declared
> that the abuses ought to be corrected, that this king's departure
> should be deferred until they were so and that a provisional Junta
> of Government should be formed for the interval before the
> arrival of the constitution.'

After the euphoria of 26 February, there were misgivings about
new arrangements that were to come into effect. Rebels like
Padre Macamboa felt the proposed constitutional reforms did not
go far enough. Under the new system, Brazil would resubmit to
rule from Portugal, after years of relative autonomy. There was in
any case still no constitution in place – everyone was waiting for
the Portuguese version of the Spanish document to be drawn up.
In the meantime, the interim government led by the Portuguese-
born philosopher, Silvestre Pinheiro Ferreira, a former adviser to
the king, was running the new government much like the old,
taking decisions without any public consultation.

It was in this atmosphere – a mixture of anger and regret, of
remorse and disgust – that the interim administration convened
an assembly of the electors – merchants, landowners, lawyers –
who had been charged with choosing members of the new
parliamentary body, the *cortes*. The discussion would be wide-
ranging, covering Dom Pedro's powers as regent, the selection
of his ministers and future political arrangements in Brazil. It was
to be held on 21 April 1821, the day before Easter, in Rio's new
commercial exchange building, an airy structure overlooking
the bay. Makeshift stands were installed and from the court's

original idea of a small, discreet gathering, the event turned into a public forum – a mass meeting at possibly one of the most sensitive times in the city's history. Sitting in the stands were dissidents like Padre Macamboa and the even more radical Luís Duprat, a twenty-year-old firebrand, the son of a French tailor. Wiry, with Robespierre-style glasses, he came well-prepared with passionate revolutionary rhetoric.

The exchange building was packed when the presiding judge called the gathering to order. He got no further than reading out the names of Dom Pedro's ministers before he was drowned out by cries for the immediate implementation of the Spanish constitution. From then on the formal agenda was swept away, hijacked by Padre Macamboa and his comrades, Duprat firing up the crowd with stirring, anti-monarchist speeches. A resolution was carried on the implementation of the Spanish constitution and when this reached the palace, Dom João was again thrown into emergency session with his advisers. Once more they gave in to the demands, but this time around, it seemed as though the situation was running out of control.

As the night wore on in the heady atmosphere of the exchange building, the discussion turned to the rumours that gold was being hidden aboard the royal fleet. Duprat declared that Brazilian gold should not be allowed to be spirited out of the country and dispatched an ageing general, Joaquim Xavier Curado, the highest ranking officer present, to seal the port. He pushed off into the bay, but only managed to relay the order to one of the forts guarding the harbour's entrance, before being arrested by loyalist troops.

'There are so many different versions of this event,' wrote Thornton back to London, 'that I should find it difficult to give your Lordship any account with which I would satisfy myself.' Thornton was referring to the labyrinthine politicking that continued into the small hours of 22 April 1821. Rio was in the process of fragmentation; everything was up for grabs and everyone rushed to defend what they perceived as their future interests. There may even have been involvement in the anti-monarchist wing from members of the court itself – those angling for Dom João to stay on in Rio, even if it meant forcing him to do so against his will. For most of the courtiers, the idea of landing in revolutionary Lisbon was not a prospect they relished.

It was four o'clock in the morning when loyalist troops, commanded by Dom Pedro, assembled and marched into the centre of Rio. They lined up, twenty-five columns wide, bayonets fixed. A single shot was fired against them, a soldier fell, followed by a deafening roar as the battalion let loose with fifty rounds into the packed exchange building. The troops then entered, wielding their bayonets and dispersed the crowds. '. . . Common people were indiscriminately killed,' an anonymous memoir related, 'and a larger number, having jumped into the sea to escape, met the death they had tried to avoid amidst the waves . . . The cadavers were clandestinely taken to the navy arsenal and there they were secretly buried.' Duprat and Macamboa were captured, as their followers fled for their lives. The brutality with which this key meeting was broken up was in some ways fitting. It was one last statement of absolutist power, a reminder of how, in the last resort, the Portuguese had maintained their South American colonies.

By eight o'clock that morning, the court had revoked the decree implementing the Spanish constitution forced on them by the assembly, arguing that it was made 'on the orders of evil-intentioned men who desired anarchy'. It was the court's last official act in Rio. The city was seething in the aftermath of the Easter Day violence, and courtiers rushed to complete the preparations for Dom João's departure. This time, there would be no processions, floats, fireworks or triumphal arches, no *beija-mão* ceremony for the king to see off his vassals. Instead, there would be silence, bar the hushed voices of those organising the loading of provisions as a stream of crates were carried down to the dock area and loaded on to the fleet. Among the cargo were coffins carrying the remains of Queen Maria I, her sister Dona Maria Anna and the Spanish Infante, Dom Carlos, on their final journeys of repatriation.

Most of the court boarded in near darkness in the pre-dawn

gloom of 25 April – three days after the exchange building massacre. Only Dona Carlota braved the crowds of curious foreigners and stunned Brazilians. She descended the ramp and stepped on to the royal galley, bidding farewell to a long and unhappy period in her life. She would miss little about Rio and if various, perhaps apocryphal, parting shots are anything to go by, vented her bitterness on a people who had hosted the royal family for over a decade. 'Finally, I am going to a land inhabited by real men,' she is quoted as saying, joking that she would be blinded back in Europe 'because I have lived thirteen years in darkness, seeing only blacks and mulattos.'

Before the royal squadron pulled out into the bay, Dom Pedro and Dona Leopoldina visited the king on board the fleet. It was an emotional farewell. The last weeks had been highly charged, the future uncertain. If the royal family was leaving for a Portugal in revolt, Dom Pedro would face an equally difficult situation in Rio. Fatherly advice was in order and dutifully given, words that would have remained lost for ever, were they not later recalled in a letter from Pedro. 'I still remember and will always remember what you told me two days before you left: If Brazil breaks away, let it be under you who respects me rather than any of those adventurers.'

For Dona Leopoldina, the departure aroused complex emotions. Two months before she had been preparing to sail for Europe; now she would find herself staying on in Rio in even more difficult circumstances. Soon after the king's departure she wrote to her father in Austria: 'This packet boat will carry news of many things that will strike you as unbelievable. Even for me, it all seems like a dream. The reality, meanwhile, is that I must stay here in Brazil, and that I am separated from my wonderful father-in-law [Dom João] which, for many reasons, is extremely difficult and painful for me.'

The thirteen-strong royal squadron carrying over 4,000 courtiers cruised out towards the bar, but then stopped and anchored opposite the Sugar Loaf Mountain, by the fort of Santa Cruz. There it paused, and from the safety of the fleet Dom João 'received the Compliments of his Court on the Occasion of the

Day, which was the Anniversary of the Queen's Birth', a ceremonial gesture that ended the years of royal celebrations in the city. The following day, the squadron set sail in perfect conditions on a breeze 'which continued so long through the Day . . . that it must have cleared the land before the evening'. Rio's unexpected encounter with the Portuguese court was over as abruptly as it had begun.

Thirteen years before, as nobles, courtiers, priests and servants fought for berths on the ships that queued to flee Lisbon, few imagined that their decision to join the fleet would lead to such an extended stay in the tropics. A good proportion of the men and women who had arrived with the court had already perished, far from their homeland; of those who had survived, some were heading home, but many more, like Marrocos, would stay on.

Dom João's prolonged stay had left an indelible mark on the city. Thirteen years had seen his botanical gardens transformed from miniature seedlings into strange and beautiful plants, his own *palma mater* still towering over the various botanical experiments which he had initiated. After slave workers surreptitiously took its seeds and sold them off, the palms propagated throughout the city, changing Rio's skyline in ways that seemed predestined. Slender, gently arching trunks sprouted from the hilltops, playing off against the neoclassical columns of the new buildings which had been put up during the court's stay.

Dom João, his advisers and former government ministers, were once more in the open sea, travelling, this time, in the opposite direction, bound for Europe. As the fleet cut through an Atlantic swell, on a small island to their south, a man lay dying in his bed. They were ten days out from Rio when Napoleon Bonaparte slipped away, after his long years of exile on St Helena. The death of the man who had driven the court out of its kingdom closed the door on an era. Yet in many respects the courtiers' position was now even worse than when, years before, the decks had been filled with traumatised refugees fleeing Napoleon's invading army. Back then, in spite of the privations, the court had been looking to the future. They had been heading towards a land where their power could be reborn, their failing empire renewed.

There had been discussions on board between politicians and bureaucrats about how this might be carried out, and once landed, the measures taken had at first been sweeping and fast paced. But the very character of the court they created in Rio worked against the realisation of their dreams. The careful copying of institutions which had existed in Lisbon doomed the venture from the outset. Rio had grown and changed, while the court dug in, refusing to react to the wave of new ideas that was moving across Europe and South America. This had been no new beginning, but an extended pause – a moment of delusion in an era of protracted imperial decline.

On the return journey, the predominant emotion was fear. There were detailed discussions about which route should be followed back to Europe. The idea of a stopoff in Bahia was floated, but thought to be too risky. So concerned was Dom João about the situation in Portugal that he tried to institute one last delaying tactic. The plan was, according to the British envoy in Rio, to dock in the mid-Atlantic at the Azores 'not merely it is said for the Purposes of Refreshment it must stand in need after such a long Voyage but also of hearing the Intelligence of Lisbon'. It would have been a dangerous move, but as they approached the archipelago, a stiff breeze pushed them past it. The fleet sailed on to Portugal.

After years of waiting, those in Lisbon were almost the last to hear of the royal family's imminent arrival. Just two days before the fleet was due to dock, ships which had left Rio after the royal convoy, but were arriving ahead of it, brought the momentous news. There were hurried preparations for the court's reception – a gala event based on an ancient protocol dating back to the birth of the Portuguese Empire. Expectant crowds thronged the port. The royal convoy eased its way into the Tagus on 4 July 1821 and anchored in view of the main square. The atmosphere was tense, the air filled with conflicting emotions – a mix of the old and the new. Lisbon was now under the control of a revolutionary government, set on a constitutional path, yet many were awed by the return of their king. The square was strewn with flowers, but also, more ominously, lined with

regiments of soldiers, standing to attention. Even before Dom
João had disembarked, it was clear that his ancient powers had
been usurped. His vessel was boarded in the port and he was
made to sign the decree he had tried to avoid in Rio, in which
he agreed to ratify the new constitution. But members of the
delegation, those who had risen up against the yoke of absolute
rule, fell to their knees when they first set eyes on Dom João,
requesting to kiss his hand.

Lisbon nobles and foreign dignitaries joined the delegates on
board to meet the royals. More than a decade had elapsed since
they had last seen the returning exiles: the young were now
middle aged, the middle aged elderly. Dom Miguel, who had
left as a six-year-old boy, returned at the age of nineteen, fit and
tanned from Rio. His sisters, children on departure, were now
young women. And it was not just differences in age that
surprised the Lisbon nobles – many of the clothes worn by
the Rio court belonged to another era. Weather-beaten courtiers dressed in ruffs, knee-breeches and powdered wigs strolled
about the decks, their appearance more eighteenth than nineteenth-century. Princess Maria Benedita, now seventy-four, was
wearing a black robe embroidered with diamonds, looking, in
the words of the French ambassador Hyde de Neuville, 'just like
a picture that had stepped out of its frame'.

José Trazimundo, who as a five-year-old boy had witnessed
the flight from Lisbon, was now eighteen, and he was allowed
on board as an aide-de-camp of one of the revolutionary
generals. From old age, he looked back on what was an
unforgettable day. 'Entering the foredeck of the ship,' he
recalled, 'I witnessed a . . . scene that is engraved on my
memory, in spite of the fact that it took place forty-one years
ago.' He too was shocked by the royals, thirteen years on: 'we
stayed together on the gangway, from where we could just see
king Dom João VI, whose bearing and expression surprised me
by its lack of elegance and its ugliness.' Dom João was wearing a
uniform, 'more thickly embroidered with gold than any I had
ever seen; decorated with numerous orders, both Portuguese
and foreign, with a plumed hat, leaning on a gold headed cane,

and from time to time taking a few steps to and fro.' He spotted Dona Carlota from a distance, who, even before setting foot in Portugal, was up to her old tricks:

> 'I could not make out Queen Carlota very well. I only saw her hand and her fan, gesticulating, but I saw perfectly well the person she was talking to: the deputy Borges Carneiro [a radical liberal]. I found out later that they were both talking indiscreetly about the reign of Dom João VI . . . It seems as if the king heard it all, pretending, however, that he didn't hear anything. Later, he was the first to complain about such indiscretion, repeating many of the phrases used by both the queen and the deputy.'

Trazimundo remained on board, transfixed, 'reduced to a profound silence'. No one recognised him, nor did he know anyone, although he did manage to pick out a courtier, one Antonio Telles da Silva, finding him 'very changed and aged'. The following day Dom João disembarked. He walked up the ramp, with court officials in train. At its top he was given the keys to the city as the crowds burst into applause for the return of their prodigal monarch. 'On all sides,' ran the official description of the homecoming, 'the people exceeded themselves in acclamations and cheers, competing with each other to show their joy; it seemed as if they wanted to compensate for the tears they had shed on 29 November, 1807.' For a brief moment it must have seemed to Dom João as if he had stepped back into a Lisbon that had changed little during his absence, that he might somehow be able to seamlessly resume his reign over the vassals whom he had abandoned for so long. But he would be quickly disabused of these ideas. On his first day back in Lisbon his trusted advisers, many of whom were lifelong companions – among them Vilanova Portugal, Joaquim José de Azevedo, and his chamberlain and confidant Lobato, as well as the Count of Palmela – were dismissed by the rebel authorities in Lisbon and sent from the city. On the same day, Dom João stammered his oath to the constitution, as he returned, neutered, to the Old World and its troubles.

FIFTEEN

The Aftermath

Dom João's worst fears would be realised in the last years of his life. The court's prolonged exile had stored up problems in Portugal, echoed throughout post-Napoleonic Europe. A liberal/royalist rift ran deep through the country. The liberals themselves were divided – some viewing the revolution as merely a means to secure the return of the royal family and the end of rule from the tropics, others looking towards a radical break from the past. In the first months after his return, Dom João played along with the prevailing mood, adapting to the life of a constitutional monarch, appointing ministers but no longer playing an active role in politics. He lodged in the centre of Lisbon in the seventeenth-century convent of Bemposta, while Dona Carlota looked on from the palace of Queluz.

It was not long before she would be courting controversy once more. In November 1822, with dissatisfaction growing from conservative factions, a delegation was sent out to Queluz to make Dona Carlota sign up to the constitution. Dona Carlota refused, creating a sensation around the country – the constitutionalists had been rebuffed by someone at the very heart of the monarchy. It was a shrewd move on the part of Dona Carlota. Overnight, she became the focal point of the coming counter-revolution. She would lose the throne and be forced into exile for her refusal to recognise the

constitution, but even so, she remained defiant. In a famous
(and perhaps apocryphal) letter, she wrote to Dom João about
her decision:

'. . . tonight I received from the hands of your ministers a decree
to leave your kingdom. And since I am ordered into exile, Your
Majesty obliges me to leave the throne that you called me to. I
forgive you from the bottom of my heart and I feel pity for Your
Majesty; all my hatred and disgust will be reserved for those
around you who have deceived you. In exile I will be freer than
Your Majesty in your palace. I take with me my liberty: my heart
is not enslaved; it never bowed down to arrogant subjects who
had the hide to impose laws on Your Majesty and who want to
force me to swear an oath that I don't believe in . . . yet again,
Dom João, you will adapt to the new situation, in spite of always
declaring your predilection for the colony.'

In the event, she would avoid what would have been her second
exile from Portugal. With pressure mounting on her to leave,
Dona Carlota said that she was too ill to travel. Doctors
confirmed that she was suffering from a pulmonary condition
dating from Rio, as well as kidney problems that had recently
brought on life-threatening attacks. Her sentence was com-
muted to the more pleasant prospect of her old villa at Ramalhão. And it was there, in amongst the Brazilian ceiling
frescoes, the citrus groves and ferns, that she brooded, biding
her time.

Years of overspending during Dom João's reign had left Rio
bankrupt. The outflow of capital that accompanied the royal
family back to Lisbon had brought on the crisis and the new
regent, Dom Pedro, began cutting back on his father's follies.
The court had owned over 1,000 horses when Dom João left for
Europe. All but 156 were sold off. The small army of royal stable
hands were dismissed and slave labour used instead. Other
extravagances fell by the wayside. The world of sacred music
and opera which Dom João had built up over his stay was

dismantled, with the bloated salaries of the Italian *castrati* the first
to go. Neukomm followed them back to Europe, leaving
behind him a reduced choir run by José Maurício and Marcos
Portugal on poverty wages. The *coup de grâce* would come later,
in March 1824, when the royal theatre burnt down. The
botanical gardens also fell on hard times. By day their exotic
crops were left abandoned, suffocated by fast-growing tropical
weeds. At night they were vandalised, their herbs pulled up to be
used in religious ceremonies.

Politically, Dom Pedro faced pressures on all sides. The
Lisbon deputies, intent on curbing the powers that Brazil had
gained during the court's stay, were calling for his return to
Europe to make a grand tour of France, England and Spain, in
preparation for his eventual ascent to the Portuguese throne. In
Brazil, he was caught between the conflicting demands of the
provinces and the Portuguese troops stationed there; while in
Rio, his unpopularity over the attack on the exchange building
lingered. Almost immediately, he was forced on to the back foot
when an insurrection led by Portuguese garrisons in Rio
reduced him to the figurehead of a government chosen by
the military. Just six months after the departure of the royal
family, he was writing in despair to his father in Lisbon: 'I beg
Your Majesty, by all that is most sacred in the world, to please
relieve me of this job, that surely is going to kill me with the
constant scenes of horror, some already in view and others much
worse to come, that I have always before my eyes.' He longed to
kiss his father's hand, he wrote, taking his place 'at the foot of His
Majesty' back in Portugal.

By the end of the year, the Lisbon *cortes* had managed to
alienate deputies sent out from the Brazilian provinces, and was
moving towards reinstating the old colonial system. There was
outrage on the streets of Rio, encapsulated by the words of José
Bonifácio de Andrada e Silva, a progressive, European-educated
Paulista, who would end up leading the independence movement. His arguments were in essence the same as those that had
been used in Portugal against Brazil only a year before. Must the
Brazilian people, asked Bonifácio, 'after being accustomed to

prompt recourse for twelve years, go and suffer like contemptible colonials the delays and chicanery of the tribunals of Lisbon, across 2,000 leagues of ocean . . . ?' The shoe was on the other foot, the prospect of bowing to the dictates of Lisbon now unthinkable in a country that had come of age during the court's stay.

It was at this point that Dom Pedro's position in Brazil shifted. His regency began to be viewed as a bulwark against the imperial demands of the Lisbon *cortes*. When, at the end of 1821, Lisbon abolished the administrative bodies that had been set up by Dom João on his arrival in Brazil, the situation came to a head. After weeks of political agitation, crowds gathered in Rio's central square and a petition of 8,000 signatures was presented to Dom Pedro, demanding that he resist pressure from Portugal and remain in Brazil. In a response that laid down the battle lines between colony and mother country, the prince defied Lisbon. 'Since it is for the good of all and the general happiness of the nation,' he said on 9 January 1822, 'I am ready. Tell the people that I am staying.' Two days later, while Dom Pedro was at the theatre, Portuguese troops stationed in Rio rampaged through the streets, smashing windows as they went. The next twenty-four hours saw a tense stand-off between Portuguese units and ragtag bands of *cariocas*, armed with pistols, fowling pieces and farm implements. Dom Pedro was so uncertain of his position that he had already sent Dona Leopoldina with their children out to Santa Cruz and had asked the captain of the HMS *Doris*, docked in the harbour, for passage for himself and his family, should he be forced out of Rio. But the Portuguese were the first to waver, pulling back their forces to the other side of the bay, before, under the threat of force from Dom Pedro, boarding transports back to Europe.

By mid-1822, disturbing reports were arriving from Lisbon. Dona Carlota was making her move, supporting her son Dom Miguel in a play for the throne. 'Your mother is for Miguel,' wrote Dom João, 'and I, who love you can do nothing against the *carbonari* [revolutionaries] who hate you.' There was also

growing uncertainty around Brazil. In a series of epic journeys
on horseback, Dom Pedro rode out deep into the surrounding
provinces – first to Ouro Preto in Minas Gerais, and then to
São Paulo – garnering support for his administration. And it
was on the way back to São Paulo, after a visit to the port of
Santos, that the iconic scene of Brazilian nationhood took
place. Suffering from a bout of diarrhoea, Dom Pedro made an
unscheduled stop by a stream called Ipiranga. There, as he
buttoned up his trousers, he was met by a messenger who had
ridden out from São Paulo with urgent mail. He brought with
him an assortment of letters – one from Dona Leopoldina,
another from José Bonifácio, as well as official notices from the
cortes in Lisbon. Read together, the picture was clear. Seven
thousand troops were being prepared in Lisbon for Brazil; both
Dona Leopoldina, who had become an ardent and influential
supporter of the independence movement, and José Bonifácio
argued that the point of no return had been reached. On 7
September 1822, Dom Pedro tore the Portuguese insignia from
his uniform and threw it to the ground. Drawing his sword he
proclaimed: 'Independence or death! We have separated from
Portugal!'

The trip to São Paulo was significant for Dom Pedro for
another reason. It was there that he met the woman who would
play a major role in his life in the years to come: Domitila de
Castro, a beguiling, dark-featured twenty-four-year-old. The
affair was passionate, and became more and more public as time
passed. Back in Rio, Dom Pedro set her up in a house near the
palace and had two children by her, one of whom died young.
He acknowledged their surviving daughter, granting her the
Brazilian title of the 'Duchess of Goiás' and insisting that on
palace visits she was referred to as 'Her Majesty'. Dona Leopoldina suffered in silence, confiding only to palace attendants: 'I
can endure anything except seeing that little girl on the same
level with my children; and I tremble with anger when I see her;
it is the greatest of sacrifices for me to receive her.' Much later,
Dom Pedro would even take Domitila on a three-week cruise
up the coast to Salvador. While Dona Leopoldina brooded in

her stateroom, Dom Pedro strolled on deck with his mistress on his arm, calling her by her pet name 'Titília'.

Late in 1826, Dom Pedro headed south to inspect troops in Rio Grande do Sul, still engaged in the never-ending battle over the Banda Oriental. He sailed on board the *Pedro Primeiro*, one of the ships (then called the *Martins de Freitas*), which decades before had been used in the evacuation of Lisbon. From its decks he wrote two virtually identical letters – one to Dona Leopoldina and the other to Domitila – each expressing his undying love and affection. While the letters made their way back up the coast towards Rio, Dona Leopoldina miscarried, and then came down with a series of 'nervous attacks'. Her physicians prescribed 'dusting powders, massages, leeches, baths, laxatives, antispasmodics [and] emetics', but whether from the cure or the disease, she died in the mid-morning of 11 December 1826.

The loss of Brazil tarnished the reputation of the liberals in Portugal. There was a widespread perception that they had mishandled the situation, and that an absolutist regime would not have lost Portugal her richest colonial holdings. In May 1823 the liberals were swept from power when the country was engulfed in the first of its many counter-revolutionary uprisings, led by Dom Miguel and engineered from the wings by Dona Carlota. Dom João was able to survive the revolt, known as the *Vilafrancada*, by reluctantly placing himself at its head. With the restoration, the order for Dona Carlota's exile was revoked, Dom João decreeing that 'his much loved and esteemed wife' should take up her rightful position as Queen of Portugal in the palace of Queluz. The reunited royal couple were fêted with old-fashioned deference and lavish celebrations in the streets, but the underlying situation was tense, Dom João's position, flanked by a wife and son of uncertain loyalty, fragile.

A second revolt, the *Abrilada* (April 1824), was a more violent affair. Once again orchestrated by Dona Carlota, Dom Miguel's forces ran riot in the city, rounding up and executing liberal opponents as they tried to flee Lisbon. With pressure mounting on him to abdicate in favour of his son, Dom João cowered in the convent of Bemposta, while out in the streets his political allies were being slain. This was the second low-point of Dom João's reign, reminiscent of his plight seventeen years earlier, when in frantic meetings with Strangford, Araújo and his palace advisers, he had fought for his survival. And this time around his response would be similar. In a faint echo of autumn 1807, Dom João rushed down to the docks in an unmarked carriage and sought refuge on a British ship, the HMS *Windsor Castle*.

From there, he requested a meeting with his errant son, Miguel. In what was a wholly unexpected turnaround, Miguel obeyed, and once on board broke down, begging his father's forgiveness. Dom Miguel spent the night confined to the stern of the ship and was taken into exile to Austria the following day. It was a crushing defeat for Dona Carlota, and this time Dom João and his ministers were determined to contain her. The aftermath of the rebellion spawned the climactic confrontation between husband and wife, who had lived through half a century of simmering, yet unexpressed hatred. In a long letter to Fernando VII in Madrid, Dom João was uncharacteristically frank:

'what pains me most in the current circumstances, is to see that moves against me emanate from those closest to me . . . I consider my wife, the queen, Your Majesty's sister, to be the most culpable, and the primary instigator of the intrigues and conspiracies which have been contrived against me. Since 1806, there has been convincing evidence of the queen's ambitious schemes, and the undignified ways in which she has tried to implement them, reaching the point in which she wanted me to declare myself unfit to govern. I won't go into the wealth of evidence of the ill-will and betrayals, culminating recently in the seducing of my gullible young son, Dom Miguel, enticing him, it seems, into the notorious acts of rebellion which I managed to put down only with the greatest effort – Your Majesty yourself

has in your hands letters written by the queen . . . which
demonstrate very clearly her culpable interference in the business
of the government . . .'

He went on to ask Fernando to write to Dona Carlota,
suggesting that she go into voluntary exile, to Spain, or perhaps
France or Italy. But Dona Carlota resisted all attempts to
remove her, again claiming ill health – 'I am suffering rheumatic attacks, great pain and a fever that has taken away all
movement in my leg,' she wrote in her defence. Rounding on
Dom João, she challenged her enemies to prosecute her: 'I
demand that they try me, with full judicial process, because this
is what the law says, and nobody can be punished without a
hearing and without proof of the crime,' adding that it was
'unseemly for the king to take such strong measures against me
prior to a formal hearing.'

Dona Carlota ended up back in the rococo palace of
Queluz, under close surveillance. Police, disguised as court
attendants, watched her every move, making daily reports on
her meetings and conversations. For a time Dona Carlota
slipped into obscurity. She paid less and less attention to her
appearance – her hair was dishevelled, and she could be seen
wandering through the palace and its grounds in loose, sack-
like dresses. Although not yet fifty, Dona Carlota was by now
seriously ill, and her long struggle to wrest power from her
husband was almost over.

Dom João would spend the rest of his days in constant fear of
further violence. They were also consumed by negotiations that
distressed him – the settlement of the Brazil question. Portugal
had refused to recognise Brazil's independence, but under
concerted pressure from Britain, was at last at the negotiating
table. The settlement was the final chapter in the increasingly
surreal relations between Portugal and her former colonial
territories. Under the agreement, brokered by the British diplomat Sir Charles Stuart, Brazil would pay Portugal compensation for the loss of her colony. A list was drawn up of all the

property, and a portion of the debts, left behind by the royal family on its departure from Rio four years before. On the bill were silverware, furniture and equipment from the royal household, the royal library, half of the debt run up to the British, warships, cargo, ammunition, and the salaries and pensions of regiments which had been stationed in Brazil. The grand total owed to Portugal was £2,000,000, of which £250,000 would go directly to Dom João for the disposal of the network of properties he had acquired during his stay in Rio. It was a treaty steeped in irony. One last shipment of treasure would cross the Atlantic from Brazil to Portugal – the payment of a bill for the court's expenses during its extended exile in Rio.

The negotiations also dealt with the thorny issue of the Portuguese throne, now split between the Old and New Worlds. On the signing of the treaty, the separation would become official, with a branch of the Braganças setting up permanently in the Americas. Dom João reserved his right to the title of 'Emperor of Brazil', but devolved the powers that it entailed to his son, Dom Pedro, with succession through his descendants. Surrounded by unstable, revolutionary republics, Brazil would progress through much of the nineteenth century with a system not unlike Britain's – a monarchy replete with a titled nobility, and a parliamentary system of government. It would be held together by the long reign of Dom Pedro's son, Dom Pedro II, a figure who, like Queen Victoria for Britain, came to embody Brazil's nineteenth-century aspirations.

On a freezing November day, Dom João signed the treaty in his office in the Mafra monastery complex. He now appeared older than his fifty-nine years. A much heavier man than in his Brazilian days, his leg problems still plagued him and he walked with great difficulty. He had taken to wearing an unkempt grey beard, which, along with his ragged clothing, gave him a tramp-like air. Dom João was pained by the recognition of Brazilian independence. His son's declaration had been followed by a mop-up operation, with residual Portuguese forces being chased out of Brazilian waters by a small fleet headed by the British mercenary, Lord Cochrane. In one instance the Portuguese had been pursued all the way across the Atlantic to the very mouth of the Tagus, where four vessels were burnt – a humiliating end to three centuries of colonial rule. The imperial dreams which had driven the early stages of the relocation – the idea of a dual, transatlantic kingdom – were now over.

On 4 March 1826, four months after signing away Brazil, Dom João left his second residence, the Bemposta convent in the centre of Lisbon, for a carriage ride. He was going to view a religious procession, but stopped off on the way to eat. He had his favourite dish – a chicken, basted in butter, finished off with a piece of cheese and some oranges. Four hours later he vomited up what would be his last full meal. On his return to the convent he suffered convulsions and collapsed. Attended by his physicians, his condition deteriorated over the following week. Dona Carlota was asked whether she wanted to see her husband but said she was too unwell to travel, even though she was staying only a few miles away in Queluz. Later that week, the king died.

Dom João was one of the few European monarchs to reign continuously through the Napoleonic era – 'the only one who ever tricked me' in Napoleon's own words, written during his exile years on St Helena. In retrospect, the Brazilian venture had been a success – overnight, the organs of a functioning state had been implanted in the colony, making the progression towards independence relatively smooth. It became a gradual process – from the opening of the ports in 1808, to the achievement of status as co-kingdom with Portugal in 1815, to the departure of the royal family in 1821 and Dom Pedro's *grito do Ipiranga* (cry of Ipiranga) in 1822. Brazil had largely been spared the violence that accompanied the independence of its neighbours, and had held together as the single gigantic nation which survives to this day.

The more immediate legacy of his rule was a constitutional crisis. With Dom Pedro Emperor of Brazil, his brother, Dom Miguel in exile in Austria and their mother, Dona Carlota still lusting after power, who would succeed Dom João on his death?

Dom João, an avoider of conflict to the last, ducked the whole issue. As he lay dying, he named his daughter Maria Teresa as temporary regent, adding vaguely that the succession would pass to 'Dom Pedro or one of his descendants'. Dom Pedro tried to clear up the ambiguities by taking the Portuguese throne and then abdicating in favour of his seven-year-old daughter, Maria da Glória, whom he promised in marriage to Dom Miguel. But when Maria da Glória arrived in Europe to take the throne, another counter-revolution – a carbon copy of the last – was under way. With Dona Carlota's support, Dom Miguel had returned from exile and declared himself absolute king. Hearing of this worrying turn of events, Dom Pedro branded his brother a traitor and recalled his daughter to Brazil.

And with the new crisis, one character who had played a vital role during the court's early years of exile returned for a curtain call. Lord Strangford was sent back to Rio to negotiate with Dom Pedro for Maria da Glória's return. In the intervening years he had served as a diplomat in Sweden and Russia and was seen by the Prime Minister, the Duke of Wellington, as the perfect choice. It was a delicate mission – 'You have not got an easy job, but you have a most important one,' wrote his colleague Sir Charles Bagot at the time. 'As to being back by Christmas, dream not of it. Your Christmas dinner of boiled monkeys and pine-apples will be eaten in Rio; but you may be back next summer . . .' Strangford was, not surprisingly, still unpopular in Rio and his attempts, along with those of the Austrian ambassador Baron von Marschall, to influence Dom Pedro met with some char-acteristically plain talking from the Emperor: 'The two sons of bitches thought they were going to take me to the cleaners,' Dom Pedro is alleged to have said, 'but I told them to get lost.' After several unpleasant months in Rio, Strangford sailed for London, having made no headway.

Dona Carlota did not have long to enjoy the success of her favourite son. She died alone in her bed at Queluz, two years after Dom Miguel seized the throne. Her last act was the signing of a will in which she remembered the palace attendants who had served her down the years. Her legacy, a family and a country at war, lived on in a fitting coda: in 1831, Dom Pedro returned to Portugal to lead the liberals in a battle to oust the *Miguelista* absolutists. The war raged for years, as Portugal was torn apart yet again. Dom Pedro's eventual victory only temporarily steadied a country that, decades on, was still feeling the effects of its thirteen-year abandonment.

Epilogue

Rio continued to expand through the nineteenth century, but its infrastructure improved only incrementally. The centrally-located *Campo de Santana* was made over as a miniature Bois de Boulogne with grottos, ponds and woods; a tunnel was driven through the granite mountains to the south of the city centre, opening the ocean-facing suburbs of Copacabana and Ipanema to development. The botanical gardens were rescued and revamped with, among other features, an imposing avenue of palms.

In the early twentieth century, the subtle topographical changes that Dom João's era had initiated – the landfills, the draining of swamp areas, the razing of low hills – were magnified into giant earth-moving exercises. Towering hills were removed, flattening out Rio's centre; more and more of the bay was reclaimed and a network of tunnels was bored through the city's mountain enclosures. Labourers destroyed whole neighbourhoods to make way for a series of boulevards which carved through the city centre. *Avenida Central* (present-day *Rio Branco*) brought a Parisian air to the capital. Monumental yet elegant, the thirty-metre-wide thoroughfare was lined with the cultural institutions of the day – the municipal theatre, the national library and the museum of fine arts – and framed in the distance by a monument of a different kind: a profile of the Sugar Loaf Mountain. Away from the centre, *Avenida Atlântica* swept

along the Copacabana beachfront, showcasing views long hidden behind walls of rock and forest. Promenades and landscaped
parks ushered in Rio's *belle époque*. By the 1920s, Rio was
enjoying a well-deserved reputation as one of the world's
premier pleasure cities.

The redesign of the city cleared the centre of its traditional
residents, the Afro-Brazilian street hawkers and small traders
who, in the time of Dom João, had shared the narrow alleyways
of old Rio with Portuguese noblemen, princes and ministers.
The rubble created by the demolition project ended up as
material for the graceful *Avenida Beira-Mar* along the Flamengo
and Botafogo beaches. There, bourgeois *cariocas* spent their
afternoons ambling along the reconstituted stonework which
had once housed the city's poor.

The ravages of twentieth-century development buried this
momentary elegance under block after block of hastily
constructed office and apartment buildings. There were
demographic reversals on the surrounding hillsides. Once
the breezy locales of the mansions and villas beloved of
Dona Carlota, they became refuges of the dispossessed: the
slaves freed into poverty after abolition, the poor driven
from the city centre. Clusters of dwellings grew up steep
hillsides, over hillocks and into the mountains, in a patch-
work of mud alleys and makeshift sheds. These were the
favelas, the slum sentinels of the new Rio. They would
progressively encircle affluent suburbs, hemming in the elite
who had created them.

Almost two centuries have passed since Rio so unexpectedly
played host to thousands of courtiers who poured across the
Atlantic to Brazil. In amongst the high-rise buildings and the
rickety redbrick slum dwellings, vestiges of this period remain –
the *Paço Real*, until the 1970s an anonymous telegraph office, has
been restored and is now a stylish arts centre, with a bookshop
and a wicker-chaired café. São Cristóvão has fared less well; its
run-down rooms and corridors now house a 1950s-style natural
history museum, with browning dinosaur skeletons and rows of
specimens under murky plate glass. In the courtyard stands a

series of headless classical statues; outside are the scrubby remains of what used to be a formally laid out garden.

Perhaps the most vivid reminder of the court's lengthy stay in the tropics is to be found on the shelves of the *Biblioteca Nacional* – the modern incarnation of the *Biblioteca Real*, which was freighted out of Lisbon during the Peninsular Wars. The climate made early inroads into the collection – on opening one white-ant-infested box, Marrocos described its contents as being reduced to 'vast carpets of powder'. But those that survived can still be found in the city to this day. It remains a superb collection, which includes an extremely rare two-volume Mo-guncia Bible dating from 1462, produced in Mainz by appren-tices to Gutenberg, alongside other riches from around Europe which, long after the departure of the royal family, have ended up permanently marooned in Brazil.

Dom João's *palma mater*, planted amid much ceremony when the court was still finding its feet in Rio, lived on as a memorial to his time in Rio. It survived through the nineteenth and well into the twentieth century, as the once rural site of the botanical gardens was engulfed by urban developments. The palm might well have lived even longer if it had not been hit by a single bolt of lightning in the early 1970s. It stayed upright, but withered and died. A part of its trunk was salvaged for display, an obscure link back to a Rio de Janeiro that has been virtually effaced by modernity, but that remains lodged in the *carioca* imagination.

Notes

Preface

p.1 On the building of Mafra, see António Filipe Pimentel, *Arquitectura e poder: o Real Edifício de Mafra*, Universidade de Coimbra, Coimbra, 1992, passim.

p.2 On the Brazilian gold rush, see Charles Ralph Boxer, *The Golden Age of Brazil: Growing Pains of a Colonial Society, 1695–1750*, Carcanet, Manchester, 1995, pp.30–83.

p.3 For a discussion of royalty, empire and the history of the royal tour, see David Cannadine, *Ornamentalism: How the British saw their Empire*, Penguin, London, 2001, pp.21–23; 114–120.

Chapter One: Exodus

p.7 On the life of Lord Strangford, see Rose Macaulay, *They Went to Portugal*, Penguin, Harmondsworth, 1985, pp.359–378; Edward Barrington de Fonblanque, *The Lives of Lord Strangford*, Cassell Petter & Galpin, London, 1877, pp.107–203.

pp.8–9 *I would rather divulge it to another than Lord Strangford* Henry Peter Brougham, *The Life and Times of Henry Lord Brougham*, 3 vols, William Blackwood and Sons, Edinburgh & London, 1871, vol 1, pp.368–369.

p.9 *respect either for common society or from those he has to do business with* Brougham, *Life*, vol 1, pp.368–369.

p.9 *like Helen and Hermione* Macaulay, *Portugal*, p.367.

p.12 *down to the last nail* Robert Blakeney, *A Boy in the Peninsular War*, Greenhill Books, London, 1989, p.12.

p.13 *would become known as the Peninsular Wars* Also known to the Spanish and Portuguese as the War of Independence.

p.14 *We have not as yet been able to secure a firm passage* Pedro Gomes to his father-in-law, the Count of Cunha, 2 November 1807, in Ângelo Pereira, *D. João VI, Príncipe e Rei*, 4 vols, Imprensa Nacional da Publicidade, Lisbon, 1953, vol 1, p.171.

p.14 For a detailed summary of the political manoeuvring of the court in the months leading up to the French invasion, see Alan K. Manchester, 'The Transfer of the Court to Brazil', in Henry H. Keith and S. F. Edwards, eds., *Conflict and Continuity in Brazilian Society*, University of South Carolina Press, Columbia, 1969, pp.148–153.

p.15 *little grey-black wicked eyes and his delightful wit* Marcus Cheke, *Carlota Joaquina: Queen of Portugal*, Sidgwick and Jackson Limited, London, 1947, p.16.

p.15 *a man of very mild but resolute character* Laure Junot Abrantès, *Memoirs of the Duchess D'Abrantès*, 8 vols, Henry Colburn and Richard Bentley, London, 1831, vol 4, p.99.

p.15 *I have had much conversation with M. d'Araújo* Strangford to Canning, Lisbon, 8 September 1807, Foreign Office (FO) 63, codex 55, no.55.

p.16 *a great and powerful empire* Strangford to Canning, Lisbon, 8 September 1807, FO 63, codex 55, no.55.

p.16 *the willing, or at least unresisting Vassal of France* Strangford's version of the Mafra meeting and its aftermath can be found at Strangford to Canning, Lisbon, 26 September 1807, FO 63, codex 55, no.63.

p.19 *his Majesty's government will be most thoroughly and manifestly justified* Strangford to Canning, Lisbon, 14 October 1807, FO 63, codex 55, no.71.

p.19 *Junot … entered Spain* Jean-Baptiste Antoine Marcellin de Marbot, *The Memoirs of Baron de Marbot*, 2 vols, Longmans, Green & Co., London, 1988, vol 1, p.295.

p.20 *Five times he made to sign* Macaulay, *Portugal*, p.359.

p.20 *impoverished, in want of everything* Pereira, *Príncipe e Rei*, vol 1, p.181.

p.21 *the court official Joaquim José de Azevedo was woken by a messenger* see Manchester, 'The Transfer of the Court to Brazil', p.153.

p.22 *If you looked to one side* Ângelo Pereira, *Os filhos d'El-Rei D. João VI*, Imprensa Nacional da Publicidade, Lisbon, 1946, p.123.

p.24 *holding back tears* For the many differing versions of Dom João's embarkation, see Lilia Moritz Schwarcz, *A Longa Viagem da Biblioteca dos Reis: do terremoto de Lisboa à Independência do Brasil*, Companhia das Letras, São Paulo, 2002, p.215.

p.25 *Don't drive so fast, they'll think we are fleeing!* Tobias Monteiro, *História do Império: a Elaboração da Independência*, Briguiet, Rio de Janeiro, 1927, p.59.

p.25 *Everyone wanted to board* Octávio Tarquínio de Sousa, *História dos fundadores do império do Brasil,* 10 vols, Olympio, Rio de Janeiro, 1972, vol 2, p.30.

p.25 *others were not so fortunate* Schwarcz, *Biblioteca,* p.213.

p.26 *on my return from the Belém docks* Manuel de Oliveira Lima, *Dom João VI no Brasil,* Topbooks, Rio de Janeiro, 1996, p.53. In the original, Joaquim José de Azevedo describes his own experiences in the third person. This has been converted into the first person for descriptive immediacy.

p.26 *My aunts immediately sent two carriages* Marques de Fronteira e d'Alorna, *Memórias do Marques de Fronteira e d'Alorna,* 6 vols, Imprensa da Universidade, Coimbra, 1932, vol 1, p.31.

p.27 *I learned that the greater part of the Royal Family* Strangford to Canning, HMS *Hibernia,* 30 November–2 December 1807, FO 63, codex 56, no.103.

p.27 *Everything depended on the degree of encouragement* Macaulay, *Portugal,* p.372.

p.28 *The wind swept in strongly from the bar* Fronteira e d'Alorna, *Memórias,* vol 1, p.32.

Chapter Two: The Journey

p.30 *We may never know how many had managed to board the fleet* Estimates have traditionally ranged from 8,000 to 15,000 (see Manchester, 'The Transfer of the Court to Brazil', pp.176–177, note 28), although recent research has argued that there may have been far fewer (see *Jornal do Brasil: Idéias,* 9 December 2000, '*Civilizados e radicais no século*').

p.31 *It is not possible to describe* Sousa, *História,* vol 2, p.38.

p.32 *The state we were in* Charles J. Esdaile, *The Peninsular War: a new history,* Allen Lane, London, 2002, p.27.

p.32 For accounts of the voyage to Brazil see Kenneth Light, *The Migration of the Royal Family of Portugal to Brazil in 1807/1808,* Rio de Janeiro, 1995; Antônio Marques Esparteiro et al., 'Transmigração da Família Real para o Brasil' in *História Naval Brasileira,* 2 vols, Ministério da Marinha, Rio de Janeiro, 1979, vol 2, pp.323–368; Thomas O'Neill, *A concise and accurate Account of the Proceedings of the Squadron under the command of Rear Admiral Sir W. S. Smith, in effecting the escape and escorting the Royal Family of Portugal to the Brazils …,* London, 1807.

p.33 *the weather so thick* Light, *Migration,* Reports and Letters (i).

p.34 *The mainmast broke* Pereira, *Príncipe e Rei,* vol 1, p.184.

p.34 *in the form of a blue lamp* Kenneth Light, 'A Viagem da Família Real para o Brasil, 1807–1808', in *D. João VI: um rei aclamado na América,* Museu Histórico Nacional, Rio de Janeiro, 2000, p.111.

p.35 *Dona Carlota paid a visit* A. J. de Mello Moraes, *História de Transladação da Corte Portugueza para o Brasil em 1807–1808*, Rio de Janeiro, 1872, p.63.

p.35 On the composition of the squadron see Manchester, 'The Transfer of the Court to Brazil', p.158; Schwarcz, *Biblioteca*, p.216.

p.35 *crowd of large armed merchant vessels; several armed brigs; thirty-six sail in all* John Barrow, *The Life and Correspondence of Admiral Sir William Sidney Smith*, 2 vols, Richard Bentley, London, 1848, vol 2, pp.264, 269.

p.35 *perhaps 1,600 according to the highest estimates* Monteiro, *Império*, p.59.

p.35 *The fleet left the Tagus in such haste* Strangford to Canning, HMS *Hibernia*, 30 November–2 December 1807, FO 63, codex 56, no.103.

p.36 *Rainha de Portugal – needs twenty-seven casks of water* Schwarcz, *Biblioteca*, p.213.

p.36 *the women, from Dona Carlota down, lined up to have their heads shaven* Monteiro, *Império*, p.59.

p.36 *Luiz Edmundo's romantic portraits* see Luiz Edmundo, *A Corte de Dom João no Rio de Janeiro (1808–21)*, 3 vols, Imprensa Nacional, Rio de Janeiro, 1939, vol 1, p.66.

p.37 *the number of persons who followed* O'Neill, *Proceedings*, pp.60–61. O'Neill's account is vivid but in some parts unreliable. He includes, for instance, an imaginary encounter between Junot and Dom João before the Portuguese fleet sets sail. This extract, though, is O'Neill's transcript of a letter he received in Rio from a Portuguese officer.

p.37 *yet Providence, in the midst of our distress granted us one blessing – few felt the effects of illness* They were, indeed, lucky. British troop transports of the era allowed for an average of one death in thirty on long voyages, although the rate could be far higher. See Robert Hughes, *The Fatal Shore*, Pan Books, London, 1987, p.144.

p.37 *One had left a teapot behind in Lisbon* Pereira, *Os filhos*, pp.114–115.

p.38 *in the most violent terms* Valentim Alexandre, *Os Sentidos do Império: Questão Nacional e Questão Colonial na Crise do Antigo Regime*, Edições Afrontamento, Porto, 1993, p.173.

p.39 *that other, smaller-scale royal flight* see Terry Coleman, *Nelson*, Bloomsbury, London, 2002, pp.182–185.

p.41 *whether through miscalculation or intention* There is a major debate about whether Cabral knew of Brazil before he set out. Although it is not inconceivable that he had some idea that there might be a land mass somewhere in the region of Brazil, there is no indication that the Cabral fleet had planned to visit this ill-defined territory *en route* to the East.

p.41 *without there being strong or adverse weather* Eduardo Bueno, *A viagem do descobrimento: A verdadeira história da expedição de Cabral*, Objetiva, Rio de Janeiro, 1998, p.46.

p.41 *long seaweeds sailors call 'botelho'*; *birds they call 'belly-rippers'* C. D. Ley, ed., *Portuguese Voyages 1498–1663: Tales from the Great Age of Discovery*, Phoenix Press, London, 2000, p.42.

p.41 *the birth certificate of Brazil* H. B. Johnson, 'Portuguese settlement, 1500–1580', in Leslie Bethell, ed., *Colonial Brazil*, Cambridge University Press, Cambridge, 1987, p.6.

p.42 *He merely threw them a red cap* An English translation of Caminha's letter can be found in Ley, *Voyages*, pp.41–59; for the original Portuguese and a discussion of the letter, see Henrique Campos Simões, *As Cartas do Brasil*, Editora do UESC, Ilhéus, 1999, passim.

p.44 *There is some evidence that Caminha's letter made the return trip to Brazil* Simões, *As Cartas*, p.39.

p.44 *the docks appeared empty* Mello Moraes, *Transladação*, p.67.

p.47 *roads shall be opened* H. V. Livermore, *A History of Portugal*, Cambridge University Press, Cambridge, 1947, p.397.

p.48 *Such a large number of people have come* Schwarcz, *Biblioteca*, p.223.

p.48 *Respecting the Lisbon business* Brougham to Earl Grey Albany, 31 December 1807, in Brougham, *Life*, vol 1, p.395.

p.49 *I have … a perfect recollection* William Napier, 'A reply to Lord Strangford's "Observations"', *History of the War in the Peninsula*, 4 vols, London, 1848, vol 1, p. xxii.

p.49 *Everyone is agreed that the choice of a minister for Brazil* Brougham to Earl Grey Albany, 31 December 1807, in Brougham, *Life*, vol 1, p.396.

Chapter Three: The Lisbon Court

p.51 *She doesn't do what she's told* Sara Marques Pereira, *D. Carlota Joaquina e os 'Espelhos de Clio': actuação política e figurações historiográficas*, Livros Horizonte, Lisbon, 1999, p.29.

p.51 *Our beloved Carlota pleases me greatly* Marques Pereira, *Espelhos*, p.30.

p.52 *she is very clever* Pereira, *Príncipe e Rei*, vol 1, pp.47–48.

p.52 *without any shame whatsoever* Ibid., vol 1, pp.47–48.

p.52 *the curious birds and flowers last sent from the Brazils* William Beckford, *Recollections of an excursion to the monasteries of Alcobaça and Batalha*, Centaur Press Ltd, Fontwell, 1972, pp.202–209.

p.53 *the most hideous specimen of ugliness* Abrantès, *Memoirs*, vol 4, p.230.

p.54 *When I entered the Princess of Brazil's [Dona Carlota's] drawing room* Ibid., vol 4, p.234.

p.55 *neglected quinta of orange trees* Beckford, *Recollections*, p.197.

p.55 *The beings who wandered about this limbo* Ibid., p.215.

p.55 *purity and elegance* Ibid., pp.213–214. This quote sounds a little too good to be true, anticipating, albeit obliquely, the royal flight to Brazil, and may also be a case of Beckford's memory playing tricks on him.

p.55 *fifteen or twenty unhappy aspirants* Ibid., p.215.

p.57 *conviction that she was irrevocably doomed* Ida Macalpine and Richard Hunter, *George III and the Mad-Business*, Pimlico, London, 1991, p.96.

p.57 *she eats barley and oyster stew* Olga S. Opfell, *Queens, Empresses, Grand Duchesses and Regents: Women Rulers of Europe, A.D. 1328–1989*, McFarland, Jefferson N.C., 1989, p.175.

p.57 *I have the displeasure to tell you* Edmundo, *A Corte*, vol 1, p.151.

p.57 *Her Majesty has frequently exclaimed* F. Winslow, *Physic and Physicians*, 2 vols, London, 1839, vol 2, p.175.

p.58 *Conqueror, under God, of Diseases* Macalpine and Hunter, *Mad-Business*, pp.104–6. On Queen Maria's mental decline, see Caetano Beirão, *D. Maria I 1777–1792*, Impresa Nacional de Publicidade, Lisbon, 1944 pp.399–420.

p.58 *either madly or hypocritically religious* Macalpine and Hunter, *Mad-Business*, pp.104–106.

p.59 For descriptions of Dom João, see Pereira, *Príncipe e Rei*, vol 1, passim; A. J. de Mello Moraes, *Chronica Geral do Brasil*, 2 vols, Rio de Janeiro, 1886, vol 2, pp.154–158.

p.61 *conjugal guerrilla war* Marques Pereira, *Espelhos*, p.53.

p.61 *little hard evidence to prove Dona Carlota's amorous escapades* see Monteiro, *Império*, p.85, note 2.

p.61 *reported in a London newspaper* Edmundo, *A Corte*, vol 1, p.239.

p.63 *Our man [Dom João] is worsening by the day* Francisca L. Nogueira de Azevedo, *Carlota Joaquina na Corte do Brasil*, Civilização Brasileiro, Rio de Janeiro, 2003, p.37.

p.63 *the Prince's mind is deteriorating by the day* Dona Carlota to Carlos IV, 13 August 1806, Queluz, Marques Pereira, *Espelhos*, p.65.

p.64 *mortified by domestic problems* Monteiro, *Império*, p.82.

p.64 On Palmela see Cheke, *Carlota*, pp.69–75. Dom Pedro de Sousa e Holstein became successively Count, Marquis and Duke of Palmela (sometimes spelt Palmella). For clarity and consistency, I have, following common usage in the literature, referred to him simply as 'Palmela' throughout – even here, where his title is anachronistic.

p.64 *The same ignorance, servile ambition and degradation* Cheke, *Carlota*, pp.70–73.

p.65 *he watched from his window* see Palmela's testimony in Edmundo, *A Corte*, vol 2, pp.612–613.

p.65 *Dear mother, I cannot willingly fling myself into a well* Cheke, *Carlota*, p.19.

p.66 *Mother of my heart, my life, my soul* Azevedo, *Carlota*, p.25.

p.67 *On the 20th of this month* Pereira, *Príncipe e Rei*, vol 1, p.183.

Chapter Four: 'Emperor of the West'

p.69 *a fortress in the Midlands* Paul Johnson, *Napoleon*, Weidenfeld & Nicolson, London, 2002, p.68.

p.70 For accounts of Portuguese maritime exploration in the fifteenth century see Peter Russell, *Prince Henry 'the Navigator' A Life*, Yale University Press, New Haven, 2000, passim; C. R. Boxer, *The Portuguese Seaborne Empire, 1415–1825*, Carcanet, Manchester, 1991, pp.15–38; Malyn Newitt, ed., *The First Portuguese Colonial Empire*, University of Exeter, Exeter, 1986, pp.1–35.

p.72 *a nineteenth-century Midlands factory floor* Descriptions of the working of a sugar mill and their modern industrial aspect are taken from Stewart B. Schwartz, 'Plantations and Peripheries, *c.*1580–*c.*1750', in Bethell, ed., *Colonial*, pp.67–81.

p.74 *mementoes from the great hulk* John Correia-Afonso, ed., *Intrepid itinerant: Manuel Godinho and his journey from India to Portugal in 1663*, Oxford University Press, Oxford, 1990, p.26.

p.75 For biographical details on António Vieira, see C. R. Boxer, *The Dutch in Brazil 1624–1654*, Clarendon Press, Oxford, 1957, pp.271–273; Thomas Cohen, *The Fire of Tongues: António Vieira and the Missionary Church in Brazil and Portugal*, Stanford University Press, Stanford, 1998, passim.

p.75 *Vieira's religious and political beliefs* Kirsten Schultz, *Tropical Versailles: Empire, Monarchy, and the Portuguese Royal Court in Rio de Janeiro, 1808–1821*, Routledge, New York, 2001, p.16.

p.75 *would assign a place for a palace* Schwarcz, *Biblioteca*, p.194.

p.76 On the Brazilian gold rush see A. J. R. Russell-Wood, 'The gold cycle, *c.*1690–1750', in Bethell, ed., *Colonial*, pp.190–243; Boxer, *Golden*, pp.30–83.

p.76 *Nothing like it had been seen before* Boxer, *Golden*, p.47.

p.76 *Whites, Coloured, and Blacks* Ibid., p.41.

p.78 *I consider, perhaps dreamily* D. Luís da Cunha, *Instruções Inéditas de D. Luís da Cunha e Marco António de Azevedo Coutinho*, Coimbra University Press, Coimbra, 1929, pp.211–212.

p.78 *he assured me* Ibid., pp.211–212.

p.79 On the Treaty of Madrid (1750), see Boxer, *Golden*, pp.293–297.

p.79 *tried to isolate Brazil* For a list of decrees passed by Lisbon to restrict commercial activity in Brazil outside of colonial export crops, see Norbertino Domingos Bahiense, *Martins e a revolucão Pernambucana de*

1817, Instituto Histórico e Geográfico do Espírito Santo, Espírito Santo, 1974, pp.42–43.

p.80 On Pombal, see Kenneth Maxwell, *Pombal, Paradox of the Enlightenment*, Cambridge University Press, Cambridge, 1995.

p.80 *thoughts again turned to transferring the capital to Brazil* Luiz Norton, *A Corte de Portugal no Brasil*, Companhia Editora Nacional, São Paulo, 1979, p.5.

p.80 *have clandestinely attempted the usurpation of the entire state of Brazil* John Hemming, *Red Gold: the conquest of the Brazilian Indians*, Papermac, London, 1995, p.496.

p.81 *the dominions in Europe* Kenneth Maxwell, 'The Generation of the 1790s and the Idea of Luso-Brazilian Empire', in Dauril Alden, ed., *Colonial Roots of Modern Brazil*, University of California Press, Berkeley, 1973, p.137.

p.81 *Your highness should order all your warships to be armed* Schwarcz, *Biblioteca*, p.195.

p.82 *The only way left to defend* Pereira, *Príncipe e Rei*, vol 1, p.131–132.

p.82 *The reluctance to remove was universal* Macaulay, *Portugal*, p.365.

p.83 *And it wouldn't just be the names of the months that would change* Anon., *Plano sabio, profferido no Parlamento de Inglaterra pelo ministro de estado Mr. Pitt, sobre a continuação da guerra com a França, e trasladação do throno de Portugal para o novo império do Brasil. Com Licença da Meza do Desembargo do Paço*, Lisbon, 1808, p.12.

p.83 *Brazil … had not been untouched by the ideas of the age* see Maxwell, 'The Generation of the 1790s and the Idea of Luso-Brazilian Empire', passim.

p.84 *I have something of great consequence* Paulo Bonavides and Roberto Amaral, *Textos políticos da História do Brasil*, 9 vols, Senado Federal, Subsecretaria de Edições Técnicas, Brasilia, 1996, vol 1, p.161.

p.84 *an elaborate show trial in Rio* Schultz, *Versailles*, p.49.

p.85 *everyone would become Frenchmen* Maxwell, 'The Generation of the 1790s and the Idea of Luso-Brazilian Empire', p.119.

Chapter Five: A New World

p.86 *Dom Marcos de Noronha e Brito … had received a bewildering array of orders* Schwarcz, *Biblioteca*, pp.234–238.

p.87 *It was two minutes to three in the afternoon* Luiz Gonçalves dos Santos, *Memórias para servir à História do Reino do Brasil*, 2 vols, Livraria Editora Zélio Valverde, Rio de Janeiro, 1943, vol 1, p.208.

p.90 *from the far off Tagus* Schultz, *Versailles*, p.39.

p.90 *Dona Carlota could not contain her disappointment* On the various versions of Dona Carlota's behaviour on arrival, see Monteiro, *Império*, p.74.

p.92 *and not just short letters* Pereira, *Os filhos*, pp.139–141.

p.93 *pomp and magnificence never seen before in the city* dos Santos, *Memórias*, vol 1, p.263.

p.93 *perhaps he had a certain audience in mind* Records of the Brazilian reaction to the Portuguese court's arrival and residence are, unfortunately, scant. Dos Santos's lengthy memoir is a blow by blow account of events, festivals, appointments etc., but it is fawning in the extreme and contains little personal commentary, in contrast to John Luccock's memoirs, *Notes on Rio de Janeiro, and the southern parts of Brazil taken during a residence of ten years in that country, from 1808 to 1818*, London, 1820, and the Portuguese archivist Luiz Joaquim dos Santos Marrocos's candid letters home (see Chapter 8).

p.94 *now even the United States was barred* Paul W. Schroeder, *The Transformation of European Politics 1763–1848*, Oxford University Press, Oxford, 1994, pp.435–438.

p.94 *The best vehicle which the rich colony of Brazil* Luccock, *Notes*, pp.96–97.

p.94 *a garrison town, though without walls* Luccock, *Notes*, p.79.

p.95 *Captain Cook ... had likened it to Liverpool; Watkin Tench ... compared it to Chester or Exeter* Jean Marcel Carvalho França, ed., *Visões do Rio de Janeiro Colonial: antologia de textos, 1531–1800*, Olympio, Rio de Janeiro, 1999, p.189.

p.95 *Beyond these limits* Luccock, *Notes*, p.39.

p.96 *Ponha-se na Rua* Lilia Moritz Schwarcz, *As Barbas do Imperador: D. Pedro II, um monarca nos trópicos*, Companhia das Letras, São Paulo, 1998, p.584, note 6.

p.96 *prudently poor* Luccock, *Notes*, p.100.

p.97 *a full apparatus of state was in operation* For a summary of the setting up of the bureaucracy in Rio, see Manchester, 'The Transfer of the Court to Brazil', pp.168–173.

p.97 *replicas ... with 'do Brasil' tacked on to their names* Manchester, 'The Transfer of the Court to Brazil', p.168.

p.99 *Cariocas ... would soon be familiar with the royal family in their midst* For descriptions of the royal family's public life in Rio, see A. J. de Mello Moraes, *Chronica*, vol 2, pp.142–158; and Edmundo, *A Corte*, vol 3, passim.

p.100 *It is very curious to notice* Carlos H. Oberacker Jr, *A Imperatriz Leopoldina*, Conselho Federal de Cultura, Rio de Janeiro, 1973, p.168.

p.102 On the history of the botanical gardens, see João Barbosa Rodrigues, *Hortus Fluminensis*, Rio de Janeiro, 1894, passim; Anyda Marchant, 'Dom João's Botanical Garden', *The Hispanic American Historical Review*, vol 41, no.2, May 1961, pp. 259–274.

p.103 *a free loan to the treasury* Luiz Joaquim dos Santos Marrocos, '*Cartas de*

Luiz Joaquim dos Santos Marrocos', Anais da Biblioteca Nacional do Rio de Janeiro, vol 56, Rio de Janeiro, 1934, pp.22–23.

Chapter Six: The War Years

p.107 *We are still here* Pereira, *Príncipe e Rei*, vol 3, pp.61–63.

p.107 *prevail upon Mr. Canning* Ibid., vol 3, pp.61–63.

p.107 *You will endeavour on all occasions* Canning to Strangford, London, 17 April 1808, FO 63, codex 59 no.1.

p.108 *He had almost made up His mind* Strangford to Canning, Rio de Janeiro, 24 July 1808, FO 63, codex 60, no.1.

p.108 *I hope that soon I will be writing to you as a Count* Pereira, *Príncipe e Rei*, vol 3, p.64.

p.109 *to declare in favour of the Prince Regent* Alan K. Manchester, *British Preëminence in Brazil: Its Rise and Decline*, University of North Carolina Press, Chapel Hill, 1933, p.114.

p.109 On disputes over the Banda Oriental, see Manchester, *Preëminence*, pp.109–112.

p.111 *Mother of my heart; I am your sister* Azevedo *Carlota*, p.25.

p.112 *Your brother and I are the best possible friends* Pereira, *Príncipe e Rei*, vol 3, pp.67–74.

p.114 *While the procession was walking* Esdaile, *Peninsular*, p.92.

p.115 *honourable only to the enemy; total ruin of a great cause; all England has been deceived in its opinion of Sir Arthur Wellesley* Gordon Kent Thomas, *Wordsworth's Dirge and Promise: Napoleon, Wellington and the Convention of Cintra*, University of Nebraska Press, Lincoln, 1971, pp.23–25.

p.115 *Dom João … first heard of the Portugal campaign through newspaper reports* Alexandre, *Os Sentidos*, p.187.

p.117 *Our beards were long and ragged* Michael Glover, *The Peninsular War 1807–1814: A concise military history*, Penguin Books, London, 2001, p.82.

p.118 *the fine balustrades [were] broken* Esdaile, *Peninsular*, p.194.

p.119 *… when Your Highness is called on* Pereira, *Os filhos*, p.151.

p.119 *Your plan of appearing in Río de La Plata* Marques Pereira, *Espelhos*, p.93.

p.119 *my love; my darling sweetheart; your loving wife* See letters in Marques Pereira, *Espelhos*, passim; Pereira, *Os filhos*, passim; Pereira, *Príncipe e Rei*, passim.

p.120 *He felt himself deeply wounded* Strangford to Canning, Rio de Janeiro, 9 October 1808, FO 63, codex 60, no.20.

p.120 *the batteries of Rio de Janeiro should fire on her* Manchester, *Preëminence*, p.123.

p.120 *I have not found His Majesty's Minister Plenipotentiary* Tom Pocock, *A*

Thirst For Glory: the Life of Sir Sidney Smith, Aurum Press, London, 1996, p.210.

p.121 *diamonds of little value and other cheap stones* Azevedo, *Carlota*, p.132.

p.123 *We have spared neither house* A. H. Norris and R.W. Bremmer, *The Lines of Torres Vedras*, The British Historical Society of Portugal, Lisbon, 1980, p.16.

p.124 *Old people, lame and sick people* Glover, *Peninsular*, p.139.

p.125 *subsisting on British handouts* Richard Wellesley, *Letter Books*, 14 vols, vols 9–10, Despatches of Lord Wellesley to Percy Clinton Sydney Smythe, Ms. 49987–8, British Library, 1810–1812, Wellesley to Strangford, 29 October 1810, Ms. 49987, no.19.

p.126 *Dom João had begun ordering the shipment of bulky court paraphernalia* Mello Moraes, *Chronica*, vol 2, p.133.

p.126 *almost finished the embarkation of the Royal House's treasures* Schwarcz, *Biblioteca*, p.266.

p.126 On the Marquis of Loulé see Oliveira Lima, *Dom João*, pp.588–589; Schultz, *Versailles*, pp.158–159.

p.127 *I waited for my king and at a distance* Schultz, *Versailles*, p.159. By this stage (1817) Dona Maria I had died and Dom João was king (see Chapter 9).

p.128 *The genius of Brazil* Luccock, *Notes*, p.253.

p.128 *a large and excellent orchestra erupted* dos Santos, *Memórias*, vol 1, p.337.

Chapter Seven: A British Invasion

p.130 *royal protocol … was enforced with a ruthlessness* Neill Macaulay, *Dom Pedro: the struggle for liberty in Brazil and Portugal*, Duke University Press, Durham, 1986, p.42.

p.130 *Thomas Sumter … was stopped by Dona Carlota's guards* Oliveira Lima, *Dom João*, p.181.

p.131 *branding her husband 'a pimp'* Oliveira Lima, *Dom João*, p.187.

p.131 *Dom João was slipping into an easy routine* See Mello Moraes, *Chronica*, vol 2, pp. 154–158; Macaulay, *Dom Pedro*, p.48; Schwarcz, *Biblioteca*, p.290.

p.132 *Your brother is alone in this court* Pereira, *Príncipe e Rei*, vol 3, p.75.

p.133 *one mingled mass of cashmeres* Herbert Heaton, 'A Merchant Adventurer in Brazil', *Journal of Economic History*, 6:1, pp.1–23, May 1946, p.8.

p.133 On the British trade invasion see Heaton, 'A Merchant Adventurer in Brazil'; Gilberto Freyre, *Ingleses no Brasil: Aspectos da influência britânica sobre a vida, a paisagem e a cultura do Brasil*, José Olympio, Rio de Janeiro, 1948, pp.147–281; John Mawe, *Travels in the Interior of Brazil, Particularly in the Gold and Diamond districts of that country …*, Philadelphia, 1816, pp. 110–112. For a summary of Luccock's life see Heaton, 'A Merchant Adventurer in Brazil', passim.

p.134 *sufficient for several years; a man wants a greatcoat* Heaton, 'A Merchant Adventurer in Brazil', pp.9, 13.

p.134 *when you hear of a vessel named Rapid or Active* Ibid., p.11.

p.135 *prevailed upon a Gent; selling beat iron by the quintal* Ibid., pp.11–12.

p.135 *Cheese was made in the district of Minas-Geraes* Luccock, *Notes*, p.47.

p.135 *civilised Indians* Luccock, *Notes*, p.273.

p.135 *the English have become masters* Heaton, *A Merchant Adventures in Brazil*, p.8.

p.136 On the treaty, its passage and the fallout in Rio, see Manchester, *Preëminence*, pp.77–108.

p.136 *being in the same mind* Strangford to Wellesley, Rio de Janeiro, 12 March 1810, FO 63, codex 83, no.17.

p.136 *We have won everything* Pereira, *Príncipe e Rei*, vol 3, p.84.

p.137 *portrait of His Majesty [George III] enriched with diamonds* Wellesley, *Letter Books*, Wellesley to Strangford, 27 November 1810, vol 9, Ms. 49987, no.20; 8 May 1811, vol 10, Ms. 49988, no.10.

p.137 *With the abolitionist cause gathering pace in Europe* On the long road to abolition in Brazil, see Leslie Bethell, *The Abolition of the Brazilian Slave Trade: Britain, Brazil and the slave trade question, 1807–1869*, Cambridge University Press, Cambridge, 1970, passim.

p.137 *the very child and champion of the slave trade* Leslie Bethell, *George Canning and the Independence of Latin America*, The Hispanic and Luso-Brazilian Councils, London, 1970, p.14.

p.138 *anything unpleasant had occurred among the British* Luccock, *Notes*, p.95.

p.138 *in a case that caused consternation within the court* Schultz, *Versailles*, p.215.

p.139 *whose Union Jacks, Red Lions, Jolly Tars* Elizabeth Mavor, ed., *The Captain's Wife: the South American journals of Maria Graham 1821–23*, Weidenfeld & Nicolson, London, 1993, p.61.

p.139 *The Brazilians are in general jealous and discontented* Strangford to Wellesley, Rio de Janeiro, 15 November 1810, FO 63, codex 86, no.86.

p.139 *insults daily offered to their Prejudices* Strangford to Wellesley, Rio de Janeiro, 15 November 1810, FO 63, codex 86, no.86.

p.139 *all sorts of exchange rates and algorithms* Schultz, *Versailles*, p.216.

p.139 *It is customary for the English* Jacques Arago, *Narrative of a voyage around the World ...*, Treuttel and Wurtz, London, 1823, p.72.

p.140 *Strangford's ... heavy-handed interventions in the ongoing fight for the Banda Oriental* See Manchester, *Preëminence*, pp.126–134.

p.140 *Your brother will hardly have time to write to you* Pereira, *Príncipe e Rei*, vol 3, p.78.

p.141 *The situation in this court is truly singular* Strangford to Castlereagh, Rio de Janeiro, 31 December 1813, FO 63, codex 148, no.151.

p.142 *The hatred of the Natives of Brazil* Strangford to Castlereagh, Rio de Janeiro, 20 February 1814, FO 63, codex 167, no.9.

p.142 *that connection with England* Strangford to Castlereagh, Rio de Janeiro, 20 February 1814, FO 63, codex 167, no.8.

p.143 *My Lord, I should fail in my Duty* Strangford to Castlereagh, Rio de Janeiro, 20 February 1814, FO 63, codex 167, no.9.

p.143 *impatient to visit His Native Country* Strangford to Castlereagh, Rio de Janeiro, 6 April 1814, FO 63, codex 167, no.23.

p.144 *all the world knew the sovereign's word was false* Strangford in Manchester, *Preëminence*, p.103.

p.144 *would serve in the eyes of the Portuguese Nation* Strangford to Castlereagh, Rio de Janeiro, 31 December 1814, FO 63, codex 169, no.126.

p.144 *two song books which he had borrowed* Marrocos, *Cartas*, p.18.

p.145 *At times he abused my confidence* Edmundo, *A Corte*, vol 2, pp.542–543.

p.145 For a colourful account of restoration Europe, see J.B. Priestley, *The Prince of Pleasure and his Regency 1811–20*, Penguin Books, London, 2002.

p.147 *addresses of exultation and gratitude … poured in* Luccock, *Notes*, p.569.

p.147 On the involved negotiations at the Congress of Vienna, see Oliveira Lima, *Dom João*, pp.303–334.

Chapter Eight: The Archivist

p.150 *My father … I am writing this* Marrocos, *Cartas*, pp.29–30.

p.151 *If I had known the state* Ibid., p.31.

p.151 *The royal palaces suffered extensive damage* Schwarcz, *Biblioteca*, p.264.

p.152 *Brazil's climate was more pestilent than Mozambique* Marrocos, *Cartas*, p.38.

p.152 *in one year alone* Ibid., p.60.

p.152 *Dom João was forced to suspend* Ibid., p.66.

p.152 *violent nervous fever* Macaulay, *Dom Pedro*, p.40.

p.152 *The Infanta D. Maria Anna has been sick for many days with a stomach spasm* Sousa, *História*, vol 2, p.64.

p.153 *land of savages* Marrocos, *Cartas*, p.68.

p.153 *You have to punish them* Ibid., p.42.

p.153 *he has been given a dozen palmatoadas* Ibid., p.73.

p.153 *when I think about the negative aspects* Ibid., pp.112–113.

p.154 *I sincerely confess* Ibid., p.61.

p.154 *I am so scandalised by this country* Ibid., p.112.

p.155 *Should they return; Only plain common goods* Heaton, 'A Merchant Adventurer in Brazil', p.14.

p.156 *I don't know what His Highness's reply* Marrocos, *Cartas*, p.200.

p.156 *The current assembling of our warships* Ibid., p.223.

p.156 *António de Araújo is undertaking major works* Ibid., p.208.

p.157 *the Baron of Rio Sêcco is building a superb palace* Ibid., p.111.

p.157 *you say that there [in Lisbon] they are readying the palace* Ibid., p.222.

p.157 *orders have been given to examine the roads* Ibid., pp.222–223.

p.158 *We are continuing to see large-scale works* Ibid., p.216.

p.158 *I am living with a carioca* Ibid., p.213.

p.158 *After reaching the age of thirty-two* Ibid., p.177.

p.159 *Brazil has opened my eyes* Ibid., p.204.

p.159 *in no way in keeping* Ibid., pp.249–253.

p.159 *I find it incredible* Ibid., p.322.

p.160 *I don't want her brought up* Ibid., p.320.

p.160 *I have bought a black wet-nurse ... for the price of 179$200 réis* Ibid., p.369.
179$200 *réis* means 179 *milréis*, 200 *réis*, where one *milréis* = 1,000 *réis*.
At the time Marrocos was writing, one *milréis* was roughly equivalent to one US dollar. See Stanley Stein, *Vassouras: A Brazilian Coffee County, 1850–1900*, Harvard University Press, Cambridge, Mass, 1957, p.293.

p.161 *been thinking about for some time* Cartas, p.368.

p.161 *this is the moment to decide* Ibid., p.383.

Chapter Nine: The Vicissitudes of Exile

p.163 *the fountain head* Malyn Newitt, *Lord Beresford and the Governadores of Portugal*, 2001, p.6.

p.163 *The state of affairs here is indeed very critical* Beresford to Sir David and Lady Elizabeth Pack, in Newitt, *Beresford*, p.10.

p.163 *I see much danger* Beresford to Lady Elizabeth Pack, in Newitt, *Beresford*, p.11.

p.164 *because of the inevitable travails of a long journey* Pereira, *Os filhos*, p.182.

p.164 *a thousand and one contingencies* Ibid., p.182.

p.165 *There is now no doubt* Marrocos, *Cartas*, pp.257–258.

p.166 *There have been moments of relief* Ibid., p.583.

p.167 *The departure was spectacular* Ibid., p.285.

p.167 *and out through the heads* dos Santos, *Memórias*, vol 2, p.528. In Marrocos's version of events (*Cartas*, p.285), Dona Carlota accompanied the fleet as it left the bay by land until Praia Vermelha, from where she watched the ships disappear over the horizon.

p.168 *she died in Madrid* Macaulay, *Dom Pedro*, p.70.

p.168 *land of monkeys and blacks* Oberacker, *A Imperatriz*, pp.34–35.

p.168 *she still moved house regularly* Sousa, *História*, vol 2, p.65; Monteiro, *Império*, p.86.

p.169 *an incident that suggests corners were being cut* Monteiro, *Império*, p.85.

p.169 *Her Royal Highness was so attentive* Marrocos, *Cartas*, p.165.

p.170 *Dona Carlota ... granted his slave girl her freedom* Arago, *Narrative*, pp. 88–
        89. Mary C. Karasch, *Slave life in Rio de Janeiro*, Princeton University
        Press, Princeton, 1987, p.339, wrongly attributes this act to Dom João.

p.171 *repeatedly misspelling it 'Migel'* Macaulay, *Dom Pedro*, p.33.

p.171 *My Mother and my Senhora* Ibid., p.47.

p.171 *my brother Miguel and I* Roderick J. Barman, *Citizen Emperor: Pedro II
        and the Making of Brazil, 1825–91*, Stanford University Press, Stan-
        ford, 1999, p.15.

p.172 *Italians, French, Spanish Americans* Sousa, *História*, vol 2, p.77.

p.173 *his hand was ripped apart in an explosion* Marrocos, *Cartas*, p.339.

p.173 *an incident involving Dona Carlota* Mello Moraes, *Chronica*, vol 2, p.176.

p.173 *Dom João himself was not free from scandal* Macaulay, *Dom Pedro*, p.69.

Chapter Ten: A Subtropical Rome

p.176 *It is impossible to describe* Marrocos, *Cartas*, p.444.

p.176 *I still hate them* Ibid., p.223.

p.177 *a new colony just outside Rio called Nova Friburgo* The scheme was not a
        success. Sickness broke out on board the Rio-bound boat, and scores
        died before even setting foot in Brazil. Promised land and slaves to
        work it, the Swiss were issued with hoes and seeds on arrival.
        Farquhar Mathison, a traveller, came across the settlement some
        years after it had been established and found only rows of empty
        houses surrounded by abandoned farmland. Of the original 700,
        only 300 remained, the rest having fled to more established farming
        districts or ended up back in Rio. See Desmond Gregory, *Brute New
        World: The Rediscovery of Latin America in the Early Nineteenth Century*,
        British Academic Press, London, 1992, pp.162–163.

p.177 *the city's administrators went so far as to propose* See Viana's recom-
        mendations in *Gabinete de Dom João VI*, Arquivo Nacional, Rio de
        Janeiro, Caixa 1; Maço 2; no.25, 22 August 1810.

p.178 *not quite of European tint* C. F. Philipp von Martius and Johann Baptist
        von Spix, *Travels in Brazil in the years 1817–1820*, 2 vols, Longman
        Hurst & co., London, 1824, vol 1, p.62.

p.179 *a slave orchestra and choir ... performed for the royal family* Schwarcz,
        Barbas, pp.222–225.

p.179 *Their whole gait announces effeminacy* Macaulay, *Dom Pedro*, p.68.

p.180 *cuisine heavily influenced by their colonial heritage* Schwarcz, *Barbas*, p.290.

p.180 *notably fastidious in the cleanliness* Luiz Edmundo, *Rio in the time of the
        Viceroys*, J. R. de Oliveira, Rio de Janeiro, 1936, p.186.

p.180 *As a rule the Brazilians* Ibid., p.186.

p.181 *not washing was a point of honour* Ibid., p.184–185.

p.181 *the carnivalesque world immortalised by Jean-Baptiste Debret* See Jean-Baptiste Debret, *Voyage pittoresque et historique au Brésil, ou, Séjour d'un artiste français au Brésil, depuis 1816 jusqu'en 1831*, 3 vols, Firmin Didot Frères, Paris, 1834–1839, passim.

p.182 On slavery in Brazil, see Robert Edgar Conrad, *Children of God's Fire: A Documentary History of Black Slavery in Brazil*, Princeton University Press, Princeton, 1983, passim; Robert Edgar Conrad, *World of Sorrow*, Louisiana State University Press, Baton Rouge, 1986, passim; Joseph C. Miller, *Way of Death: Merchant Capitalism and the Angolan Slave Trade*, James Curry, 1988, passim; for Rio see Karasch, *Slave*, passim.

p.182 *A stranger unacquainted with the slave trade* Peter Fryer, *Rhythms of Resistance: African musical heritage in Brazil*, Pluto, London, 2000, p.6.

p.183 *he acquired two pairs of slaves* João Capistrano de Abreu, *Chapters of Brazil's Colonial History 1500–1800*, Oxford University Press, Oxford, 1997, p.51.

p.183 *the archivist Marrocos became typical* Marrocos, *Cartas*, p.377.

p.183 *mouthing Ave Marias mechanically* Luccock, *Notes*, p.64.

p.184 *Many of the negro slaves are remarkably well formed* James Henderson, *A History of Brazil; comprising its geography, commerce, colonization, aboriginal inhabitants ...*, London, 1821, p.74.

p.184 *One of the things that always excites* Jurandir Malerba, *A corte no exílio: civilização e poder no Brasil às vésperas da independência (1808–1821)*, Companhia das Letras, São Paulo, 2000, p.141.

p.184 *The smell and heat in the room* Karasch, *Slave*, p.38.

p.185 *Expecting that the Slave trade* Conrad, *God's Fire*, p.31.

p.185 *The court passed a series of measures* Conrad, *Sorrow*, p.58.

p.186 *whipping them in the streets* Schultz, *Versailles*, p.125.

p.187 *an urban economy ... had grown up around the use of slaves in Rio* Karasch, *Slave*, p.205.

p.187 *In a fascinating set of legal cases* Schultz, *Versailles*, pp.165–176.

p.188 *runaways who have reached the spirit land* Conrad, *God's Fire*, p.124.

Chapter Eleven: The Turning Point

p.189 *Several fine alleys of bread-fruit trees* Martius and Spix, *Travels*, vol 1, p.221.

p.190 On the history of the royal library, see Schwarcz, *Biblioteca*, passim.

p.191 *acclamation* Coronations had been abandoned in Portugal after King Sebastião was killed in 1578 on the battlefield in Morocco. See Macaulay, *Dom Pedro*, p.66.

p.191 *a violent Paralytic Affliction* Strangford to Castlereagh, Rio de Janeiro, 31 December 1813, FO 63, codex 148, no.151.

p.191 *It is in fact somewhat surprising* Cheke, *Carlota*, p.52.

p.191 *full of good intentions* Oliveira Lima, *Dom João*, p.571.

p.193 *The freedmen and the slaves* Ibid., p.501.

p.194 *Death to aristocrats Documentos Históricos*, 110 vols, Biblioteca Nacional do Rio de Janeiro, 1953, vol 102, pp.12–13; Emilia Viotti da Costa, *The Brazilian Empire: Myths and Histories*, University of North Carolina Press, Chapel Hill, 2000, p.8.

p.194 *half-castes, mulattoes and Creoles Documentos Históricos*, vol 102, pp.12–13; Costa, *Empire*, p.11.

p.194 *an astounding event* Roderick J. Barman, *Brazil: The Forging of a Nation, 1798–1852*, Stanford University Press, Stanford, 1988, p.57.

p.195 *to mount a rescue operation from Recife to free Napoleon*, see J.A. da Costa 'Napoleon I au Brasil', *Revue de Monde Latin*, vol 8, pp.205–16.

p.195 *a similar process could have produced four giant states* Barman, *Nation*, pp.40–41, divides what could have been in a different way: a loyalist Amazon basin, a split between Pernambuco and Bahia, with the rest forming a single 'Republic of Brazil'.

p.196 *natives with their bows and arrows* Oliveira Lima, *Dom João*, p.515.

p.198 *undisguised hatred* Marrocos, *Cartas*, pp.22–23.

p.198 *to become a Count in Portugal* Manchester, 'The Transfer of the Court to Brazil', p.182, note 104.

p.200 *The suffering of our people* Alexandre, *Os Sentidos*, p.404.

p.200 *Your Majesty should be well informed* Ibid., p.406.

p.200 *News has been put about* H. J. D'Araújo Carneiro, *Cartas Dirigidas a S. M. El Rey D. João VI desde 1817*, Cox & Baylis, London, 1821, p.6.

p.201 *goes against a habit formed by two centuries* Alexandre, *Os Sentidos*, p.362.

p.201 *turning Brazil into a 'Negroland'* Kenneth Maxwell, *Why was Brazil Different? The Contexts of Independence*, Working Papers on Latin America, The David Rockefeller Center for Latin American Studies, Cambridge, Mass., 2000, p.17.

Chapter Twelve: Dona Leopoldina

p.203 *pleasing ... He is not extraordinarily handsome* Oberacker, *A Imperatriz*, p.70.

p.204 *the Portuguese are the slowest people in the world* Gilberto Ferrez and Robert C. Smith, *Franz Frühbeck's Brazilian Journey*, University of Pennsylvania Press, New York, 1960, p.15.

p.204 *I have never seen a more spoilt and foolish child; My little Archduchess is ... a child* Oberacker, *A Imperatriz*, pp.94, 103.

p.205 *She has a very large and handsome dining room* Ferrez and Smith, *Frühbeck*, p.16.

p.205 *Johann Baptist Emanuel Pohl … had a chance to look around Dona Leopoldina's cabins* Ibid., p.16.

p.205 *a considerable number of cows* Ibid., p.16.

p.206 *I found them very kind* Oberacker, *A Imperatriz*, p.57.

p.206 *I have always had a particular affinity to America* Ibid., p.56.

p.207 *an ugly doll representing Napoleon* Ibid., p.16.

p.207 *When news of the wedding* Ibid., p.60.

p.207 *Europe has now become unbearable* Ibid., pp.57–58.

p.208 *Antarctic France* A colony set up in the bay of Rio de Janeiro in 1555 by the eccentric noble Nicolas de Villegagnon. It started with high hopes, but was riven by religious dissent and broke apart three years later, to be definitively dislodged by the Portuguese in 1560. See Hemming, *Red Gold*, pp.119–138.

p.208 *the ambassador assures me* Oberacker, *A Imperatriz*, p.63.

p.208 *I will conduct myself with all possible modesty* Ibid., pp.75–77.

p.208 *The only thing that frightens me* Ibid., p.65.

p.208 *the voyage doesn't scare me* Ibid., p.74.

p.208 On the journey to Brazil, see Ferrez and Smith, *Frühbeck*, passim.

p.209 *At one moment the ship lay on one side* Oberacker, *A Imperatriz*, p.106.

p.210 *He [Pedro] was sitting in front of our princess* Ibid., p.111.

p.211 *Apart from the semi-Asian court* Ibid., p.166.

p.212 *any provincial German noble* Ibid., p.121.

p.212 *kept half-full chamber pots* Monteiro, *Império*, p.89.

p.212 *the arms, shoulders and backs of the women* Schwarcz, *Biblioteca*, p.334.

p.213 *The queen and all the princesses* Oberacker, *A Imperatriz*, p.119.

p.213 *bawdy verses, illustrated by pornographic doodles* Macaulay, *Dom Pedro*, p.312, note 37.

p.213 *calling his mother a 'bitch'* Ibid., p.189.

p.213 *There'll be no shortage of people* Ibid., p.118.

p.214 For an account of the *Viagens Filosóficas* and Ferreira's expedition, see William Joel Simon, *Scientific Expeditions in the Portuguese Territories (1783–1808)* …, Instituto de Investigação Científica Tropical, Lisbon, 1983, passim; Alexandre Rodrigues Ferreira, *Viagem Filosófica pelas capitanias do Grão Pará, Rio Negro, Mato Grosso e Cuiabá, 1783–1792*, Conselho Federal de Cultura, Rio de Janeiro, 1971, passim.

p.215 *All are untouched* Simon, *Expeditions*, p.126.

p.217 *The country is entrancing, full of delicious spots* Bertita Harding, *Amazon Throne*, Harrap & Co, London, 1942, p.71.

p.217 *a few completely frank words* Oberacker, *A Imperatriz*, p.127.

p.217 *You are indeed right* Ibid., p.164.

p.218 *She was very kind* Ibid., p.167.

p.218 *would develop a loathing of Portuguese doctors* Ibid., p.136.

p.218 *I only receive letters from Italian boats* Ibid., pp.179.

p.218 *There is nothing that I desire with more ardour* Ibid., p.179.

p.219 *he had the kindness to tell me* Ibid., p.132.

p.219 *has pleased everyone in the extreme* Marrocos, *Cartas*, p.305.

p.219 *the life style, in which people never go to the theatre* Oberacker, *A Imperatriz*, p.176.

p.219 *Those who don't know her* Ibid., p.182.

p.220 *I think of you all the time* Ibid., p.182.

p.220 *I must confess with total honesty* Ibid., p.182.

Chapter Thirteen: Danger Signals

p.221 *There was trouble across Brazil's borders* On the highly complex situation in the rest of South America during the court's stay in Rio, see David Bushnell, 'The Independence of Spanish South America', in Leslie Bethell, ed., *The Independence of Spanish South America*, Cambridge University Press, Cambridge, 1987, pp.95–154; Edwin Williamson, *The Penguin History of Latin America*, Allen Lane, London, 1992, pp.195–228.

p.223 *the first sovereign to be crowned in the New World* dos Santos, *Memórias*, vol 2, p.616.

p.224 *The hesitation at the first and second arches* Luccock, *Notes*, p.572.

p.224 *I have to warn that the news* Marrocos, *Cartas*, p.315.

p.226 *Ideas of revolution were widespread* Isabel Nobre Vargues, 'O processo de formação do primeiro movimento liberal: a Revolução de 1820', in José Mattoso, ed., *História de Portugal*, 8 vols, Editorial Estampa, 1993, vol 5, *O Liberalismo*, p.57.

p.227 *the fight for independence had started in Portugal, not Brazil* Maxwell, *Different*, p.10.

p.227 *The idea of the status of a colony* Ibid., p.10.

p.227 *Things will never return to how they were before* Beresford to Palmela in Pereira, *Os filhos*, pp.286–287.

p.228 *The King answered with an appearance of great Anxiety* Thornton to Castlereagh, Rio de Janeiro, 18 November 1820, FO 63, codex 229, no.60.

p.228 *Delay is the radical fault of this government* Barman, *Nation*, p.61.

p.229 *If it [Brazil] separates and cuts off communication* Ibid., p.69.

p.230 *his Royal Person or one of his sons* Francisco Adolfo de Varnhagen, *História da Independência do Brasil*, Brasilia, 1972, p.42.

p.230 *There are beautiful villas* Norton, *A Corte*, p.85.

p.232 *the disgraceful events that I witnessed* Duque de Palmella, *Despachos e Correspondência do Duque de Palmella colligidos e publicados por J.J. Dos Reis e Vasconcellos*, 4 vols, Imprensa Nacional, Lisbon, 1851, vol 1, p.142.

p.232 *the hatred and slanders* Edmundo, *A Corte*, vol 2, p.621.

p.232 *Unfortunately, he doesn't want to take a decision* Oberacker, *A Imperatriz*, p.205.

p.232 *... if you do not succeed* Ibid., p.200.

p.233 *this is painful for the princess royal* Ibid., p.200.

p.233 *I found her very agitated* Ibid., p.200–201.

p.233 *who will be born at sea* Ibid., p.200–3.

p.234 *he proposed to the king a set of principles* Macaulay, *Dom Pedro*, p.76.

p.235 *copies were left outside the palace* Schultz, *Versailles*, p.239.

Chapter Fourteen: The Return

p.236 For accounts of the court's last months in Rio see Barman, *Nation*, pp. 65–80; Macaulay, *Dom Pedro*, pp.70–86; Schultz, *Versailles* pp.235–247; Varnhagen, *História* pp.35–94.

p.236 *Treasonous pamphlets and satirical verses* Schultz, *Versailles*, pp.247–265.

p.237 *except for modifications that local circumstances* Macaulay, *Dom Pedro*, p.78.

p.238 *to observe, protect and perpetually maintain* Ibid., p.80.

p.240 *Reports were spread of the Discontent of the People* Thornton to Castlereagh, Rio de Janeiro, 3 May 1821, FO 63, codex 227, no.30.

p.241 *There are so many different versions of this event* Thornton to Castlereagh, Rio de Janeiro, 3 May 1821, FO 63, codex 227, no.30.

p.242 *Common people were indiscriminately killed* Schultz, *Versailles*, p.247.

p.242 *on the orders of evil-intentioned men* Macaulay, *Dom Pedro*, p.85.

p.243 *Finally, I am going to a land inhabited by real men* Debret, *Voyage*, vol 3, p.268.

p.243 *I had lived thirteen years in darkness, seeing only blacks and mulattos* Mello Moraes, *Chronica*, vol 2, p.208.

p.243 *I still remember and will always remember* Schwarcz, *Biblioteca*, p.355.

p.243 *This packet boat will carry news* Oberacker, *A Imperatriz*, pp.211–212.

p.243 *received the Compliments of his Court on the Occasion of the Day* Thornton to Castlereagh, Rio de Janeiro, 27 April 1821, FO 63, codex 227, no.5.

p.244 *which continued so long through the Day* Thornton to Castlereagh, Rio de Janeiro, 27 April 1821, FO 63, codex 227, no.5.

p.245 *not merely it is said for the Purposes of Refreshment* Thornton to Castlereagh, Rio de Janeiro, 27 April 1821, FO 63, codex 227, no.5.

p.246 *just like a picture that had stepped out of its frame* Cheke, *Carlota*, p.87.

p.246 *Entering the foredeck of the ship* Fronteira e d'Alorna, *Memórias*, vol 1, p.241.

p.247 *I could not make out Queen Carlota very well* Ibid., vol 1, p.241.

p.247 *the people exceeded themselves in acclamations* Pereira, *Príncipe e Rei*, vol 4, p.175.

Chapter Fifteen: The Aftermath

p.249 *tonight I received from the hands of your ministers* Schwarcz, *Biblioteca*, p.360. According to Marques Pereira, this oft-quoted letter is apocryphal, although a copy does exist, signed '*Rainha*' (Queen), in the Ajuda library, Lisbon. See Marques Pereira, *Espelhos*, p.172, note 73.

p.249 *Dom Pedro ... began cutting back* Macaulay, *Dom Pedro*, pp.96, 176.

p.250 *I beg Your Majesty* Ibid., p.101.

p.250 *after being accustomed to prompt recourse* Ibid., p.106.

p.251 *Since it is for the good of all* Ibid., p.107.

p.251 *Your mother is for Miguel* Ibid., p.117.

p.252 *I can endure anything* Ibid., p.199.

p.253 *dusting powders, massages, leeches* Ibid., p.202.

p.254 *what pains me most* Marques Pereira, *Espelhos*, p.157.

p.255 *rheumatic attacks, great pain* Ibid., p.159.

p.257 *the only one who ever tricked me* Robert Harvey, *Liberators: Latin America's struggle for independence*, John Murray, London, 2000, p.469.

p.258 *You have not got an easy job* Fonblanque, *Strangford*, p.161.

p.258 *The two sons of bitches* Macaulay, *Dom Pedro*, p.227.

Epilogue

p.260 On Rio's transformation during the nineteenth and twentieth centuries, see Arquivo Geral da Cidade, *Memória da Destruição: Rio – Uma História que se perdeu (1889–1965)*, Arquivo da Cidade, Rio de Janeiro, 2002, passim; Teresa Meade, *'Civilizing' Rio: reform and resistance in a Brazilian city, 1889–1930*, Pennsylvania State University Press, Penn., 1997, passim; Jeffery Needell, *A tropical belle époque: elite culture and society in turn-of-the-century Rio de Janeiro*, Cambridge University Press, Cambridge, 1987, passim.

p.262 *vast carpets of powder* Schwarcz, *Biblioteca* p.282.

Select Bibliography

Abrantès, Laure Junot, *Memoirs of the Duchess D'Abrantès*, 8 vols, Henry Colborn and Richard Bentley, London, 1833.

Abreu, João Capistrano de, *Chapters of Brazil's Colonial History 1500–1800*, Oxford University Press, Oxford, 1997.

Alexandre, Valentim, *Os Sentidos do Império: Questão Nacional e Questão Colonial na Crise do Antigo Regime*, Edições Afrontamento, Porto, 1993.

Anon., *Plano sabio, profferido no Parlamento de Inglaterra pelo ministro de estado Mr. Pitt, sobre a continuação da guerra com a França, e trasladação do throno de Portugal para o novo império do Brasil. Com Licença da Meza do Desembargo do Paço*, Lisbon, 1808.

Arago, J, *Narrative of a voyage around the World ...*, Treuttel and Wurtz, London, 1823.

Arquivo Geral da Cidade, *Memória da Destruição: Rio – Uma História que se perdeu (1889–1965)*, Arquivo da Cidade, Rio de Janeiro, 2002.

Azevedo, Francisa L. Nogueira de. *Carlota Joaquina na Corte do Brasil*, Civilização Brasiliera, Rio de Janeiro, 2003.

Bahiense, Norbertino Domingos, *Martins e a revolucão Pernambucana de 1817*, Instituto Histórico e Geográfico do Espírito Santo, Espírito Santo, 1974.

Barman, Roderick J., *Citizen Emperor: Pedro II and the Making of Brazil, 1825–91*, Stanford University Press, Stanford, 1999.

Barman, Roderick J., *Brazil: The Forging of a Nation, 1798–1852*, Stanford University Press, Stanford, 1988.

Barrow, John, *The Life and Correspondence of Admiral Sir William Sidney Smith*, 2 vols, Richard Bentley, London, 1848.

Beckford, William, *Recollections of an excursion to the monasteries of Alcobaça and Batalha*, Centaur Press Ltd, Fontwell, 1972.

Beirão, Caetano, *D. Maria I 1777–1792*, Impresa Nacional de Publicidade, Lisbon, 1944.

Bethell, Leslie, ed., *Colonial Brazil*, Cambridge University Press, Cambridge, 1987.

Bethell, Leslie, ed., *The Independence of Spanish South America*, Cambridge University Press, Cambridge, 1987.

Bethell, Leslie, *The Abolition of the Brazilian Slave Trade: Britain, Brazil and the slave trade question, 1807–1869*, Cambridge University Press, Cambridge, 1970.

Bethell, Leslie, *George Canning and the Independence of Latin America*, The Hispanic and Luso-Brazilian Councils, London, 1970.

Blakeney, Robert, *A Boy in the Peninsular War*, Greenhill Books, London, 1989.

Bonavides, Paulo and Amaral, Roberto, *Textos políticos da História do Brasil*, 9 vols, Senado Federal, Subsecretaria de Edições Técnicas, Brasilia, 1996.

Boxer, Charles Ralph, *The Golden Age of Brazil: Growing Pains of a Colonial Society, 1695–1750*, Carcanet, Manchester, 1995.

Boxer, Charles Ralph, *The Portuguese Seaborne Empire, 1415–1825*, Carcanet, Manchester, 1991.

Boxer, Charles Ralph, *From Lisbon to Goa, 1500–1750*, Variorum Reprints, London, 1984.

Boxer, Charles Ralph, *Four Centuries of Portuguese Expansion, 1415–1825: A Succinct Survey*, Witwatersrand University Press, Johannesburg, 1961.

Boxer, Charles Ralph, *The Dutch in Brazil 1624–1654*, Clarendon Press, Oxford, 1957.

Brandão, Raúl, *El Rei Junot*, Atlântida, Coimbra, 1974.

Brougham, Henry Peter, *The Life and Times of Henry Lord Brougham*, 3 vols, William Blackwood and Sons, Edinburgh & London, 1871

Browne, Captain Thomas Henry, *The Napoleonic War Journal of Captain Thomas Henry Browne, 1807–1816*, Bodley Head for the Army Records, London, 1987.

Bueno, Eduardo, *A viagem do descobrimento: A verdadeira história da expedição de Cabral*, Objetiva, Rio de Janeiro, 1998.

Bushnell, David, 'The Independence of Spanish South America', in Bethell, ed., *The Independence of Spanish South America*, Cambridge University Press, Cambridge, 1987, pp. 95–154.

Calmon, Pedro, *O Rei do Brasil*, Olympio, Rio de Janeiro, 1935.

Cannadine, David, *Ornamentalism: How the British saw their Empire*, Penguin, London, 2001.

Carneiro, H. J. D'Araújo, *Cartas Dirigidas a S. M. El Rey D. João VI desde 1817*, Cox & Baylis, London, 1821.

Cheke, Marcus, *Carlota Joaquina: Queen of Portugal*, Sidgwick and Jackson Limited, London, 1947.

Cohen, Thomas, *The Fire of Tongues: António Vieira and the Missionary Church in Brazil and Portugal*, Stanford University Press, Stanford, 1998.

Coleman, Terry, *Nelson*, Bloomsbury, London, 2002.

Conrad, Robert Edgar, *World of Sorrow*, Louisiana State University Press, Baton Rouge, 1986.

Conrad, Robert Edgar, *Children of God's Fire: A Documentary History of Black Slavery in Brazil*, Princeton University Press, Princeton, 1983.

Correia-Afonso, John, ed., *Intrepid itinerant: Manuel Godinho and his journey from India to Portugal in 1663*, Oxford University Press, Oxford, 1990.

Costa, Emilia Viotti da, *The Brazilian Empire: Myths and Histories*, University of North Carolina Press, Chapel Hill, 2000.

Cunha, D. Luís da, *Instruções Inéditas de D. Luís da Cunha e Marco António de Azevedo Coutinho*, Coimbra University Press, Coimbra, 1929.

Debret, Jean-Baptiste, *Voyage pittoresque et historique au Brésil, ou, Séjour d'un artiste français au Brésil, depuis 1816 jusqu'en 1831*, 3 vols, Firmin Didot Frères, Paris, 1834–1839.

Dropmore Papers, *An outline of a scheme to transport the Prince Regent of Portugal, or his son, to Brazil and to send a military force to assist the emancipation of Spanish and Portuguese America and the opening up of South America to British trade*, British Library Manuscripts, vol CCCCXXXI, Ms. 59285, 1805–before 25 June 1806.

Edmundo, Luiz, *A Corte de Dom João no Rio de Janeiro (1808–21)*, 3 vols, Imprensa Nacional, Rio de Janeiro, 1939.

Edmundo, Luiz, *Rio in the time of the Viceroys*, J. R. de Oliveira, Rio de Janeiro, 1936.

Esdaile, Charles J., *The Peninsular War: a new history*, Allen Lane, London, 2002.

Esdaile, Charles J., *Spain in a Liberal Age: from Constitution to Civil War, 1808–1939*, Blackwell, Oxford, 2000.

Esparteiro, Antônio Marques et al., 'Transmigração da Família Real para o Brasil' in *História Naval Brasileira*, 2 vols, Ministério da Marinha, Rio de Janeiro, 1979 vol 2, pp. 323–368.

Ferreira, Alexandre Rodrigues, *Viagem Filosófica pelas capitanias do Grão Pará, Rio Negro, Mato Grosso e Cuiabá, 1783–1792*, Conselho Federal de Cultura, Rio de Janeiro, 1971.

Ferrez, Gilberto and Smith, Robert C., *Franz Frühbeck's Brazilian Journey*, University of Pennsylvania Press, New York, 1960.

Ferrez, Marc, *O Rio Antigo do fotógrafo Marc Ferrez: paisagens e tipos humanos do Rio de Janeiro 1865–1918*, Editora Ex Libris, Rio de Janeiro, 1985.

Fonblanque, Edward Barrington de, *The Lives of Lord Strangford*, Cassell Petter & Galpin, London, 1877.

França, Jean Marcel Carvalho, ed., *Visões do Rio de Janeiro Colonial: antologia de textos, 1531–1800*, Olympio, Rio de Janeiro, 1999.

Francis, David, *Portugal 1715–1808: Joanine, Pombaline and Rococo Portugal as seen by British diplomats and traders,* Tamesis, London, 1985.

Freyre, Gilberto, *Ingleses no Brasil: Aspectos da influência britânica sobre a vida, a paisagem e a cultura do Brasil*, José Olympio, Rio de Janeiro, 1948.

Fronteira e d'Alorna, Marques de, *Memórias do Marques de Fronteira e d'Alorna*, 6 vols, Imprensa da Universidade, Coimbra, 1932.

Fryer, Peter, *Rhythms of Resistance: African musical heritage in Brazil*, Pluto, London, 2000.

Garcia, Rudolfo, ed., *Correspondência entre Maria Graham e a Imperatriz Dona Leopoldina e cartas*, Biblioteca Nacional, Rio de Janeiro, 1940.

Glover, Michael, *The Peninsular War 1807–1814: A concise military history*, Penguin Books, London, 2001.

Graham, Maria, *Journal of a Voyage to Brazil and residence there, 1821–23*, London, 1824.

Gregory, Desmond, *Brute New World: The Rediscovery of Latin America in the Early Nineteenth Century*, British Academic Press, London, 1992.

Guedes, Max Justo and Lombardi, Gerald, eds., *Portugal Brazil: The Age of the Atlantic Discoveries*, Bertrand Edition, Franco Maria Ricci, Brazil Cultural Foundation, Lisbon, 1990.

Harding, Bertita, *Amazon Throne*, Harrap & Co, London, 1942.

Harvey, Robert, *Liberators: Latin America's struggle for independence*, John Murray, London, 2000.

Hayter, Alethea, ed., *The Backbone: diaries of a military family in the Napoleonic wars*, Pentland, Edinburgh, 1993.

Heaton, Herbert, 'A Merchant Adventurer in Brazil', *Journal of Economic History*, 6:1, May 1946, pp.1–23.

Hemming, John, *Red Gold: the conquest of the Brazilian Indians*, Papermac, London, 1995.

Henderson, James, *A History of Brazil; comprising its geography, commerce, colonization, aboriginal inhabitants* ..., London, 1821.

Hughes, Robert, *The Fatal Shore*, Pan Books, London, 1987.

João VI, Dom, *Gabinete de Dom João VI*, Caixas 1–6, Arquivo Nacional, Rio de Janeiro, 1808–21.

Johnson, H. B., 'Portuguese settlement, 1500–1580', in Bethell, ed., *Colonial Brazil*, Cambridge University Press, Cambridge, 1987, pp.1–38.

Johnson, Paul, *Napoleon*, Weidenfeld & Nicolson, London, 2002.

Karasch, Mary C., *Slave life in Rio de Janeiro*, Princeton University Press, Princeton, 1987.

Karasch, Mary C., 'Rio de Janeiro: from colonial town to imperial capital', Robert Ross and Gerard Telkamp, eds., *Colonial Cities: essays on urbanism in a colonial context*, Comparative studies in overseas history, vol 5, Nijhoff, Dordrecht, 1985.

Ley, Charles David, ed., *Portuguese Voyages 1498–1663: Tales from the Great Age of Discovery*, Phoenix Press, London, 2000.

Light, Kenneth, 'A Viagem da Família Real para o Brasil, 1807–1808' in *D. João VI: um rei aclamado na América*, pp.108–113, Museu Histórico Nacional, Rio de Janeiro, 2000.

Light, Kenneth, *The Migration of the Royal Family of Portugal to Brazil in 1807/1808*, Rio de Janeiro, 1995.

Livermore, H. V., *A History of Portugal*, Cambridge University Press, Cambridge, 1947.

Luccock, John, *Notes on Rio de Janeiro, and the southern parts of Brazil taken during a residence of ten years in that country, from 1808 to 1818*, London, 1820.

Macalpine, Ida and Hunter, Richard, *George III and the Mad-Business*, Pimlico, London, 1991.

Macaulay, Neill, *Dom Pedro: the struggle for liberty in Brazil and Portugal*, Duke University Press, Durham, 1986.

Macaulay, Rose, *They Went to Portugal*, Penguin, Harmondsworth, 1985.

McLynn, Frank, *Napoleon: a biography*, Pimlico, London, 1997.

Malerba, Jurandir, *A corte no exílio: civilização e poder no Brasil às vésperas da independência (1808–1821)*, Companhia das Letras, São Paulo, 2000.

Manchester, Alan K., 'The Transfer of the Court to Brazil', Henry H. Keith and S. F. Edwards, eds., *Conflict and Continuity in Brazilian Society*, University of South Carolina Press, Columbia, 1969, pp.148–190.

Manchester, Alan K., *British Preëminence in Brazil: Its Rise and Decline*, University of North Carolina Press, Chapel Hill, 1933.

Marbot, Jean-Baptiste Antoine Marcellin de, *The Memoirs of Baron de Marbot*, 2 vols, Longmans, Green & co., London, 1988.

Marchant, Anyda, 'Dom João's Botanical Garden', *The Hispanic American Historical Review*, vol 41, no.2, May 1961, pp. 259–274.

Marques Pereira, Sara, *D. Carlota Joaquina e os 'Espelhos de Clio': actuação política e figurações historiográficas*, Livros Horizonte, Lisbon, 1999.

Marrocos, Luiz Joaquim dos Santos, '*Cartas de Luiz Joaquim dos Santos Marrocos*', Anais da Biblioteca Nacional do Rio de Janeiro, vol 56, Rio de Janeiro, 1934.

Martius, C. F. Philipp von and Spix, Johann Baptist von, *Travels in Brazil in the years 1817–1820*, 2 vols, Longman Hurst & co., London, 1824.

Mattoso, José, ed., *História de Portugal*, 8 vols, Editorial Estampa, Lisbon, 1993.

Mavor, Elizabeth, ed., *The Captain's Wife: the South American journals of Maria Graham 1821–23*, Weidenfeld & Nicolson, London, 1993.

Mawe, John, *Travels in the Interior of Brazil, Particularly in the Gold and Diamond districts of that country* ..., Philadelphia, 1816.

Maxwell, Kenneth, *Why was Brazil Different? The Contexts of Independence*, Working Papers on Latin America, The David Rockefeller Center for Latin American Studies, Cambridge, Mass., 2000.

Maxwell, Kenneth, *Pombal, Paradox of the Enlightenment*, Cambridge University Press, Cambridge, 1995.

Maxwell, Kenneth, 'The Generation of the 1790s and the Idea of Luso-Brazilian Empire', Dauril Alden, ed., *Colonial Roots of Modern Brazil*, University of California Press, Berkeley, 1973.

Meade, Teresa, *'Civilizing' Rio: reform and resistance in a Brazilian city, 1889–1930*, Pennsylvania State University Press, Penn., 1997.

Mello Moraes, A. J. de, *Chronica Geral do Brasil*, 2 vols, Rio de Janeiro, 1886.

Mello Moraes, A. J. de, *História de Transladação da Corte Portugueza para o Brasil em 1807–1808*, Rio de Janeiro, 1872.

Miller, Joseph C., *Way of Death: Merchant Capitalism and the Angolan Slave Trade*, James Curry, London, 1988.

Monteiro, Tobias, *História do Império: a Elaboração da Independência*, Briguiet, Rio de Janeiro, 1927.

Napier, William, 'A reply to Lord Strangford's "Observations" ' *History of the War in the Peninsula*, 4 vols, London, 1848.

Needell, Jeffery, *A tropical belle époque: elite culture and society in turn-of-the-century Rio de Janeiro*, Cambridge University Press, Cambridge, 1987.

Newitt, Malyn, 'Lord Beresford and the *Governadores* of Portugal', 2001.

Newitt, Malyn, ed., *The First Portuguese Colonial Empire*, University of Exeter, Exeter, 1986.

Norris, A. H. and Bremmer, R. W., *The Lines of Torres Vedras*, The British Historical Society of Portugal, Lisbon, 1980.

Norton, Luiz, *A Corte de Portugal no Brasil*, Companhia Editora Nacional, São Paulo, 1979.

Oberacker, Carlos H. Jr, *A Imperatriz Leopoldina*, Conselho Federal de Cultura, Rio de Janeiro, 1973.

Oliveira Lima, Manuel de, *Dom João VI no Brasil*, Topbooks, Rio de Janeiro, 1996.

O'Neill, Thomas, *A concise and accurate Account of the Proceedings of the Squadron under the command of Rear Admiral Sir W. S. Smith, in effecting the escape and escorting the Royal Family of Portugal to the Brazils...*, London, 1807.

Opfell, Olga S., *Queens, Empresses, Grand Duchesses and Regents: Women Rulers of Europe, A.D. 1328–1989*, McFarland, Jefferson N.C., 1989.

Palmella, Duque de, *Despachos e Correspondência do Duque de Palmella colligidos e publicados por J.J. Dos Reis e Vasconcellos*, 4 vols, Imprensa Nacional, Lisbon, 1851.

Pereira, Ângelo, *Os filhos d'El-Rei D. João VI*, Imprensa Nacional da Publicidade, Lisbon, 1946.

Pereira, Ângelo, *D. João VI, Príncipe e Rei*, 4 vols, Imprensa Nacional da Publicidade, Lisbon, 1953.

Pimentel, António Filipe, *Arquitectura e poder: o Real Edifício de Mafra*, Universidade de Coimbra, Coimbra, 1992.

Pocock, Tom, *A Thirst For Glory: the Life of Sir Sidney Smith*, Aurum Press, London, 1996.

Prado, Caio Jr, *The Colonial Background of Modern Brazil*, University of California Press, Berkeley & Los Angeles, 1971.

Presas, José, *Memórias Secretas de D. Carlota Joaquina*, Tecnoprint, Rio de Janeiro, 1996.

Priestley, J. B., *The Prince of Pleasure and his Regency 1811–20*, Penguin Books, London, 2002.

Rodrigues, Ana Maria, ed., *D. João VI e o seu tempo*, Comissão Nacional para as Comemorações dos Descobrimentos Portuguêses, Rio de Janeiro, 1999.

Rodrigues, João Barbosa, *Hortus Fluminensis*, Rio de Janeiro, 1894.

Russell, Peter, *Prince Henry 'the Navigator' A Life*, Yale University Press, New Haven, 2000.

Russell-Wood, A. J. R., *A World on the Move: the Portuguese in Africa, Asia, and America, 1415–1808*, Carcanet, Manchester, 1992.

Santos, Luiz Gonçalves dos, *Memórias para servir à História do Reino do Brasil*, 2 vols, Livraria Editora Zélio Valverde, Rio de Janeiro, 1943.

Saramago, José, *Journey to Portugal: A Pursuit of Portugal's History and Culture*, Harvill, London, 2000.

Schroeder, Paul W., *The Transformation of European Politics 1763–1848*, Oxford University Press, Oxford, 1994.

Schultz, Kirsten, *Tropical Versailles: Empire, Monarchy, and the Portuguese Royal Court in Rio de Janeiro, 1808–1821*, Routledge, New York, 2001.

Schultz, Kirsten, 'Royal Authority, Empire and the Critique of Colonialism: Political Discourses in Rio de Janeiro (1808–1821)' in *Luso-Brazilian Review*, XXXVII, 2000, pp.7–31.

Schwarcz, Lilia Moritz, *As Barbas do Imperador: D. Pedro II, um monarca nos trópicos*, Companhia das Letras, São Paulo, 1998.

Schwarcz, Lilia Moritz, *A Longa Viagem da Biblioteca dos Reis: do terremoto de Lisboa à Independência do Brasil*, Companhia das Letras, São Paulo, 2002.

Schwartz, Stewart B., 'Plantations and peripheries, c.1580–c.1750', Bethell, ed., *Colonial Brazil*, Cambridge University Press, Cambridge, 1987, pp. 67–81.

Simões, Henrique Campos, *As Cartas do Brasil*, Editora do UESC, Ilhéus, 1999.

Simon, William Joel, *Scientific Expeditions in the Portuguese Territories (1783–1808)* ..., Instituto de Investigação Científica Tropical, Lisbon, 1983.

Sousa, Octávio Tarquínio de, *História dos fundadores do império do Brasil*, 10 vols, Olympio, Rio de Janeiro, 1972.

Souza, Iara Lis Carvalho, *Pátria Coroada: O Brasil como Corpo Político Autônomo 1780–1831*, Editora Unesp, São Paulo, 1998.

Tavares, Francisco Muniz, *História da revolução de Pernambuco de 1817*, Governo do Estado, Casa Civil de Pernambuco, Recife, 1969.

Thomas, Gordon Kent, *Wordsworth's Dirge and Promise: Napoleon, Wellington and the Convention of Cintra*, University of Nebraska Press, Lincoln, 1971.

Tostes, Vera Lúcia Bottrel, ed., *D. João VI: um rei aclamado na America*, Museu Histórico Nacional, Rio de Janeiro, 2000.

Vargues, Isabel Nobre, 'O processo de formação do primeiro movimento liberal: a Revolução de 1820' José Mattoso, ed., *História de Portugal*, 8 vols, Editorial Estampa, Lisbon, 1993, vol 5, *O Liberalismo*, pp.45–63.

Varnhagen, Francisco Adolfo de, *História da Independência do Brasil*, Brasilia, 1972.

Wellesley, Richard, *Letter Books,* 14 vols, vols 9–10, Despatches of Lord Wellesley to Percy Clinton Sydney Smythe, Ms. 49987–8, British Library, 1810–1812.

Williamson, Edwin, *The Penguin History of Latin America*, Allen Lane, London, 1992.

Index

Abel, Charles 182
Abreu, Capistrano de 41
absolutism 229, 231, 259
Acre 10
Aeneid (Virgil) 36
Africa: slave trade 46, 73, 137, 138, 182
Afro-Brazilians 180, 181, 206, 209
Aguiar, Dom Fernando José de Portugal, Marquis of 141, 143
Ajuda Museum 214
Ajuda Palace 20, 25, 58, 158; *see also* royal library
Alexander I, Tsar of Russia 179, 225
Alfonso de Albuquerque (ship) 34, 36, 90
Algarve 19, 78
Alorna, Marquis of 81
Amazon, River: disputed territories 77; expeditions 208, 213, 214–6
American War of Independence 83
Americas: idea of relocation to 70, 76; wealth of resources 76, 202; *see also* North America; South America
Amsterdam 80
Ana de Jesus Maria (daughter of Dona Carlota) 24, 62
Andalusia 105, 121
Angola 77–8, 102, 138, 174, 201, 214; *see also* Luanda
Angostura 222
anthropology: Austrian mission to Brazil 203

anti-British feeling 139–40, 142
anti-colonialism 227
anti-monarchism/anti-royalism 83, 145, 192–3, 235, 241–2
Antonil, André João 76
Arago, Jacques 139–40
Aranjuez 105
Araújo, Antônio de 22, 23, 27, 60, 62, 97; dealings with Strangford 7, 15–16, 18, 20; on board *Medusa* 34, 39, 67; and Rodrigo de Sousa Coutinho 38, 39; opposition to trade treaty 132–3; return as minister 141, 142, 143, 145, 156, 177, 191
architecture 46, 177
Arcos, Dom Marcos de Noronha e Brito, Count of 86
Argentina *see* Buenos Aires; Río de La Plata
Army of the Andes 222
Arrábida, Friar (Mafra librarian) 36
art *see* French Artistic Mission
Artigas, José Gervasio 140, 141, 226
Atlantic: Portugal's trade and empire 71–4
Augusta (transport ship) 203, 204
Austerlitz 11, 47
Austria 172, 203, 254; in Napoleonic Wars 11, 206–7; *see also* Congress of Vienna; Vienna

Austria (transport ship) 203
Austrian court: and Dona Leopoldina's impending marriage 207, 218; and Portuguese court 211–12
Azevedo, Joaquim José de (court official) 21–2, 26, 103, 156–7, 247
Azores 245

Bagot, Sir Charles 258
Bahia 37, 46, 68, 71, 80, 142, 192, 194, 227; revolution 232, 234
Banda Oriental (disputed territory) 109–10; and Dona Carlota's ambitions 118, 122; battle for 140, 141, 162, 192, 200, 226, 253
Bank of Brazil 198–9, 239
Banks, Sir Joseph 216
Barreto, José de (merchant) 20–1
batuque (dance) 92
Bayonne 10, 19, 104
Beckford, William 52–3, 55
Bedford, HMS (British warship) 31, 33, 34
beija-mão 100, 212, 238
Belém 214, 216, 234
Belgian Congo 3
Belgium 3, 206
Bemposta convent 254, 257
Beresford, Maj. Gen. William Carr 125–6, 142, 144, 162–3, 167, 199, 222, 226–7
Berlin Decree 11, 12
Bezerra, João Paulo 191
Biblioteca Nacional 262

Acknowledgements

I would like to thank my brother Hugo for his optimism and encouragement when this book was no more than a rough mental sketch. Several years down the line, his editorial input proved invaluable. Roderick J. Barman, Alfeu França, Neill Macaulay, Malyn Newitt, Steve Nugent, Kirsten Schultz and Landeg White took the time and trouble to plough through an entire early draft, and offer their thought-provoking comments and corrections. At Bloomsbury, thanks goes to my editors Rosemary Davidson, Victoria Millar, Nicola Barr and Margaret Stead for their detailed feedback, as well as Liz Calder for her enthusiastic backing of this project from the outset. On the pictorial side, Elisa Guerra in Rio de Janeiro photographed some of the plates.

All my family have been a bedrock of support throughout – especially my parents in Sydney and Helen and Paul Godard in Nîmes, whose characteristic blend of relaxed hospitality and superb Provençale cuisine eased me through some difficult writing sessions. Among the many who have helped, supported, and fed me over the years in Rio, with true *carioca* 'carinho', are Ana Claudia, Christian, Adriana, Cat, Aydano, Luciana, Milton, Guta, Léo, Maria Alice, Edyomar, Bá, Lara, Zenir, Cézar, Lívia and 'tios' Alfeu, Dea, Aimar, Roberto, Leny and Leila. To them, I hope this book goes some way towards reciprocating the warmth and friendship they have offered me over this last decade.

London, 2004

LIST OF ILLUSTRATIONS WITH CREDITS

COVER IMAGE: *A bureaucrat promenades with his family*, Jean-Baptiste Debret. This famous Debret watercolour depicts the promenade of a wealthy bureaucrat's family. According to custom, the head of the family leads off the march, followed by his offspring, the youngest first; then comes the (pregnant) mother and a procession of slaves: her lady-in-waiting, her wet-nurse and the wet-nurse's own slave. Bringing up the rear is the master's servant and two young apprentice slaves 'who will grow up to the crack of a whip', with the cook standing in the doorway (Jean-Baptiste Debret, *Voyage pittoresque et historique au Brésil, ou, Séjour d'un artiste français au Brésil, depuis 1816 jusqu'en 1831*, 3 VOL 3, Firmin Didiot Fréres, Paris, 1834–39, p. 126–7.) Courtesy of Museus Castro Maya.

COLOUR INSERT

1. *Dom João VI* by José Inácio S. Paio (1824), Palácio Nacional de Mafra, courtesy of Instituto Português do Património Arquitectónico (IPPAR).

2. *Dona Carlota Joaquina*, anon., Palácio Nacional de Ajuda, courtesy of IPPAR.

3. *Dom Pedro*, drawing, Jean François Vautier; engraving, Badoureau, Palácio Nacional de Ajuda, courtesy of IPPAR.

4. *Percy Clinton Sydney Smythe, sixth Viscount of Strangford*, courtesy of the National Portrait Gallery, London.

5. *Embarkation for Brazil*, Nicolas Louis Albert Delerive, Museu Nacional dos Conches, courtesy of Instituto Português de Museus.

6. *Allegory of the virtues of Dom João VI*, Domingos António de Sequeira, 1810, Palácio Nacional de Queluz, courtesy of IPPAR.

7. *Entrance to Rio harbour* from João Maurício Rugendas, *Viagem Pitoresca através do Brasil*, Biblioteca Histórico Brasileira, São Paulo, plate 1/6, courtesy of Canning House Library, London.

8. *Rio harbour* from João Maurício Rugendas, *Viagem Pitoresca através do Brasil*, Biblioteca Histórico Brasileira, São Paulo, plate 1/7, courtesy of Canning House Library, London.

9. *View from in front of São Bento Monastery* from João Maurício Rugendas, *Viagem Pitoresca através do Brasil*, Biblioteca Histórico Brasileira, São Paulo, plate 3/12, courtesy of Canning House Library, London. Photo: Elisa Guerra.

10. *Public Punishment* from João Maurício Rugendas, *Viagem Pitoresca através do Brasil*, *Biblioteca Histórico Brasileira*, São Paulo, plate 4/15, courtesy of Canning House Library, London.

11. *Slave woman portraits* from Jean-Baptiste Debret, *Viagem Pitoresca e histórica ao Brasil*, 3 vols, Bibiloteca Histórica Brasileira, São Paulo, 1949, vol 2, plate 22, courtesy of Canning House Library, London. Photo: Elisa Guerra.

12. *A Brazilian lady at home* from Jean-Baptiste Debret, *Viagem Pitoresca e histórica ao Brasil*, 3 vols, Bibiloteca Histórica Brasileira, São Paulo, 1949, vol 2, plate 6, courtesy of Canning House Library, London. Photo: Elisa Guerra.

13. *Dinner in Brazil* from Jean-Baptiste Debret, *Viagem Pitoresca e histórica ao Brasil*, 3 vols, Bibiloteca Histórica Brasileira, São Paulo, 1949, vol 2, plate 7, courtesy of Canning House Library, London. Photo: Elisa Guerra.

14. The Archduchess Leopoldina, miniature, around 1817 from *Viagem ao Brasil nas aquarelas de Thomas Ender 1817–18*, Kapa Editorial, Petrópolis, 2000, vol 1, p. 22. Photo: Elisa Guerra.

15. *The disembarkation of the princess royal Dona Leopoldina* from Jean-Baptiste Debret, *Viagem Pitoresca e histórica ao Brasil*, 3 vols, Bibiloteca Histórica Brasileira, São Paulo, 1949, vol 3, plate 32, courtesy of Canning House Library, London. Photo: Elisa Guerra.

16. *The departure of Dona Carlota* from Jean-Baptiste Debret, *Viagem Pitoresca e histórica ao Brasil*, 3 vols, Bibiloteca Histórica Brasileira, São Paulo, 1949, vol 3, plate 46, courtesy of Canning House Library, London. Photo: Elisa Guerra

17. *The disembarkation of the King Dom João VI accompanied by a parliamentary deputation, on 4 July 1821*, engraving, Constantino de Fontes, courtesy of *Museu da Cidade*, Lisbon.

A NOTE ON THE AUTHOR

Patrick Wilcken grew up in Sydney. While editing the books website for the *Daily Telegraph*, he spent lengthy periods in Rio de Janeiro. More recently, he has contributed Brazil-related reviews and features to the *Times Literary Supplement*, the *Guardian* and *Index on Censorship*. This is his first book.

A NOTE ON THE TYPE

The text of this book is set in Bembo. This type was first used in 1495
by the Venetian printer Aldus Manutius for Cardinal Bembo's
De Aetna, and was cut for Manutius by Francesco Griffo. It was one
of the types used by Claude Garamond (1480–1561) as a model for
his Romain de L'Université, and so it was the forerunner of what
became standard European type for the following two centuries.
Its modern form follows the original types and was designed
for Monotype in 1929.